D0297560

TORNADO BOYS

TORNADO BOYS

THRILLING TALES FROM THE MEN AND WOMEN WHO HAVE OPERATED THIS INDOMITABLE MODERN-DAY BOMBER

IAN HALL

GRUB STREET • LONDON

Published by
Grub Street
4 Rainham Close
London
SW11 6SS

Copyright © Grub Street 2016

Reprinted 2019

Copyright text © Ian Hall 2016

A CIP record for this title is available from the British Library

ISBN-13: 9-781-910690-13-0

Printed and bound in India by Replika Press Pvt. Ltd.

CONTENTS

INTRODUCTION

Ian Hall

The Tornado GR1 was conceived as a tactical nuclear bomber, a low-level interdictor for the Cold War era. Its crews knew their job, which was to demonstrate the expertise, equipment and readiness required to deter the Warsaw Pact from attacking NATO nations. But when it had been in service for little over a quarter of its life a series of extraordinary transformations began. The Tornado force participated in live combat – far from the anticipated theatre of operations. The Warsaw Pact collapsed. The aircraft was upgraded to GR4 standard, outwardly almost indistinguishable but with combat capability undreamt of in the early days. Tornados would continue, for many years, on operations as different as chalk from cheese from those for which the aircraft had been designed.

This volume, a compendium of tales by those who have flown, serviced, supported and commanded Tornado operations, gives a flavour of the many and varied aspects of the Tornado GR1/GR4 world over the years. Most of the contributors are people I met during my own, single Tornado tour, and many of them went on to experience the extraordinarily diverse nature of the aircraft's eventual tasking.

CHAPTER 1

TO BE, OR NOT TO BE

'Mother Riley's Cardboard Aeroplane' and 'Must Refurbish Canberra Again' were phrases commonly coined to represent 'MRCA'. There seemed to be more than a degree of scepticism around the RAF as the Tornado was prepared for service entry. This was to some extent understandable. Vulcan people would not have regarded it a worthy successor to their mighty jet; not least, it possessed only a fraction of the range and payload. Buccaneer crews were very much attached to their steeds, and fiercely loyal to the ethos of the fleet. And yet the Tornado was to replace both types.

And even when, by the late 1970s, the Tornado was approaching service acceptance, RAF people could have been forgiven if they weren't rushing to place bets on its entry into service. After all, many of them had grown weary of seeing exciting projects being derailed by changes of the political mind. TSR2 – cancelled as its test phase was about to accelerate; F-111 – the order cancelled before the first airframe had been delivered; P1154, the supersonic Harrier – cancelled before metal had been cut; likewise with the Anglo-French Variable Geometry machine (AFVG). The last had foundered partly due to difficulties in reconciling the plans of two different nations. Even though the international concept had subsequently been proven with the successful delivery of the Jaguar, Puma and Gazelle, there still remained a suspicion that the Anglo-German-Italian Tornado could yet founder.

Amidst the doubt, though, there were those who remained optimistic. Members of the international project staffs and testing teams were already seeing at first hand the immense potential of the new aircraft, and were determined to bring it to fruition. Among them was Dick Bogg, a friend of many years' standing who, through a later series of command postings, became a stalwart of the Tornado world.

AIR COMMODORE DICK BOGG (RETD)

In the summer of 1971 I was at Boscombe Down working as a trials officer flying the navigation and weapon aiming system trials on the Phantom FGR2. One Wednesday afternoon, as I climbed out of the Phantom, I was asked to report to my wing commander who announced calmly, "Tomorrow, you are to attend an interview in London for a job with the MRCA." There was not a deal of choice in the matter, but I had to ask him, "What's

MRCA?" He explained that I was on the short list for an avionics test appointment in the flight-test department of the international project office in Munich for the new, secret Multi-Role Combat Aircraft, still on the drawing board but having recently entered the development phase. In the space of five minutes I learned that it was being progressed jointly by West Germany, Italy and the United Kingdom (Belgium, Canada and the Netherlands having already pulled out) as a single replacement for ageing F-104 Starfighters, Vulcans, Canberras and Buccaneers. The new aircraft would have all manner of state-of-the-art sophistication and was already being nicknamed 'the all-electric jet'. It was Europe's biggest ever military project and was set to topple American dominance in the field; thus the political and industrial stakes were high.

Next afternoon I reported to the MoD in Whitehall for my interview with the head of the programme's systems engineering division. There were two other candidates, one civilian, one military. It was unusual for an RAF flight lieutenant to undergo such a job interview and I found it somewhat daunting. There was a general chat, followed by probing questions on navigation and weapon aiming system testing, statistics and suchlike. It made for an interesting forty-five minutes, following which I was asked to report straight back to work.

I arrived back at Boscombe at 5.30pm, whereupon my boss immediately told me that I'd got the job; I was to start work in Munich on Monday! I was to leave the RAF on loan to NATO, essentially becoming a 'civilian' on contract. All very odd. Also, I couldn't believe that a selection had been made, approved by the MoD and agreed by the RAF's personnel department – all in the space of two hours. Although I managed to negotiate a short delay, it was still a whirlwind departure from the RAF, and I soon found myself living in a Munich hotel. The day I arrived was the start of *Oktoberfest* – timing impeccable!

I was to work for the NATO MRCA Development and Production Management Agency (NAMMA), and in the city the next morning I began my first ever day of work in civilian clothes. My new boss was a German civil servant flight test engineer. There was also another German in the flight-test section and we would be getting a young Italian air force captain in due course. I renewed acquaintanceship with my earlier interviewer, Mr Wason Turner, and was taken to meet the GM and his deputy. The former was a Luftwaffe two-star general while the latter was an RAF air commodore, both also on loan.

NAMMA shared an office block with Radio Free Europe, the broadcaster to east European countries; there were many stony-faced characters in the vicinity, and it seemed incongruous, at the height of the Cold War, for the government agency supervising the most secret NATO programme of the period to be sharing a building with RFE. Security was important, but one day when the DGM was holding a meeting in his office the door burst open and in rushed a German major. He clicked his heels and shouted that there was a bomb scare – the DGM would have to evacuate his office. With true British phlegm, the DGM looked over his half-moon glasses at his colleagues, responding with: "I don't think we need to worry about a bomb, do you gentlemen?" The meeting continued.

In my arrival interviews I was told repeatedly that the job of NAMMA staff was to be impartial, to evaluate on the basis of presented facts, even if conclusions ran counter to national prejudices. This was a challenging concept, but I soon learned that it was the only way to secure credibility, and most NAMMA people were able to play a straight bat. There were also, of course, national representatives who would fight for national interests – and it often appeared that our boxing ring had more than four corners.

It became evident that, although the development phase had been approved, in the longer term the MRCA project was still at a rather uncertain stage. I soon learned to be optimistic, reflecting the style of the GM, who gave weekly pep talks to the whole staff so that everyone from telephonist to senior officer knew of the programme's trials and tribulations.

Whatever the politics, and they were considerable, NAMMA was charged with managing the programme and for interfacing with the numerous contractors. Our intermediary was Panavia, the manufacturing consortium formed in March 1969 between Aeritalia, British Aircraft Corporation and Messerschmitt-Bölkow-Blohm. It was a real step forward that NAMMA occupied the same building as Panavia – the face-to-face contact with our opposite numbers was invaluable. There was no question that MRCA represented the most ambitious international collaborative programme ever. There were bound to be risks, turmoil, argument and frustration, but the dedicated NAMMA and Panavia teams would do much to bolster national cohesion and resolve as this brave concept progressed.

The next day I was taken to the MBB factory on the outskirts of Munich to see the MRCA itself – although the most advanced item at that time was a full-scale wooden mock-up. Amidst tight security I entered a guarded section of the factory to view the new design. I was struck by the huge, ugly fin, like a vast shark's; I was told it was necessary for low-level, high-speed stability, but I immediately thought that its size would make it a dead giveaway, visible for miles.

With so many types to be replaced by the MRCA, sceptics dubbed it the multi-role 'compromise' aircraft. While the aim was to produce a single model for all roles (strike/attack, counter air, interdiction, reconnaissance, air defence, close air support) the four participating air arms (the German navy was involved, too) had their own particular requirements. There were fierce debates on whether a single-seat variant could be produced, mainly for the IAF, while the Marineflieger stuck out for a long time for a different radar for its aircraft. Gradually, other national differences emerged, some quite understandable (weapons, and electronic warfare equipment, for example) but others, such as on radios, seemingly ludicrously damaging to commonality. In the end a single airframe shape had been chosen – although, much later, the UK 'stretched' its interceptor. That would, by the way, become the ADV (air defence variant), while the generic attack model was known as the IDS (interdictor/strike).

The aircraft would be powered by two Turbo-Union RB199 turbofans. These new engines (also products of a tri-national consortium) were designed for high fuel efficiency, hence long range at transonic speeds, and also provided high thrust with reheat for take-off and combat manoeuvring. But the most striking design aspect of MRCA was its wing. To meet the conflicting requirements of low-speed control and high-speed efficiency, a variable-geometry arrangement was adopted, with wings pivoting from 25° to 67°.

To permit low-level penetration in all weathers, the aircraft would be equipped with an automatic terrain-following system using a separate radar antenna in the nose to detect ground obstructions ahead, coupled to an autopilot that would maintain a constant ground clearance height. For the first time, European air forces would have the same operational capability whatever the time of day and regardless of weather – a crucial element of the dream. There would be a triplex fly-by-wire flight control system giving redundancy and great safety, and offering smooth handling at all weights and at any speed and altitude. Additionally, one of the most comprehensive avionics suites seen on any combat aircraft would be fitted; there would be radar, doppler, inertial, laser, low-light television (later cancelled) and TACAN, all controlled by a digital main computer. I simply could not believe the specified figures, and couldn't wait to see those accuracies confirmed in practice.

All very exciting, but I didn't have long to familiarise myself with the basic concepts because, in my second week, there was a meeting of the international FTG (flight test group), of which I was to be the secretary. I was somewhat daunted by this group's august composition. There were members from the national air staffs, project offices and flight test centres. In addition, there was strong representation from Panavia, MBB, BAC and Aeritalia. All in all, a full conference room.

There appeared to be two main topics for my introductory three-day meeting. The first was to discuss the draft flight test programme for the yet-to-be-built aircraft. There would be nine prototypes for Panavia (a reduction from the ten originally planned), plus six pre-series aircraft for national testing; the programmes for all fifteen had to be balanced and harmonised. The fundamental principle of the MRCA programme was work sharing, based on the numbers each country initially aimed to buy. The Germans would take 420 aircraft, the British 420 and the Italians 100. Those numbers would eventually change slightly, but the agreed work-sharing arrangement was set at 42½%, 42½%, 15%. This arrangement was applied to all aspects of the programme, including equipment orders and involvement in the flight test programme. Regarding the latter, the FTG had to devise a programme that divided testing of both prototype and pre-series aircraft as nearly as possible according to the agreed ratios.

The meeting's second task was to tackle the *Oktoberfest*. Even with our huge numbers we wouldn't significantly alter the amount of beer consumed – but at least we could try! We agreed that, as good personal relationships go a long way to easing professional frictions in the conference room, it was important to bring together government and contractor representatives in a social environment. Panavia had reserved a large booth in one of the enormous beer tents, but the amount of noise our large party made, even in reheat, was drowned by the cacophony of the essential German oompah band and 2,000 other guests.

Notwithstanding the doubts surrounding the MRCA programme, two events that first autumn gave cause for optimism. First, the contract was awarded for the aircraft's radar. This was, perhaps, the most lucrative equipment contract of all and had been contested fiercely by all participants, with American companies also bidding. Rightly, the participating nations would prefer to buy German, British or Italian, and the eventual selection of the American Texas Instruments radar was a difficult decision. But with that selection made the programme began to look more secure.

Another positive was the first staff outing, when the GM took the whole NAMMA team to the MBB factory in Augsburg. The purpose of the visit was to see the first piece of metal being cut. Work had just started on the manufacture of the wing centre-box section, the enormously strong structure that would hold the wings to the fuselage. The centre-box was hewn from a single piece of metal on an enormous milling machine, and it was extraordinary to witness its transformation from a simple chunk of metal into the heart of a flying prototype.

Just as critical to the success of the project would be the engine, which was a new design and, unusually for a fighter type, would have reverse thrust for retardation after landing. The first engines had already been run by Turbo-Union and I visited the company's test facilities to see one of the first reheat runs – very impressive. Later, the engine would be tested beneath a Vulcan test bed flown by Rolls-Royce.

A good example of the role of NAMMA came while the Italians were still considering the single-seat option. After taking advice from Panavia, it became clear that the cost increment of developing the variant would be exorbitant, and NAMMA was left with the task of advising the board of directors of this. There was much heated argument; the Italians would have a problem if only two-seaters were built, for they had no navigators! The day the board was discussing this I returned to my office after lunch to find two Italian generals and an air marshal sitting on my desk. Air Marshal Sir Douglas Lowe, himself a navigator, spoke first: "Dick, I want you to tell the generals about navigators," – then he left. The Italians had lost their single-seater and now had to learn, fast, what navs did, how they trained, where and for how long. It was the first time I had had such a captive audience of generals and we talked earnestly for two hours. Years later I was delighted to see that the IAF had adopted many of the suggestions we discussed that day.

In the RAF I had been used to being nobbled for various secondary duties, but as a 'civilian' I hadn't expected to do work that seemed well outside my bailiwick. However, procurement of flight test instrumentation for the pre-series aircraft (sensors, thermocouples, strain gauges and all sorts of other transducers) turned out to be a fascinating subject, and I was helped by experts from all the nations. Over a nine-month period I chaired many meetings to select the appropriate instrumentation for each aircraft, but I recall one in particular. My secretary shared an office with a German girl whose father owned a vineyard on the Mosel, and she announced that she would be bringing wine to taste one evening. I tendered my apologies as I would be in the UK, and she said she'd save some for me. The next day, during a break in the FTI meeting, I was staggered to see ten small glasses of wine lined up on my desk. So I sampled a mouthful of each in about two minutes flat and selected two that appeared to taste the best; more decisions were taken that afternoon than we'd made at the previous ten meetings!

Test instrumentation was often discussed within the FTG. Panavia intended to use telemetry to send test parameters direct to a ground station to allow engineers to observe results as they occurred. This was a well-known technique used worldwide, but for some reason there was opposition from elements within the FTG. I was surprised, for I could see the benefits that should derive, particularly in safety, and greater efficiency in utilisation of expensive test flight time. The opposition stemmed, it turned out, from an incident during the early Jaguar development programme, which some put down to poor use of telemetry. But that was years ago and, now we would use telemetry for MRCA testing.

After I had been at NAMMA for about a year I received an official-looking communication; it was one of the first of the RAF's famous 'blue letters', and told me that I was to be promoted to squadron leader. This was unexpected, particularly as I was officially 'out of the air force' during my Munich tour. I was a civilian, being promoted by the RAF! I went to Wason Turner with the letter. He was delighted, naturally, and talked immediately to the air commodore who gruffly wondered why he hadn't been told. "He'll have to go," he said; "I'm not having a squadron leader holding down a flight lieutenant's post." Turner said he didn't wish to lose me, and came up with an imaginative solution that would satisfy everyone. If he could secure national approval he would get my post in NAMMA upgraded – after all, he reasoned, the flight test programme was becoming more important with time. And by chance, he concluded, he had the ideal candidate for the 'upgraded' job. Sold! So I stayed.

I had joined NAMMA when it had about ninety people, but as confidence in the project strengthened so too did the staff numbers, reaching about 190 two years later. One office, which a Luftwaffe lieutenant colonel shared with an RAF squadron leader, threw up a remarkable coincidence. These two were veterans of the Second World War. To begin with, the atmosphere between them was somewhat stilted, particularly when it emerged that one had been a Messerschmitt pilot and the other had flown Spitfires. The ice only really thawed when the chaps discovered that they might have taken part in the same campaign, leading to an examination of logbooks and the inevitable recollection of certain flights – together with descriptive manoeuvres with hands, as only fighter pilots can. They had almost certainly been in combat against each other. Clearly both lousy shots – but they'd lived to tell the tale and, henceforth, became extremely close pals.

I wasn't directly involved with avionics equipment procurement, but had a close interest in its, at times, acrimonious selection process. Indeed my FTI procurement was simplicity itself compared to the cut-throat selection of avionics, which had to conform, as closely as possible, to the magic 42½%, 42½%, 15% work-share agreement. Sometimes national preferences did not always make the best operational or programme sense. For very good operational reasons, the German navy insisted on a different radar, but this would be an expensive addition for only 112 aircraft; integration with the rest of the systems had to be assured and separate flight tests would be needed. This was doubly awkward because the Marineflieger wanted its production aircraft first. This was the tail wagging the dog, particularly as most of the performance characteristics of 'their' radar were virtually identical to the air force radar. In the end common sense prevailed and they accepted the same radar as the rest of the programme; collaboration meant compromise in some areas.

From an early stage the nations had formed a committee to discuss with NAMMA and Panavia the layout of the cockpits, including location of instruments and switches. This was clearly a most important group of aviators and their work was vital to achieving satisfactory ergonomics, leading later to harmonisation of switchology and procedures, including navigation and attack sequences. Much of this work later proved to have been on the mark, although my personal and minor criticism was the lack of foot-operated radio transmit and mute buttons (à la Buccaneer) in the rear cockpit.

One day a colleague and I had to go to the MBB complex on the outskirts of Munich, home of the avionics engineering management team. We were frequent visitors there and were always required to sign in before entering. On this day, we were surprised to find a huge queue in the entrance lobby, so we joined the end of the line. As we got closer we saw everyone taking off their jackets and rolling up their sleeves, so we did likewise, shortly receiving an atomised spray in the upper arm. We were then asked which department we worked for, and said we did not work there at all but had merely come for a meeting. Consternation – we had been given routine flu jabs! We thanked them and proceeded to our meeting, protected for the forthcoming winter.

As equipments were gradually decided, vital checks had to be made on the aircraft's weight and centre of gravity. NAMMA employed a man whose sole job was to perform these calculations, which were vital to the eventual performance of the aircraft. But it hardly seemed full-time work and I often wondered what the weights man did when he was not weighing – until a wag said "Oh, he just sits and waits!"

Definition of the avionics system was carried out by a separate, tri-national consortium, and following each selection Panavia would get down to integrating the component into the system. Individual testing by contractors was followed by sub-system rig testing before units ever saw the real aircraft. It was fascinating to see this performed, gradually increasing the level of integration until a whole MRCA avionics system was available. Flight-standard units would be subjected to rigorous flight testing, not in an MRCA but in an interim test vehicle. The choice of this avionics 'hack' had been the source of great controversy; the UK had proposed the Buccaneer, with Germany offering the Starfighter. NAMMA strongly favoured the Buccaneer because it was large enough to accommodate all of the MRCA's extensive equipment and the necessary FTI (much of it carried on the Buccaneer's rotating bomb-door). The Starfighter was clearly too small, but the argument raged for months, finally centring on the cost of the project. The presence within NAMMA of a former RAF engineering officer with Buccaneer experience, whose arguments were decisive, led to the Buccaneer being selected – but only after the number of hacks was reduced from three to two. These, loaned by the RAF, would be converted to MRCA standard by Marshall of Cambridge, who would design a layout to incorporate as much of the MRCA avionics as space would allow while leaving intact the Buccaneer's normal flight control and flight instrumentation system.

Incorporating MRCA's sophisticated digital flight control system was out of the question, which meant that the hack would not be able to investigate MRCA's automatic terrain following, although manual terrain following would not be a problem. Nevertheless, there was lots of useful work which would yield important trials information prior to final installation on MRCA itself.

When the hack contract was eventually signed, Sir Arthur Marshall gave a celebratory party. A couple of our members were staying in a little pub nearby. After the party, we were taken to 'The Green Man' at around midnight only to find it locked with no lights on and no bell. Silently (I doubt!) we walked around the building to discover only a single window ajar, but that was on the first floor. To people trained for their initiative, there seemed to be only one solution – the smallest man would be pushed through the window and he would then come downstairs and open the main door. So, our lightest (not me) was hoisted up in a remarkable show of strength and balance, disappearing into the first floor room. As he later recalled, he was immediately struck with fear on finding himself in someone's bedroom, with a person asleep in bed. The only thing to do was to tiptoe quietly out of the room, but when he arrived at the bedroom door it was locked. He saw the key on the bedside table and quietly let himself out. Phew!

After all the political wrangling, the hack programme was up against the time stops. If it got behind that of MRCA itself there was no point in having a hack, since MRCA could perform the tests itself. However, this would have denied the avionics programme the opportunity to evaluate equipment performance early and to make any necessary changes prior to the more expensive and even more time-critical MRCA prototype programme.

An odd aspect of my NAMMA tour was that all members belonged to 'the staff

association', a NATO-wide civilian organisation that equated to union membership
– a bit odd for a military man, and I never thought much about it until we were
called out on strike! I can't remember what the problem was except that it was
not one specifically at NAMMA, but the NATO 'union' called out all civilian staff
on a one-day strike and that embraced us. The RAF officers decided on a pow-
wow with our new air commodore, Roger Topp (who had led the celebrated
Black Arrows aerobatic team – which, famously, had looped twenty-two Hunters
at Farnborough) and we decided to quietly ignore the strike call. I don't think
this stance was particularly troublesome to the (real) civilian members of staff,
but membership of the staff association took another twist later. Under NATO
regulations, all members of staff voted for representatives to attend union meetings
in Brussels. Following the election I found to my embarrassment that I was now
one of NAMMA's representatives. Now this did give me a problem, since this was
tantamount to being a 'shop steward', which definitely ran counter to my military
principles. I discussed this with the air commodore, who decided that it could be
awkward if I declined – after all, I was serving under a contract and it would not
send the right message if an RAF member thought he was different to everyone else.
But our diplomatic DGM agreed that, conveniently, I would always be 'unavailable'
whenever meetings were called in Brussels.

Throughout the first two years the pace of progress was fantastic; we could see
that real aircraft were being built and that everyone wanted the project to succeed.
In a programme of that magnitude and cost there were bound to be problems,
but collaboration was there to stay. During that time there was one man who kept
his head more than others and who kept the programme on an even keel; it was
without question Wason Turner, the chief of the system engineering division. His
engineering knowledge, his skill at defusing problems and his ability to convince
doubters were outstanding.

Turner's deputy was an Italian, General Enzo Bianchi, a rotund gentleman with
a charming accent who was loved by everyone for his scatterbrain style. One day at
Rome airport, his driver was carrying his suitcase when the general bumped into a
chum. They nattered for a while and then went their own ways – but with Bianchi
asking his driver "Tell me, was I going or coming?" He was no fool, though; he
understood far more than he let on and his questions always hit the nail on the head.

When Wason Turner left NAMMA I decided that we must mark his departure
in some formal way. Throwing caution and expense to the wind, we booked a
posh restaurant and I asked General Bianchi to say a few polite words to mark the
departure. But he declined, saying that his English wasn't up to the mark. Despite
my protestations, he was adamant. But farewell words really should come from the
deputy, so I persevered, even getting quite angry with him. Eventually he agreed,
but he was nervous and we settled on his speaking for no more than five minutes.
In case of any last-minute awkwardness I lined up a back-up speaker.

The evening was a relaxed affair, with Bianchi being characteristically mischievous in trying to speak at completely the wrong time. But finally I gave him the nod to say his few words before we adjourned to the bar, whereupon he staggered us all by delivering one of the most amusing after-dinner speeches I have ever heard. He spoke for almost half an hour about Wason's contribution to the programme in a most clever way, demonstrating a level of English comprehension none of us suspected him to possess. It was brilliant.

Several years later, as a fledgling Tornado squadron commander, I was able to invite Wason Turner to Brüggen, as the then newest squadron was officially inaugurated with the latest-build standard aircraft. I think he enjoyed the occasion as much as I did, particularly as I was able to recount his remarkable contribution to the early programme.

As well as MRCA, another construction programme was going on in Munich throughout my first two years. To prepare for the 1972 Olympic Games the city was undergoing a facelift, including to its underground railway. The shopping centre, about half a mile long, was completely dug up, a huge hole appearing ready to drop in the new railway. There was muddy chaos for months, but in true German style it was all completed in time for the games. Built too were a new Olympic stadium and tower, the former with a distinctive modernistic glass roof and the latter, with a high-speed lift to the top, offering spectacular views across the city and the distant Alps. The period of the games was fantastic, although sadly overshadowed by the terrorist killing of Israeli athletes.

There was more international sport in Munich, for in 1974 the football World Cup was staged there. After the competition, the Olympic stadium became home to the famous Bayern Munich soccer team, but there were two other well known football clubs in the city, the first being Munich 1860. The other comprised a team of international stars from NAMMA! We played most weeks throughout the year, and although the football might not have been world class, everyone enjoyed the matches enormously. Once we played a team from the Royal Bavarian Ballet, which we thought would be a walkover. But we were staggered by their fitness, and they walloped us. We also played against the retired professionals of Munich 1860 who were about to depart on a tour of South America, where they would give demonstration matches, usually prior to league or international fixtures. Since they were normally paid for their appearances, Munich 1860 were anxious that we did not try to make money out of our game – we were not to charge spectators to watch. Of course our throngs of spectators normally amounted to about twenty; we explained that we played football for fun, not money, so the game went ahead. And what a performance it turned out to be. All the 1860 players had to have played for the first team and be over thirty-five. Four were in their fifties, one was sixty, and two of them had played in the 1936 German national team! The underlying skill of these chaps was a sight to witness and in the last ten minutes they simply turned up the pressure and strode to an easy 6–3 win. It was great fun. We might have lost the football, but in the subsequent drinking, which I was pleased they eagerly accepted, we won handsomely. What a great experience, and it was good for international relations.

Elsewhere, though, interesting international hurdles had to be overcome. Under the terms of the work-sharing agreement, MBB would build the centre fuselage, Aeritalia the wings and BAC the nose and tail sections. These companies would build those parts for all 950 of the aircraft (as I mentioned earlier, numbers changed throughout the project) and then ship their pieces to the other factories to be joined together, Meccano style. This technique called for great precision all round. There was no scope for error in measurements, no mistakes over imperial and metric measure – the latter would be used exclusively, even by BAC (several years before metrication became mandatory in the UK).

The component parts were shipped around Europe, despite political hurdles placed in the way. For example the Italian wings had to go via France to Germany because neutral Austria and Switzerland would not allow military machinery to cross their borders. By this stage of the game there was little that could stop the programme, and everyone was working at fever pitch to get the first prototype into the air. The pressure was on; would the dream be realised?

At that time my boss told me that, before he had joined NAMMA, he had worked on the international Kestrel vertical take-off programme and that participants had painted a special roundel on each aircraft. So we drew a tri-national air force roundel with 120-degree segments in each of the national air force colours. It looked good, and we suggested that the idea be adopted with the 'home' nation's segment uppermost; this was agreed for each of the nine prototypes.

These were all rapidly taking shape, each with its own specific series of tasks allocated to it, with the whole being integrated into the overall test programme. The allocated tests, in turn, led to a definition of the equipment and instrumentation for that particular prototype. Much equipment would not be available from the manufacturers for the first aircraft. Some early equipments would be to a lower standard than the final versions, so care had to be taken to ensure that items incorporated were both essential to and suitable for the tests.

The first three prototypes would be concentrating on handling and performance testing, and it had been decided that the full avionics suite would not be fitted to these aircraft. It had been assumed that the full system would be installed on subsequent aircraft regardless of the tests allocated to each, but equipment availability and expense later led some to question this approach. Specifically, the first Italian prototype, P05, was planned to be fitted with the full avionics system, even though some were arguing for a minimum avionics fit. While this debate was going on I visited Aeritalia in Turin looking at FTI, and it was clear that the build was going ahead assuming full avionics, and this led to a detailed discussion in the FTG. I saw the reasoning behind a reduced fit, but by then had learned a great deal about the

The official roll-out at Manching, 8 April 1974. The aircraft is still without ejection seats. (Photo reproduced by permission of Panavia Aircraft GmbH)

MRCA' s avionics system. Few people realised at that time that 'integrated' was the operative word, and it was not a matter of simply removing an item of equipment just because the tests on the aircraft did not merit it. Rather, virtually a whole avionics system was necessary simply to fly the aircraft – basic flight instrumentation was derived from only the full avionics suite. The Italians got their way – which was another example of NAMMA' s impartiality.

The world, aviation enthusiasts and spies alike, wished to see the aircraft and make their own judgements as to its performance. While the prototypes remained in the factories, security was simple to safeguard, but as soon as the stage was reached when aircraft needed to be out of doors, it was more of a problem.

It had been decided that the first prototype would be flown in Germany at MBB's Manching airfield. However, it was being assembled in the Ottobrunn factory, 90km south of Manching, and the only way to move it was by road. So at the appropriate moment the component parts of P01 were moved in secret, somewhat ignominiously covered by tarpaulins, during the night of 12 December 1973, to be finally assembled at Manching in preparation for ground tests and first flight.

Traditionally, all aircraft have a formal roll-out ceremony, when the new machine is presented to the governments, service chiefs, the press and the world. For MRCA, that came at Manching on 8 April 1974. P01, registration number D9591, looked magnificent in its red and white livery and sporting the new roundel. Sadly no ejection seats were fitted so the cockpits looked a bit odd – during tow-out, the brakeman sat on a wooden crate! Thereafter, the pressure was on to make the first flight and to demonstrate the aircraft at international airshows.

But progress was hampered by engine problems. There had been a much publicised first flight date of December 1973, but six months later MRCA had still not got off the ground. Indeed, modified engines did not arrive at Manching until July 1974. There was still public and political opposition in some quarters and the last thing that was needed was this lengthy delay, but that's the way of development programmes.

Being a member of the flight test team gave me inside information on the extensive on-aircraft system tests and taxi tests, all building confidence prior to first flight. I was aware when these were being carried out, and it was during final engine ground tests that I took my wife to Manching where, from outside the security fence, we could see the aircraft. She had suffered the long hours and the dramas too, but had no idea what MRCA looked like. Now was a fine chance for her to gain a sneak preview; standing atop the car, she could see the aircraft. Unfortunately one of the engines failed while she was watching; thereafter, I tried never to let her see the aircraft again prior to first flight.

Finally, though, things looked more encouraging, and the well-prepared plan to call together senior government and service chiefs for the first flight was initiated. At the appointed time, all the highly paid VIPs arrived and were wined and dined by Panavia – only to have their hopes dashed as another snag caused a postponement. So the VIPs departed and Panavia worked furiously to get the aircraft ready again. The distinguished guests reconvened on 14 August 1974. At the eleventh hour a gearbox change caused frustration all round, some of the VIPs getting a little fed up despite the gin and tonic.

There had been great debate and rivalry about who would crew the first flight, but finally, later that afternoon, Paul Millett (BAC) and Nils Meister (MBB) climbed aboard. There was nothing but relief as the MRCA finally took to the air. It was the most beautiful sight I have seen, the only maiden flight I ever witnessed. It was perfect and, at that moment, the dream had been realised. Shakespeare's question was indeed answered, for MRCA was indeed 'to be' – and a huge party followed. Simultaneously I established another dream – to fly the MRCA myself.

The other prototypes were taking shape in all three countries and, in parallel with the aircraft build, there was separate production and testing of equipment to be fitted to those aircraft. I was most interested in the avionics; some units had been flown in the Buccaneer hacks, and all had been subjected to integration tests on complex avionics rigs at Warton and Munich. This latter series of tests gave us the first real chance to play with the equipment and its switches and to evaluate its performance prior to installation in MRCA.

Airborne at last. The prototype MRCA takes off from Manching on 14 August 1974.
(Photo reproduced by permission of Panavia Aircraft GmbH)

Space was found, on the first flight, for a small number of commemorative, signed, first-day covers.

Returning to the first Italian prototype, PO5, its first flight was delayed by engine snags, eventually taking place in December 1975. Sadly, this aircraft crashed after only nine flights following a problem with a pitch control computer. The damage was so severe that there was doubt whether it would be cost-effective to rebuild it. But the other nations did not wish to give up one of their prototypes so, despite the lack of decision, the Italians got on and rebuilt it. It was not, however, until March 1978 that it flew again.

In the meantime, the second Italian prototype, PO9, flew in February 1977. I later came across this aircraft at Decimomannu (Sardinia) in October 1979 while I was a flight commander on a Buccaneer squadron. I took the opportunity to visit the flight test team and persuaded them to let me show squadron members around. It happened that the Aeritalia navigator was sick, and I was asked to fly a few test flights with their test pilot; "You can remember how to switch it on, Dick – they're simple tests!" I assumed this was the Italian sense of humour again, but just imagine the subsequent furore if I had flown and something had gone wrong – front-line Buccaneer navigator flying a Panavia prototype aircraft operated by Aeritalia in Italy. It doesn't bear thinking about.

In the earlier equipment-selection process, compromise could not always be reached and the result was a loss of interoperability and commonality between the participants. Critically, weapons carriage was to become a bugbear. An early option had been conformal (aerodynamic) carriage of weapons but this approach was rightly discounted as being too expensive. The alternative was the normal and well-proven method of hanging bombs beneath the aircraft from weapons carriers. Extraordinarily, the nations could not agree on the method of suspension, and two different and incompatible methods were adopted. This meant, for example, that RAF bombs could not be hung onto a German aircraft without modification to the lug carriage system. This approach undermined the fundamental principle of interoperability and had to be addressed urgently to adopt a suitable fix. Issues such as this led inevitably to increased cost, delay and additional flight-testing.

At the end of my contract I 'rejoined' the RAF, moving to the MoD in London to set up a new MRCA office to oversee the operational introduction into RAF service. Central to this was the preparation of a formal concept of operations to be prepared within one year by a three-man team led by a group captain. We had to work extremely hard during this period, with the job being a fascinating insight into the future shape, size and disposition of what was to become the backbone of the RAF's front-line offensive capability. It was reassuring to find much later that our recommendations had been implemented just about in full.

During that year I realised that two significant things had been overlooked. First, no one had thought through how the avionics system would be programmed with flight-plan data. A tape recorder had been built into the system to allow data to be fed in by tape, but no thought had been given as to how the tape would be prepared.

New mission-planning devices were being proposed by several companies so we asked industry to produce a planning tool whose output was a magnetic tape that could be inserted directly into the aircraft's computer system. This oversight was so basic and the need for a solution so urgent that I wrote a technical specification, had it approved, and got a contract awarded after a competition, all in the space of about nine months – supersonic speed for the MoD!

Nor had anyone considered auto-TF training by front-line crews. When I asked about this I was told that there was not a problem and that MRCA would use the UK's existing and extensive low-flying system. But when I inquired about training at night and in poor weather, there was a stony silence. Many thought this was not necessary; because the aircraft was capable of such flying all by itself, the only difference between good weather, daytime flying and the opposite extreme was a simple switch in the cockpit! I argued that nothing could be further from reality, citing USAF experience with the F-111, where psychological pressures had proved intense when night fell or the weather deteriorated. Aircrews feel 'uncomfortable' close to the ground when they cannot see features and obstructions. The RAF was buying an all-weather aircraft and, I argued, crews must be permitted to train in poor weather, at night, at low level.

I needed to strengthen the case, and arranged a brief conversion course on the F-111 to gather further evidence. Training with the Americans at Upper Heyford in Oxfordshire, I was to see auto-TF at first hand, using a system similar to that installed in MRCA. The subsequent flight demonstration was eye-watering, as I was shown just how close the TF system would take an aircraft to vertical cliff faces or towers without reacting to them. I could see why there was a psychological hurdle to overcome.

I argued that we should open up part of our low-flying system for bad-weather TF flying and at night. The flight safety and air traffic control implications would need urgent study and this was initiated after I left the MoD, but I was later delighted to find that my recommendations had been accepted in full, even exceeded. In addition, Goose Bay in Canada was later used for extensive in-cloud TF flying for operational squadrons.

Two other significant events occurred during my short time in the MoD. The first, of great interest to many people, was the selection of a name for the MRCA. During its conception and development the participating nations had sought a name but had not been able to establish the common solution preferable in a collaborative programme. During my year in London, proposals were sought and NAMMA wrote a paper. Our office suggested 'Panther', and there were several others. In the end, the board of directors agreed on 'Tornado', the only name submitted that meant the same in all three languages. In fact it was a most apt name for such a potent weapons system. The second was the UK's announcement that it would build the F2 stretched fighter version with a considerably different avionics fit.

A total of 165 aircraft would be procured from within the originally announced number of UK Tornados to be purchased.

Collaboration might not have yielded the cheapest programme, although it certainly bought economy of scale. Some of the development problems, as I have noted, seemed purely political, and there were rivalries also between the participating services. Some were so severe that under conventional circumstances, the programme might have been cancelled, and it is true that, at one time or another, each of the participants would have cancelled a national programme. So the tri-national memorandum of understanding provided a certain stability, for one nation could not withdraw unilaterally.

The aircraft would enter service with all four air forces (German air, German navy, Italian and RAF), and of course there was a fierce export campaign; the Royal Saudi Air Force came on-board within the massively important *Al Yamamah* project. The big money was in production – so the final build of 977 Tornados represented an astronomic achievement for European industry and showed real competition for the US. Further vindication of the decision to collaborate.

It was an immense privilege to have been there at such an early stage. And the icing on my cake came in later flying the Tornado as both squadron and station commander. It was also wonderful to take an aircraft to Manching for a day in 1984 to participate in the annual Panavia/NAMMA day out and to renew acquaintance with so many friends, including my old boss, then chief flight test engineer for MBB. So I was lucky enough to be able to confirm at first hand that the original dreams of the early 1970s had come to pass. But the Tornado remaining the backbone of the RAF's offensive capability until nearly 2020 – an in-service life of almost forty years? No, that's something I could never have imagined in 1971 when I joined the project.

CHAPTER 2

GIANT VOICE

The first few RAF Tornado units to form took the numbers of distinguished strategic bomber squadrons: IX, 27, and 617. Many suspected that this owed something to the man who was chief of the air staff at the time; the man who, in the Vulcan's dying days, had ordered the famous 'Beetham bomber' to be launched on its epic raid against the runway at Port Stanley. But whatever the reason it reinforced the impression that the aircraft was a new V-bomber. Of course it was nothing of the sort, either in range or payload. And in any case the Vulcan's primary *raison d'être*, carrying the UK's strategic deterrent, had been passed many years earlier to the Royal Navy's Polaris submarine force.

The USAF's 'Giant Voice' competition seemed primarily to be the domain of its B-52 Stratofortresses. Even though F-111s had participated in later years, it was very much a 'strategic' event. Thus it was a surprise to many – and perhaps quite a bold move – when the Tornado, a 'tactical' aircraft, was dispatched across the pond to compete. It would be very interesting to see how it would do, and Vic Bussereau is able to tell us – because he was there.

WING COMMANDER VIC BUSSEREAU (RETD)

When P01 first took to the air I was a Phantom FGR2 navigator at RAF Brüggen on 31 Squadron – and from then on I set my sights on joining one of the early MRCA strike/attack squadrons. Perhaps I could also get involved in the aircraft's development programme first.

Luck was on my side when, almost four years after that first flight, I found myself starting a three-year tour at NAMMA in Munich, via a stint at the RAF College at Cranwell struggling through the general duties aero systems course with nineteen other students. My time in Munich passed quickly as the development programme of the Tornado continued apace. As I approached the end of my time at NAMMA I awaited my posting with some trepidation – as there were rumours that I would be posted back to the Vulcan force I had left in 1973 (there were still remnants around). However, I was greatly relieved and very pleased to find that I was to become the navigation leader on the second Tornado GR1 squadron to form. This turned out, after some indecision, to be 617 Squadron at RAF Marham.

Following refresher training and Tornado courses, I arrived in November 1982 to join 617 – still officially to reform after disbanding with its Vulcan B2s the previous December. Little did I realise the interesting times which lay ahead.

At that time the squadron had only two aircraft and two crews. Work on the new aircraft and on a brand-new HAS site had its challenges as more aircraft, crews, equipment and, significantly, release to service clearances gradually became available. The squadron officially reformed in January 1983 and we continued towards our NATO commitment in the overland strike and attack roles. Meanwhile, in the latter part of that year a rumour started doing the rounds that Tornados were to take part in the USAF's Strategic Air Command Bombing and Navigation competition (elements of which were, from time to time, known as Exercise Giant Voice) in the USA. These rumours followed a visit to the USA by a team of RAF specialists to observe the 1983 competition; one of these was Squadron Leader Alan Dyer-Perry, a 617 Squadron navigator flight commander with F-111 experience, and another was Squadron Leader Nigel Huckins, a QWI from Honington. Unbeknown to 617 at that time, Nigel had been working closely with the Tornado in-service software maintenance team (TISMT), and in particular with Howard Robinson, who was BAe's representative detached to TISMT, to explore changes to the aircraft's operational flight programme aimed at enhancing the Tornado's capabilities for the event.

The first SAC competition had been held in 1948, and it had become an annual event, barring the 1960s and 1970s when Vietnam operational commitments had prevailed. The RAF first partook with B-29 Washingtons in 1951 but did not return again until 1957, when two Vulcans and two Valiants competed. Vulcans then participated in many of the subsequent competitions.

Rumours were replaced by confirmation that 617 Squadron would represent the RAF in the 1984 competition with two teams of two aircraft, supported by Victor K2 tankers from 55 Squadron, also based at Marham. The detachment was to deploy to Ellsworth AFB in South Dakota, a large B-52 base, from the end of August to mid-October, first to familiarise both squadrons with operating in the US environment and then to compete. Our exercise was to be known as 'Prairie Vortex' – PV for short.

The competition, which would be held over a three-week period, was clearly going to be extremely challenging for 617, flying a complex aircraft that had been in service for barely two years. We would be up against B-52s, USAF FB-111s, USAFE F-111s and RAAF F-111s, some thirty-six opponents in all. Moreover, we would be flying sorties of over five hours, compared with our typical one-hour-forty-minute duration. So, unlike the other competitors, we'd require tanker support. On the plus side we would benefit from the experience of our many ex-V force navigators.

The elements of the competition for which Tornados had been entered would be flown in two phases. The first would be a daytime hi-lo-hi profile to the Nellis ranges with both simulated SAM and fighter threats on the low-level portion, which would culminate with practice bomb drops on two separate no-show targets (aimed by reference to offset features visible to radar) some twenty miles apart. Phase two would comprise two sorties, one day and one night, both of which would be hi-lo-hi-lo-hi profiles. Each sortie would include a high-level target and four low-level targets with simulated weapon releases; the accuracy of these attacks would be assessed by ground radar bomb scoring units. The low-level routes through Wyoming, Montana and South Dakota were cleared for automatic TF in cloud if necessary. In addition to weapon accuracy, timing to weapon release point and ECM effectiveness was also to be assessed.

Air-to-air refuelling (AAR) with the Victor tankers was to be an essential ingredient throughout. However, this would be especially so on phase two when the Tornados would climb out from low level after the first two targets to RV with the tankers, uplift sufficient fuel in the most expeditious manner, and then return to low level to complete a further two targets. Finally they would climb again for the transit back to Ellsworth.

Following crew changes made in early April, six crews were selected to work up for the competition. The pilots were chosen for their flying skills, particularly AAR, their airmanship and their 'big-match temperament', while the navigators needed outstanding radar expertise – and the experience and ability to work with degraded systems. Those ex-V force navigators would now prove their worth!

The work-up started immediately, with much day and night RBSU work at Spadeadam and West Freugh ranges. This was limited to the use of the only two aircraft that, at the time, had competition-specific modifications fitted, but it allowed the crews to get used to the simulated releases. This process involved the cut of a tone which was broadcast from the aircraft at the release point, and combined it with tracking information obtained by the ground radar sites and release parameters obtained from each aircraft's data-dump facility. From this information, simulated weapon impact points were determined and scores calculated.

The UK training was interrupted by a deployment, known as PV1, to Ellsworth AFB for two weeks in May. Three Tornados and two Victors plus support equipment and ground personnel were deployed, staging through Goose Bay in Canada. This allowed crews to operate against a number of the ranges to be used during the competition for simulated attacks with tone releases. Significantly, the routes chosen allowed many of the competition routes and ranges to be criss-crossed. Even though we had to remain outside thirty degrees of competition tracks, this provided an opportunity to obtain vital radar intelligence. Finally, it provided aircrew and ground crew the opportunity to identify and resolve problems when operating out of Ellsworth, proving a vital lead-in for the main detachment.

PV1 was not without its interesting moments. One lesson was that the four-external-tank fit for the Tornado GR1, with the standard of engine fitted at that time, was not compatible with AAR from Victors for crossing the Atlantic. At the typical heights for AAR, the Tornado required afterburner on one engine in order to plug in successfully and maintain contact. As the aircraft got heavier, almost full afterburner was needed on one engine. This placed unforeseen demand on Victor fuel capacity, which resulted in a fuel emergency situation on recovery to Goose Bay. We concluded that three external tanks would be better for long, medium-level transits.

My new pilot, Flight Lieutenant Steve Legg, and I enjoyed the delights of first-class travel to Ellsworth courtesy of an RAF Hercules, but we brought a Tornado back to the UK. The first leg to Goose Bay went without incident; however, the leg from Goose Bay to Marham proved far more interesting. The first refuelling bracket went smoothly, but on the second our prod missed the basket. Trying again, our probe tipped the drogue, which immediately broke off from the hose, leaving the remains of it flailing around on the end of our probe. The hose, now minus its basket, took on the appearance of a demented snake. At this point we were about halfway between Greenland and Iceland, and had concerns that part of the drogue had gone down the starboard intake, damaging the engine. The Victor crew worked out that we would be better continuing on to Iceland, and this we did without further incident, but with the remains of the drogue continuing to flap on the end of our probe. The Victor remained with us until we were within radio range of Iceland before continuing, while we made a precautionary single-engined landing at Keflavik.

A recovery Hercules arrived the following day, and technicians determined that the engine had not suffered any damage. However, Steve and I were 'invited' to continue to the UK in the Hercules while another crew flew our Tornado. An eventful episode which was made more pleasant by the night stopover in Iceland in a wooden chalet on the edge of a lava field, where we took a midnight swim in daylight in a warm-water spring. Regrettably, Steve and I had no money with us and the owner of the chalet would not accept a credit card; I recall it took several months for Marham's accounts section to reimburse him!

Back in the UK, work-up for the competition began in earnest. It was decided that OC 617 Squadron, Wing Commander Tony Harrison, would not fly in the competition as his presence on the ground would be essential. All six crews would get equal exposure to the RBSU ranges, AAR and, significantly, extended length profiles.

Despite problems with aircraft serviceability, the programme stayed largely on track. Many more simulated attacks with tone releases were carried out against no-show targets using offset bombing techniques during June, building up over July and August to full-length profiles, with 55 Squadron playing its part by providing the essential AAR support. This gave both Tornado and Victor crews the opportunity to practise the join-up technique that was devised for phase two of the competition by Alan Dyer Perry and Flight Lieutenant Dick Lotinga. This involved using Tornado radar and air-to-air TACAN, as there would be no external agency available to assist. The aircraft would converge on reciprocal headings towards a datum point and, at given split range, the Victor would turn through 180° and the Tornados would manoeuvre to roll out behind and just below the tanker. Once sufficient fuel had been taken, the Tornados, already on correct heading to re-join the low-level route, would drop off. Timing was critical, with each second early or late on target resulting in points loss, so it's easy to see how important the refuelling RV was.

Meanwhile there was much activity on the ground, with the focus on Nigel Huckins, who was detached to 617 from Honington to act as the project officer. Under his supervision, two non-competition squadron navigators started detailed planning for both the continued training in the US and the competition, while two of the competition navigators assessed the radar film from PV1. In addition, support was provided by Flight Lieutenant Mac McBeath from the Joint Air Reconnaissance and Intelligence Centre who, using a point-positioning system, started working on vertical photography supplied by the USAF in the competition briefing pack. This, combined with the information gleaned from PV1 radar film, enabled initial selection and mensuration of both radar offsets and fix points. Much of this vertical photography was of poor quality and was up to three years out of date. However, the biggest problem throughout the whole exercise was mapping, with large-scale coverage of the required areas in the US being either unavailable or difficult to obtain. TISMT support continued with assistance to develop further the aircraft software, as well as developing programmes for a computer which was used to store and analyse data produced from PV1.

The engineers were also very busy during this phase preparing the aircraft and embodying competition modifications. Eight aircraft were readied, with the intention of deploying six. A contractor working party from RAF Honington carried out laser modifications, while squadron engineers, supported by additional Marham personnel, strove to embody other required modifications. These included the provision of a groundspeed readout on the HUD, increasing the number of waypoints and fix points available, increasing offset distances to twenty nautical miles and fitting the laser ranger.

At last came the great day, 29 August, with six Tornados and four Victors deploying via Goose Bay. The second, and major, part of Prairie Vortex (PV2) had begun. In fact elements had started some ten days earlier when an advance party had left to set up the combined squadron operations, while a ground survey party had deployed to Ellsworth in early August. Comprising Nigel Huckins and navigators Flight Lieutenants Bob Sinclair and Graham Heath, and Squadron Leader Mike Ellaway, this was an invaluable part of the overall exercise. Split into two teams, they visited all four of the ranges, with exotic names such as Wibaux, Gillette, Scobie and Powell, that would be used on phase two of the competition. The teams took many photographs of likely pre-bomb fixes and radar offsets, noting details such as construction and material, likely radar characteristics, possible terrain screening and clutter around each point. Four-wheel-drive vehicles were required for some areas, and they even hired a light aircraft to cover more extreme areas. On return to Ellsworth the data was recorded and plotted, and offsets and fix points mensurated using the point-positioning system. All was now ready for the flying to start.

The main party soon settled into their new environment, with everybody living in hotels in Rapid City, a town thirty minutes drive away. While the aircrew lodged in a basic, no-frills motel, our adjutant found himself in the wonders of the Rapid City Hilton – as, he told us, he held the imprest and needed a safe in his room.

Flying commenced with academic range sorties on the strategic training ranges which were to be used. Flying against the competition targets was, as one would expect, prohibited; however, radar offsets selected as a result of the radar intelligence collected in May and the ground survey could, in many cases, be evaluated. Furthermore, to augment the inadequate vertical photographs and large-scale mapping in the offset areas, crews were briefed to take vertical photos of the areas from 5,000 feet using hand-held cameras.

By mid-September the academic range sorties were complete, the support team had reviewed all the data and crunched more numbers to refine values, and the final offset selections had been made. It was now time to test aircrew, aircraft and the work done by the support team by bringing together all the ingredients required for the competition. Aircraft performance was being assessed, as well as the scores achieved by the aircrew. It was almost time to nominate the four crews who would compete.

Although the priority for the detachment was never in doubt – to win all three of the elements of the competitions for which the Tornado had been entered – there were many opportunities to visit some of the notable features of the surrounding area and to explore the delights of Rapid City. Six of the more adventurous aircrew clubbed together to buy a car, a banger they called 'Elvira', which travelled far and wide in their hands. Others, using hire cars or vehicles provided by the USAF, visited places in and around the Black Hills. Mount Rushmore, with its carvings of four US presidents, was a must. I and other squadron navigators formed a group that became known as 'scuttle's tours' after the well-known Benny Hill character, Fred Scuttle. Our 'tour' went to Deadwood one bitterly cold Saturday; while we didn't see either Doris Day or the Deadwood stage, we did have a bowl of soup to warm up in the saloon where Wild Bill Hickok was shot in the back while playing cards. We even climbed the hill to Mount Moriah cemetery, where Hickok and Calamity Jane lie in adjacent graves.

Close by our motel was the Colonial Bar, which became very much 'our pub'. We met many interesting folks there, including a number of FBI agents who visited one evening with their wives. We also met up with a geologist who, when we suggested it would be fun to blow up the very large pumpkins which were sitting on the bar, offered us the opportunity to do just that. We went off into the hills with a couple of the large vegetables, and he produced a brown satchel containing sticks of some form of explosive. The pumpkins were wired up with a detonator, I was allowed the privilege off pushing down the handle, and up they went. A dead tree was next to explode, before we found a deep, black pool of water in which to sink one of the sticks of explosive. The plume of water produced was most satisfying! Rather alarmingly, the geologist turned up at Ellsworth on the day the Tornados finally departed for the UK – carrying, once again, the brown satchel. He tried to present two of the crews with small parcels, an offer which was politely refused. We hurriedly escorted him to Ellsworth's main gate, being highly relieved when he drove off into the distance.

Another vivid memory is of a 'scuttle's tour' into Wyoming to visit Devil's Tower, which featured in the 1978 sci-fi film *Close Encounters of the Third Kind*. On arriving at the base of the tower we unloaded kit from the car boot, and a rather reluctant navigator was made to don ropes and hard hat to be photographed posing as though about to scale the sheer face. After climbing the first fifteen feet and then giving up, some genuine climbers appeared, having just descended from the top, and remarked that it was a mighty fine day for the climb. A very embarrassing moment for me!

Returning to the competition it was now time for the final part of the work-up – the full-length training profiles. By this time the teams had been selected:

RAF 1:   Flight Lieutenant John MacDonald and Squadron Leader Alan Dyer-Perry, Flight Lieutenant Steve Legg and Squadron Leader Vic Bussereau.
Reserves: Flight Lieutenants Jim Davidson and John Huggett
RAF 2:   Squadron Leader Pete Dunlop and Flight Lieutenant Dick Middleton, Flight Lieutenants Iain Hunter and Dermot Dolan.
Reserves: Flight Lieutenants Dick Lotinga and Mike Ellaway

We practised full sorties for both phases. Phase one went without incident: Victor AAR en route; descend to low level into the Nellis ranges; release a practice bomb on each of the two targets in range 76; climb out and take on more fuel; accompany the Victor back to Ellsworth. The phase two practices, though, had some interesting moments. The route required us to auto-TF over high ground, approaching some 8,000-foot high ridges. Quite spectacular scenery, though Steve Legg and I flew about sixty per cent of our trips at night. But at last observing in daylight what we had already completed at night was a moment to remember. I must say here that the auto-TF function worked impeccably.

One issue which did concern us was the weather. Although towards the end of the detachment there were some very cold days, we also experienced some extremely high temperatures during the work-up and changes could be rapid. On one evening a sortie had to be cancelled when a cockpit canopy could not be opened because of high temperatures during the day. Those high temperatures also set off some significant thunderstorms along the routes we were to fly. One night, our met officer from Marham, who was with us, warned that we might see some big boomers.

After witnessing a spectacular thunderstorm at low level, one navigator was heard to say after landing that he had pulled down his tinted visor and continued with Dire Straits playing loudly through the cockpit voice recorder. High temperatures also caused considerable turbulence at times, an issue especially when refuelling. On one occasion when taking on fuel, Steve and I hit severe turbulence and I recall looking down on the top surfaces of the Victor as we fell out of the drogue. We were very circumspect for the remainder of that sortie.

I haven't so far mentioned the electronic warfare aspect of the competition. The Skyshadow countermeasures pod was a relatively new addition to Tornado's inventory, and 617's experience with it was limited. During the work-up the pod was programmed by the RAF Electronic Warfare Operational Support Establishment to counter the expected, simulated SAM threats. The establishment also provided on-site support at Ellsworth to maintain the pods, as well as offering much-needed guidance on employment.

The competition commenced properly in early October, with our master plan devised to ensure maximum flexibility should the prime aircraft become unserviceable at any time up to take-off. Phase one sorties brought the added spice of having to evade Canadian CF-101 Voodoo aircraft en route to the target area. But things went well, and all four crews felt confident after completion of this phase.

Phase two commenced ten days later. The first of the two sorties for each crew was supposed to be at night; however, as the slots allocated to the RAF teams were at the end of the aircraft stream, our sorties were flown in early-morning daylight. Three of the four crews reported that all seemed to go well, with radar offsets found and timing good. However, John MacDonald and Alan Dyer-Perry experienced a major problem, with only some quick thinking salvaging anything at all from their sortie. After the medium-level target and while preparing to descend, they noticed that the main computer ground position seemed to have jumped about two miles; this was something that happened occasionally in those days and was confirmed by the radar picture. The intention was to fix the computer by matching the radar picture with the moving map display – not a particularly accurate method but the best available in the circumstances. But a bigger problem then occurred when the spring-loaded fix accept/reject switch suffered a mechanical failure, losing its spring. There was now no way the fix just completed could be accepted. The only way that the computer could now be updated was to first update the inertial platform by carrying out unplanned, visual, on-top fixes and, when completed, recycle the computer to get it to accept the inertial position. While trying to sort this issue they were also doing the descent checks, making contact with the strategic training range and carrying out the appropriate weapon switchery. Thus the first target was not a success, and in Alan Dyer-Perry's words, "the score was not of competition standard – or any other standard". However, working very much as a team, they adopted a makeshift routine, not practised before, which produced excellent results on the remaining three targets as well as enabling them to make an accurate RV with their tanker before the final two low-level targets.

The last competition sortie was a daytime task against the ranges. Again the RAF were at the end of the aircraft stream, so this time, perversely, our allocated slots were at night. The only unserviceability I recall was a partial failure of the Skyshadow pod on my aircraft. However, we did have a problem when trying to RV with our tanker for the mid-point AAR slot. The join up was hampered by cloud and we finally plugged in late, still heading in the direction of the descent point. By the time we reached the point we still hadn't taken enough fuel and, to remain within the airspace allocated for AAR, the Victor had then to fly a racetrack pattern. Steve was working hard to stay plugged in throughout the turn as the aircraft's weight increased and, by the time we had the required fuel we were flying away from our descent point and had lost time. However, by increasing to maximum permitted speed we sorted out the timing by the time we reached our next low-level target. The remainder went as planned, and then it was climb to height and return to Ellsworth one last time.

All that remained was to pack up the detachment, and the Tornados and Victors left Ellsworth on 22 October, accompanied by an engineering support team. The remainder of the detachment left a few days later in a VC10. The results were to be announced at a three-day symposium at Barksdale AFB at the end of October, so, having returned to Marham, all the competing aircrew together with Tony Harrison, Wing Commander Andy Valance (OC 55 Squadron) and Group Captain Bob O'Brien (OC RAF Marham), found that they would be flying out to Barksdale with a number of the engineers from both 617 and 55 for the symposium the following week. Best uniforms were to be taken, as well as new flying suits.

We were joined there by a variety of very senior RAF officers, including the C-in-C Strike Command and the AOC No 1 Group. The symposium got under way the following day; however, the part that we were all waiting for, the results ceremony, didn't start until 2100 hours. All the competing crews assembled in a large auditorium, together with the VIPs. As the results were put up, one by one, on a vast board at the back of the stage, the suspense built. But finally came what we had all been waiting for – confirmation that 617 Squadron had done the business!

- The Curtis E LeMay bombing trophy, awarded to the bomber crew compiling the most points in high- and low-level bombing and time control, was won by Pete Dunlop and Dick Middleton, who scored 2,616 points out of a possible 2,650. Second place went to Steve and me with 2,612 points. In third place, trailing by thirty-one points, was a B-52 crew. Altogether forty-two crews had taken part.

- The John C Meyer memorial trophy, awarded to an F-111 or Tornado team compiling the highest damage expectancy from their bombing, was won by one of the two Tornado teams. Their scores were assessed on both low-level bombing and evasive tactics using ECM. The award went to Pete Dunlop and Dick Middleton in one aircraft, with Iain Hunter and Dermot Dolan in the second. They achieved a score of 90.43% (our Skyshadow pods had worked). The second RAF team of John MacDonald and Alan Dyer-Perry, and Steve and me were awarded third place with 83.08%.

- In the Mathis Trophy, competed for by twenty-one teams and awarded to the unit with the highest points for both high- and low-level bombing, RAF team two came second, while my team came sixth.

We all acknowledged that the Victor tankers had been vital to our success. Of course they could not win events for us. But such was the severity of the timing penalties that, if the Victors hadn't been where and when we needed them they could certainly have lost us the competition.

Naturally the rest of the evening and night were a bit of a blur. I seem to recall that the hotel swimming pool was the focus for quite a few hours – it seemed a good idea to have a dip in flying suits – and we certainly consumed a few beers. The following day was devoted to recovery in time for the symposium banquet, again attended by all participating crews. It came as bit of a surprise to note that there was a singalong in which we were all expected to participate – this included each Wing entertaining all present with a song. As there were no known words to the Dambusters March the RAF contingent decided to be very British and sang Jerusalem!

Best uniforms were required for the presentation ceremony, which saw Pete Dunlop, Dick Middleton, Iain Hunter and Dermot Dolan weighed down with silverware. Following a quick lunch we all boarded the VC10 for our trip back to Marham. The high jinks on the journey home are another story.

It is now thirty-four years since the Tornado GR1 entered RAF squadron service. The aircraft then represented a new era in the arena of offensive airpower, and the SAC bombing and navigation competition in 1984 was the first significant operational and international challenge for the aircraft – and indeed the first triumph. The results obtained were outstanding, remembering this was before the era of GPS and smart bombs. Prairie Vortex required a stupendous effort and consumed resources, but provided the opportunity to gain a much deeper understanding of the aircraft and its systems. It paved the way for the Tornado to be a big player for many, many years to come; we had certainly spoken with a Giant Voice.

CHAPTER 3

INTERNATIONAL TRAINING

At the time Tornado entered service collaboration was the flavour of the day, so when it came to setting up the training pattern it seemed natural to adopt an international model. The three nations would share a conversion unit located at RAF Cottesmore in the East Midlands, staffed and funded proportionally. Operationally, there were differences between the participants; not least, the various air forces planned to hang different weapons on their aircraft. Therefore the syllabus of the international unit would be limited to common aspects: initial conversion; formation and instrument flying; using the navigation system; terrain following; and so on. Students would then move on to national 'advanced' conversion units.

There were pros and cons to this pattern. Presentationally it was outstanding; politicians could point to the virtues of European cooperation, and perhaps also to economies of scale. But reaching agreement on any point, however minor, was less easy with three nations to be satisfied, while economies were, at least partly, offset by the cost to each nation of running a two-stage training process.

This mixed training pattern lasted for around twenty years before divergence in aircraft standards provided the trigger for a reversion to purely national processes, and today we find the RAF's Tornado OCU looking much like any other RAF training unit.

Curiously, when I was an MoD staff officer in the late 1980s, one of my jobs was to produce the 'EFA introduction to service' plan (the aircraft which eventually became Typhoon). During my work the assumption was that EFA would follow down the international training path, with a couple of bases in Spain being front runners for the location. I can imagine there would have been a long queue for posts as instructors in the sun! But that idea never got beyond the drawing board, with each of the four Typhoon nations going alone from the outset. Perhaps, in the end, the lessons drawn from the initial Tornado training experience had, on balance, been negative.

One of the early instructors at the international Tornado unit was Mike Crook, whom I know from Jaguar days. With both of us now being among the army of retired RAF people who have settled in Norfolk, we still see a good deal of each other at social gatherings. Mike, these days, is very much into gliding, and repeatedly tries to entice me to join him. For now, I'll settle for hearing what he has to say about training at Cottesmore.

SQUADRON LEADER MIKE CROOK (RETD)

It was July 1982 and my time on the Jaguar had, as I then thought, come to an end. In my attempts to escape a ground tour I had accepted a posting to the newly formed Tri-National Tornado Training Establishment. This was, and is, a mouthful by anybody's standards and it came to be known as the TTTE – the Triple-T-E. I was to be the deputy chief instructor and boss of the standards squadron. For political reasons the chief instructor and deputy had to come from different contributing nations, so my boss was Klaus Kahlert, a very amiable German and a capable pilot with whom I got on very well.

I arrived at Cottesmore in 1982 to start the ground school; because of the complexities of the new aircraft this was to last for a month – a length of time unknown in any other ground school I had ever attended. The course was very well designed and managed. Every morsel of information seemed to be essential, particularly when it came to the final exam; if my memory serves me there were 100 pieces of essential information, so the pass mark was 100%.

Of course the most important part of the ground school was the mandatory visit to Ruddles Brewery in nearby Oakham, all part of the course bonding process. Whilst the Germans were always very hospitable with their *Jever Pils* and the Italians with their *Chianti*, there is no doubt that Ruddles County scored highly in their estimations. As OC Standards Squadron later on, I naturally felt this to be an important part of my standardisation function, and I accompanied many such visits – although after the first few conducted tours I generally made a beeline straight for the hospitality room.

Following ground school the course progressed according to plan and we all graduated in September. Although not strictly essential for my job, I had succeeded in persuading the management that, in the interest of my street cred, I should also do the weapons conversion course which had recently been established at RAF Honington. So a further three months followed with virtually no responsibilities other than to enjoy playing with this new toy, in activities such as air combat training, simulated attack profiles and weapons sorties.

Time passed rapidly at Honington and we soon arrived at the last block of flights, the operational phase. At that point my Tornado career, and indeed my flying career overall, very nearly came to grief in a big way. One sortie involved getting airborne with four 1,000lb concrete bombs, putting the aircraft up towards maximum all-up weight. I had been fully briefed on the need for a greater rotation at lift off, with a much higher than normal angle of attack; this would be akin to my experiences of taking off in a Jaguar loaded with a recce pod, and perhaps I was lulled into a false sense of security. I do remember thinking as we rotated that the aircraft was

The international staff of the Standards Squadron at the TTTE – British, Italian and German. Mike Crook is fifth from the left.

extremely reluctant to climb away and seemed a little 'wallowy'. As we sank into the shallow dip at the western end of the runway the penny finally dropped for both me and my navigator that we had completed this manoeuvre without the benefit of take-off flaps – despite challenge and response checks, duty pilot in the tower and a check from the runway caravan at the departure point.

This attempt to expand the Tornado's flight envelope had, of course, been seen by many who had watched us disappear over the horizon and vanish into the dip, then reappear and stagger away once I got some flap selected. So we made it back for a rather one-sided conversation with Duncan Griffiths, the then boss of TWCU. Considerably chastened, I completed the course and headed back to base to take up my post; not the most auspicious of starts.

I soon settled into life at Cottesmore, and what a great place it was. The tri-national aspect of the unit had many plus points. Firstly, Taceval, early-morning callouts, and the like became things of the past, for we were not an RAF establishment and played no part in operational force generation. Secondly, it was a great social environment. Each nation seemed to take it in turns to organise a mess function to celebrate its own national food and drink, a duty-free store was established on the site for the use of our European partners, and the Germans retained a small communications aircraft. This was to ferry pilots back and forth to Germany, but the primary cargo sometimes seemed to be *schweinshaxe*, **wurst** and barrels of *pils*.

There were three training squadrons, all staffed by instructors from all nations but each with a boss from a specific nation. Courses arrived every two weeks and were allocated to one of the training squadrons. On my standards unit, the position of boss rotated through each of the contributing nations; we looked after course content, validation and changes, instructor training, check rides and so on. There was night flying year-round, so there would normally be one squadron operating earlies, one through the main part of the day and one in the night phase.

The Tornado was a bit like a big Jaguar, which I had really enjoyed flying, but also had a shed load of new technology to do many of the things that the Jaguar couldn't. It had computers and management systems – and loads of other new, buzzword bits of kit that are commonplace nowadays. The variable-geometry wings were great for manoeuvring, the engines were big and extremely powerful, and because we always flew without external stores we were operating at very light weights and enjoyed terrific power-to-weight ratios. This was always demonstrated on about the third training sortie by getting the student pilot to climb in reheat out to the east of Cottesmore. The published climb speed was 450 knots but, unless the student maintained a good instrument scan, the aircraft would inevitably go supersonic between 15,000 and 20,000 feet. That exercise also helped to generate great awareness of fuel consumption, the fuel flow meters being against the top stops.

Computers and technology did, however, bring problems. Reverse thrust was fitted to obviate the need for tail parachutes for short-field landings. In high-speed taxiing trials at Warton during the testing days, this had led to directional instability and to an aircraft departing the runway – fortunately, I believe, without severe damage. This led to the birth of the nosewheel steering computer to take out any undemanded yaw, which required a computer self-test every time the gear was selected down. Of course at Cottesmore, circuits and landings were a good part of the training day and there were frequent failures of the self-test of this computer. So two or three times a week, there would be approach-end cable engagements with the use of the emergency tail hook. From the cockpit this hook could only be selected down, but fortunately there was a cadre of big strong firemen who could manually reset it up despite the close vicinity of the jet exhausts. This happened so frequently that we managed to get the runway-out time down to about ten minutes or so.

Reverse thrust also led to amusement every now and then. On one occasion I had been on an instructional sortie with a student and he was taxiing the aircraft back to the parking slot. This necessitated running along the back of the aircraft line and then making a right-angled turn into our allocated slot where a ground crew member was signalling. We had adequate rolling momentum up to the turn but came almost to a halt having completed it. The ground crewman continued to wave us forward, so the student applied power and we immediately started rolling backwards – to the consternation of our marshaller who waved more frantically. Of course it was reverse thrust, still selected following the landing despite the after-landing checks. The selection was not, unfortunately, visible from the instructor's seat. Luckily the slot immediately behind was vacant and there was no damage other than huge embarrassment. We rectified the situation, as you would imagine, in a cool and calm manner!?

A couple of incidents highlighted interesting aspects of the computer-controlled engine management systems. The first happened as I was climbing out from low level, close to a fairly active weather front. I'd selected full dry power and we were in thick cloud in a steep climb. Suddenly, of their own accord, the engines ran down to idle. I rapidly selected a more sensible attitude and, luckily, they then ran back up to full power. This happened a couple of times more before they settled down as we broke out on top. During the debrief I was assured by the engineers that this was 'not possible' and that the aircraft had been fully checked out and screened for electromagnetic interference.

The second event had more expensive consequences. One of our pilots taxied the aircraft onto a parking slot and, during engine shut down, the engines wound up to full power and one of them was written off. It seemed possible either that the checklist sequence was not followed exactly or, perhaps more likely, electrical power was deselected before the engine RPMs had decreased sufficiently. At any rate the default 'no electrical power' engine setting seemed to be 'maximum'. There were many lessons to be learned in those early days.

The aircraft was well designed with numerous system redundancy features incorporated both for safety and survivability, and although in the early days this led to a fairly high unserviceability rate, there were few serious incidents. But one major event had occurred before my arrival when an aircraft had made a wheels up landing at RAF Coningsby. Whilst I cannot recall the cause, I believe an aircraft of one nation was involved with an instructor from another and a student from the third – which must have led to an interesting Board of Inquiry.

One of that aircraft's damaged undercarriage doors was fastened, as a trophy of sorts, above the coffee bar in the squadron adjacent to mine. I was there one morning having a coffee with an old Jaguar colleague and three of his chums who were visiting us on a landaway exercise in their Hawks. In the middle of responding to their wisecracks about the door trophy, the crash horn sounded; I joked, "That will be another wheels-up landing." We hastened outside to see, to my horror, a Tornado sliding down the runway on its belly, the reheat having just been cancelled. Fortunately no one was hurt, although my friends had more laughs about the Tornado's apparent inadequacies. It would appear that the cause this time had been the ex-Starfighter pilot preselecting gear up prior to lift off; apparently this had been the habit on the F-104 so that, once the weight-on-wheels switches released, the gear came up immediately, thus avoiding any overspeed issues due to the aircraft's rapid acceleration. Unfortunately the Tornado system didn't quite work like that, and it was also thought that the aircraft's shape possibly caused some aerodynamic suck-down back on to the runway. The take-off brief for new German and Italian students was smartly changed.

In the rear cockpit there was no indication of gear selection. In fact instruction from the rear seat was always a bit of a challenge. Unlike in the Jaguar there was no differential in seat height, so the rear occupant of a Tornado couldn't look over the head of the front seater. This often made monitoring the first approaches flown by the student pilot an interesting exercise. This was particularly the case when carrying out a 67° wing approach – which configuration was practised in case the wings should ever be stuck fully swept. At around 1,000 feet the instructor would completely lose sight of the runway owing to the very high angle of attack. The only visual way to monitor where the aircraft was going was to look out sideways at known features passing by. This was a pastime of dubious excitement, and for practice we never touched down, always doing a low-altitude go around. Fortunately the failure, to my knowledge, never occurred, which was just as well as the approach speed was up around 200 knots.

Another major challenge for the pilot instructor when training a student pilot was to manage all the avionics, the majority of which were located in the rear cockpit and normally part of the navigator's empire. Familiarity with this kit did, however, come to good use when flying with a student navigator who was having finger trouble with the inertial navigation set-up or the radar system.

One aspect of Tornado flying which was brand new to me and to all those joining the course was the terrain-following radar, bringing the ability to fly at low level at night or in cloud. This challenge emphasised the need for the two-man crew to work as a team. Initially a number of flights were flown at 500 feet above ground in good visual conditions, manually following a flight director system which was linked into the terrain-following radar so that the system would give command directions to maintain the height above obstacles ahead. This then progressed to a series of flights using the autopilot to fly the aircraft. The set height was slowly decreased, and the crew would eventually be operating at night and in cloud. To safely fly the aircraft along a planned route required considerable pre-planning; not least the route selected had to be within the aircraft's performance and manoeuvre capabilities. Of course this process was further practised at the weapons conversion unit and on operational squadrons.

Whilst I could never say that this type of operating was as enjoyable as the standard, visual, low-level flying I had been used to, it was certainly very challenging and satisfying when it all worked as planned. Needless to say this didn't always happen, which led to some adrenalin-making moments. The safety fall-back position of the system was that if computer or hardware errors were detected, the autopilot would put the aircraft into a thirty-degree climb. If the problem was of a very short duration the aircraft would then nose over back down to low level again, this being known as a closed-loop pull up. If however the problem was not resolved, the aircraft would be left in a climb and the autopilot would disconnect – the so-called open-loop pull up. The crew were then left to manually recover the situation. This failure generated a high rate of climb, which became very interesting in the middle of the night or in cloud when flying below controlled airspace, so careful route planning was needed to minimise possible issues developing. In the early days, closed-loop pull ups were relatively frequent when approaching power lines, making for an uncomfortable ride because of the negative G during the push over back to low level. The severity of these manoeuvres could be adjusted by selecting a hard, medium or soft ride which would adjust the clearance the system would give to obstacles before the aircraft started to pull up. Good team work within the crew was necessary to keep ahead of the aircraft in these situations.

It was also essential to avoid getting lost in the marvels of all this modern electronics and forgetting about the world outside. I well remember having to fast-talk the unit out of a difficult situation with a very irate Manchester air traffic control officer, who was vociferously complaining about one of our aircraft rattling across the middle of his airport at 250 feet and 450 knots. In those days the Tornado navigation system was primarily based on an inertial platform. This meant that it was necessary now and then, particularly before a target run, to take a fix to correct any errors that were developing. When I called in this particular crew for a full and frank discussion they assured me that they were exactly on the pre-planned track. Subsequent checking revealed that they were indeed exactly on the system-planned track as shown on their displays, but were paralleling the real-world track

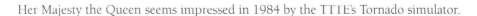

Her Majesty the Queen seems impressed in 1984 by the TTTE's Tornado simulator.

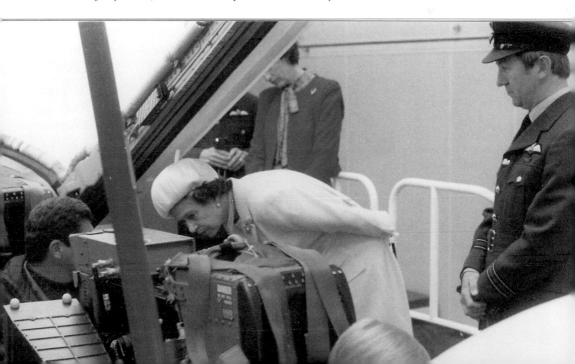

by some thirty-five miles displacement, this being an error they had introduced by an erroneous update. The conversation then became pretty one-sided, as you would imagine.

Our tri-national venture attracted a lot of VIP visits by senior officers and politicians from interested nations. One noteworthy visitor was HM the Queen in June 1984. This galvanised the station into a high state of activity to prepare for the great day, with much tidying up and practising. My role on the day was to show Her Majesty the simulator in operation, which she observed with particular interest – although she declined my invitation to become our latest trainee. Other visitors, though perhaps not so grand, were in their own way very important as well. The head brewer of the aforementioned Ruddles Brewery became an honorary member of the mess as well as of each of the squadrons, and was therefore a frequent visitor. There were of course also numerous visits by local organisations as part of the process of establishing goodwill with our neighbours – who had to put up with our extremely noisy Tornados by day and night.

One of the more unusual aspects of my job was to represent the TTTE view on checklists at regular tri-national meetings. At first sight this might seem somewhat less than interesting – discussing whether to insert a comma or debating the order of the after take-off checks. Fortuitously, however, Panavia had agreed to host these meetings in Munich. Once I discovered that they occurred twice a year, just by chance around *Karnival* time and during the *Bierfest*, I approached the task with a great deal more enthusiasm. I attended about six meetings all told, and although I'm not convinced that the flight reference cards were any better at the end of my time, the visits were most instructive.

All good things come to an end, and one day in July 1985 I was summoned for a discussion about my future. I was offered the one-time good deal of a staff college course at Greenwich. Well, I probably wasn't in a receptive frame of mind, and age certainly wasn't on my side for a glowing career, so it only took a nanosecond to decide against. I had been hoping to further my flying career with British Aerospace, because I was aware that the Tornado contract with Saudi Arabia was on the horizon, but, as is so often the case in life, timing is of the essence, and the Saudis were still weighing up the relative merits of the Mirage 2000 and the Tornado. However, every cloud has a silver lining, or so I thought then, because what BAe did offer me was a Jaguar post in Nigeria. But that's a tale to be found in *Jaguar Boys*.

CHAPTER 4

BROWN AMONG THE BATS

"We are ... hyaahh ... while the enemy is ... hyaaahh!" The ground liaison officer's (GLO) stentorian tones batter our eardrums, accompanied by expansive sweeps of his pointer across the map that covers almost the entire planning room wall in our war headquarters. Pretty much the whole of NATO's central front is depicted in large-scale detail, with a mass of coloured pins, flags, arrows and threat circles indicating the relentless progress of the bad guys. He continues: "The Second Pomeranian Foot and Mouth is advancing along an axis just south of the Baltic coast..." We listen attentively, mainly for the benefit of the foreign evaluators. Secretly, we wish the GLO wouldn't go on so.

Ground liaison officers loved that sort of thing. In my experience, although there was the odd one whose heart wasn't really in the job, by far the majority very much enjoyed their postings to RAF squadrons: their briefings to the boys; their detachments; and their expeditions and adventures. We enjoyed having them, and as you'll see from this account by Pat King there was much to occupy them on an RAF squadron apart from looking after ground aspects of our exercise scenarios.

Some GLOs made quite a career of light-blue service life, once having attached themselves to the RAF never returning to their mainstream army careers. Pat was one such; indeed we still see him amongst us, as he is a regular attendee at the monthly get-togethers of the old codgers who make up our gang of former jet pilots. In the following chapter he gives us an army view of starting up the first Tornado squadron.

MAJOR PAT KING (RETD)

In September 1982 my family and I returned from Germany, I having been short toured as a forward air controller after some genius suggested there was no place for FACs in a future European war. Following six months peacekeeping in Sinai, I was posted to RAF Honington – initially to 208 Squadron, which flew Buccaneers, but also to keep an eye on IX(B) Squadron's formation with Tornados. The latter was on the other side of the airfield in a new HAS site named Gotham City, after the bat in the squadron's badge. 208 departed after a

43

few months and my unit (self plus one NCO clerk) transferred itself full-time to IX(B). The initial Tornado unit was originally, I understand, to have been number 617 Squadron of 'Dambuster' fame, but as this first squadron was planned to move later to Germany, the powers-that-be decided that it would be more diplomatic to keep 617 on our side of the Channel. I think they were right; in my previous incarnation I admit to having been guilty of walking across the Möhne Dam loudly humming the Dambusters March!

IX Squadron made me very welcome and ordered me to get a dog, as "all majors have dogs". So I recruited a rescued springer called Jasper who loved cats, hated other dogs, and was the biggest gannet on the planet. He was also a people person, but many times in the crew room I heard cries of "Bugger off, Jasper" as he homed in on somebody eating sarnies. Squadron Leader Bruce Chappell and I devised a dog code, as Jasper did not see eye to eye with Boris, his Labrador. A call of 'dog state black' meant that Boris was in, while 'liver and white' meant Jasper was in. Jasper was extremely obedient and was nearly always off the lead, but after a close call with a police dog one evening he had to be reined in.

Don, the squadron intelligence officer (squinto), taught me my trade, as there was no GLO course available for me. He was invaluable, and I soon felt fairly confident. Indeed I developed a very good rapport with the whole station's intelligence personnel. As a first tourist with the RAF I found life strange, but quickly adjusted to everything bar happy hour on Friday evenings; those I thought rather odd, to say the least. However after a few months I began to see why they did it; it was a good way of letting off steam.

Life in the UK was OK, except that I had a forty-six-mile journey to work every day. If I couldn't hack it on a daily basis I would have moved into the mess from Monday to Friday, but it didn't come to that. Readiness and reaction times were the key; on one very important callout I managed the cross-country journey along minor roads in forty-six minutes. Even now, after twenty years retired, a night phone call has me instantly awake and reaching for my kit.

The Tornado seemed extremely temperamental to begin with. Spares were in short supply so they cannibalised one aircraft – the 'Christmas tree'. On one notorious occasion all the jets were unserviceable, which left us little option but to take an early and liquid lunch. The locals moaned about reheat noise and cracked windows, and I could sympathise; the drumming in the chest caused by the engines' racket was fearful.

I worked in the pilot briefing facility (PBF), a hardened building which constantly smelt of crap, as some ace had got its sewerage pipe gradient wrong. During exercises it became almost unbearable. Jasper didn't help; on leaving the PBF it was his custom to pee on the sandbags outside the entrance. One day he performed, only to find that the sandbags were blue; he had watered the station commander's trousers. Profuse apologies from me, only to be told by the staish that the next time he came across he would wear his immersion suit!

One of the alternative hidey-holes if we were exercise-bombed out of the PBF was the engineers' hardened facility. We would move sharply across the intervening hundred metres, following our noses – for there was a smell there, too. The waft of engineers' cigarettes and nicotine hit you like a wall; you could cut the blue smoke with a knife. They were a great bunch and I got to know a few of them quite well. They worked incredibly hard, with the late shift often working all night to get enough jets ready for the next day.

The site itself was cleverly designed, dispersed so that one attacking aircraft ought to be able to damage no more than one HAS. I helped to build the guard posts round the site, bearing in mind that all of them had to be in line of sight with each other. Jasper was a wizard at keeping the rabbit population down.

We got ready for our first Taceval when we would be tested in a war scenario. Part one, the callout and generation, went well. During my initial briefing someone asked where the British corps was on the map. I pointed out the position, adding that they would be easy to find by the cloud of blue smoke from the tanks' engines – and because their guns would be pointing east even though they'd be travelling west. Part two was going extremely well until Mike Stephens and Nigel Nickles's aircraft crashed. Nigel parachuted to safety, walked to the nearest habitation, a farm, and announced that he had just baled out and could he use their phone. But there was no sign of Mike. The aircraft had become uncontrollable; Mike had ordered Nigel to eject, saying that he would follow once he had turned out to sea. We searched a huge area of woodland and fields to find him, but it eventually became clear that his body was in the wreckage. It was my first and only crash site, and I will never forget the all-pervading smell of kerosene.

I had lost a good friend, a former A-10 exchange pilot who still used American jargon. I gather it was most probable that he had been disabled as the back-seater had ejected, and we buried him in Honington church yard. The crash site was on the Sandringham estate, and Her Majesty the Queen had a small memorial to him erected nearby, just outside Wolferton.

The Taceval was abandoned following the accident and we had to do it all over again later. Because of the nuclear aspects, a single mistake would have meant failure – but we made it. By this time I was right on top of the job, and with all those navigators around to help with the mapping we had ample manpower; I even had time to read a book.

Later there was a pleasant interlude when I helped out the Harrier detachment in the Falklands. From mid-summer in England, via equatorial Africa and Ascension Island, experiencing air-to-air refuelling in a Hercules, to mid-winter in Port Stanley, the journey itself was a great experience. Winter won the day, though, for the exercise was entirely weathered out.

When Don left, his replacement squinto was a squintess, namely Flight Lieutenant Sue Weightman. I had never worked with a servicewoman before and was extremely worried by it all, but Sue proved to be a real grafter and very easy to get on with.

Her husband was a Victor pilot, based at RAF Marham, the station known to old hands as 'El Adem with grass' (El Adem having been a bleak, Libyan airfield much used by the RAF in days gone by). She was extremely good at her intel work and we got all our briefings up to a high standard. In Goose Bay, Labrador, for an exercise, we made ourselves responsible for replenishing the crewroom treats. Then, having had a lovely day's sailing, we were the cooks for the BBQ and didn't poison anyone!

What an incredible place was Goose; we had winter, spring and summer all in one week. Huge excitement followed the thawing of the river to let the first ship up with badly needed supplies. Days later a camp fire got out of hand, with the resulting forest fire threatening to engulf the whole settlement, and we were ordered to prepare for evacuation to Gander. I got the boys up and was then sent to wake up a Herc crew who had arrived for our return to the UK. As was regularly the case, on-base accommodation was not considered adequate for transport crews, and they were in a downtown hotel. I banged them up and was told in no uncertain terms to bugger off. I returned to the squadron, to be told to go back again and emphasise the seriousness of the situation. It worked this time. When I got back the evacuation was in full planning mode, and I had visions of wobbling Tornados flying to Gander – as we had had a good evening the night before. It all panned out in the end, though, as the wind changed direction and we were stood down.

Back at Honington we had a new squadron standard presented, with all the stops pulled out to make it a fantastic spectacle. I was charged with controlling the flypast of two aircraft, timed to occur as the squadron presented arms after an advance in review order. The parade went extremely well and I duly called in the two jets who had been loitering near Thetford. With a huge roar it seemed to me that they flew over at fifty feet, wings swept, in reheat; at any rate I swear I saw the reviewing officer jump four feet in the air.

Another time we were tasked with a fly-by over the Bury St Edmunds Battle of Britain parade. I went and worked out how long I had in hand to call the jets in, by marching the route the parade would take. On the day it was foggy and you could hardly see your hand in front of your face. I called the crew in on time, but the weather intervened and the jet was 150 metres to one side, following along another street.

On another occasion the squadron had to prepare a demonstration attack for VIP visitors to the station. At the dress rehearsal, in they came from the Bury St Edmunds end, wings swept right back, looking just like a group of bats. Down they came, one in particular coming down ... and down ... and down – until we were all ducking for cover. Jasper's large ears nearly come off his head! The pilot was extremely lucky, for all the chiefs were away that day.

My old battalion asked if I could arrange some aircraft activity, and the squadron obliged with a pair to make a pass over Stanford battle area, near Thetford, as they returned to Honington. I was ready to do my FAC bit, but this time the crew found the target without me. In the evening a singleton did a re-run, which put the wind up some of the boys in the trenches. Prior to the Tornado, they hadn't been used to aircraft attacking at night.

We also supported a demonstration on Larkhill ranges, which went swimmingly. Later I took the aircrew down to the School of Infantry at Warminster for the annual fire-power demonstration. We had a thumping good night at the Bell Hotel, but then ran into bother at the ranges in the morning. None of the aircrew had combat kit with them, just turning up in cold weather flying suits. Some stuffy colonel went ballistic, but luckily an old boss of mine was running the demo – so we were able to ignore the fuss.

In late 1984 we gained a Canadian exchange pilot, Howie Cook, and his wife Colleen. As he was not vetted he could not participate in anything nuclear. He got very frustrated, and when we dined out the first boss Howie stood up and said, "Sir, if your speech is classified would you like us to leave the room?" Cheers from the boys. Later, at another Taceval, I recall Howie standing there in the middle of the mass launch. The shout came: "For f**** sake Howie, grab your kit and get ready to fly, we're a pilot short!" Whether or not his vetting had come through – and whether or not he flew – I can't remember.

Colleen got a verbal rocket from the station master, in front of us all, for wearing culottes at a dining-in night. It's hard to imagine that things were so stuffy just thirty years ago. Especially as behaviour at the time could be outrageous in all the messes. I remember one evening when an inebriated flight lieutenant was being a nuisance to some wives of RAF Regiment men. I saw their husbands go into a huddle, and the next minute they spear-chucked him out of one of the windows. An earth-covered officer came spluttering back in; the point had been well made.

Then the Buccaneer OCU gave a farewell luncheon party as a parting gesture. As we went in I noticed two beautifully made Buccaneer models hanging on the walls of the dining room, with rockets fitted under their wings. The retiring boss spoke very cheerfully about their time at Honington, and then he reached for what looked like a TV remote. "Duck, Pat", came the shout, as with a huge roar the rockets ignited, flew across the room and blew a huge hole in the kitchen door. Howls of laughter all round.

Later, we had a squadron get together to bid farewell to another outgoing boss. At one point a very pretty WRAF corporal asked to speak with him. I noticed the boys sniggering, and sure enough off came the rain coat and beret and there stood a stripper in all her glory!

Another peripheral issue, which became a pain in the butt, was when the squadron was tasked to take part in a new recruiting film. Jasper and I had small parts, but by about the third take of one scene the boys had had enough. They were to be filmed coming out of the briefing room, but on this occasion they emerged on their knees singing, "Hi ho, hi ho, it's off to work we go". Surprisingly, even the director was seen to smile. The clip came to light on Facebook in 2013 and still went down well.

Life was good, but I heard on the grapevine that a GLO vacancy was coming up at RAF Coltishall with 41(F) Squadron. Not only was Colt more convenient for my home, but 41's war assignment was to Norway. I had served three winters in the Arctic with my own battalion and several in the German Harz mountains, so the idea of getting back on skis appealed to me. Additionally, IX Squadron was about to move to Germany, something I didn't particularly fancy, so I asked the boss if I might leave for pastures new. He gave me the all clear so I left for Colt. To mutual regret, I think; they gave me a good send-off and I got my regulation tankard, which I was very chuffed about. In return I presented them with a statuette of a heavily laden infantryman, which I likened to a fully bombed-up Tornado – great when light but struggling when fully kitted out. I met the 'bats' again in Bahrain during Gulf War One, happily renewing many old friendships.

Jasper had, by this time, been dispensed with owing to increasingly bad behaviour. He had attacked most of the dogs in the village and finally threatened a guide dog. That was the last straw; I missed him badly, but he found a new life with the police where he became a really good drugs dog. As I left the squadron, squintess Sue said that she was going to get a springer pup. They're amazing dogs, so full of energy; I wonder whether she knew what she was letting herself in for?

Great memories, all of them, and I had withdrawal symptoms when I left. But it was time to move on. Now ... where are my skis?

CHAPTER 5

THE GULF CONFLICT – 'GULF WAR ONE'

Cold War warriors like me, brought up on a diet of deterrence in the European theatre, rarely thought about the possibility of actual combat. True, we would have done our duty if things had come to that, but even following the UK's unlikely involvement in the Falklands in 1982 we didn't really expect to get into a shooting war. And nor, I hazard a guess, did those who specified, designed and procured the Tornado really expect it to go into combat. But it did, with the Gulf Conflict very much marking the 'end of chapter one' for the Tornado force and the initiation of a new era. Nothing would be the same again, so let's now hear from one of the squadron commanders from what came to be known as 'Gulf War One'. He is the man who won a DSO for his leadership of the Dhahran Tornado detachment, Jerry Witts.

AIR COMMODORE JERRY WITTS (RETD)

"Got the offset. Correction's in. Take it," says AJ. The aircraft lurches left as I reselect track hold on the autopilot. It all seems very unreal, creaming along at 500 knots through the thick, velvety darkness. The HUD tells me we are 180 feet above the desert but it could just as well be 18,000, because I can't see a thing ahead, just the unwinding time-to-weapon-release circle on the symbology. Thank goodness it's flat – at least we think it is. Perhaps I should have put the night vision goggles on after all? Too late now.

"Five miles. I'm happy. Radar off."

"MASS. Late arm. Stick top live."

We recite the litany of checks just as we have done a thousand times before. But never like this. This time it's for real, and just thirty seconds ahead lies an Iraqi airfield. It's shortly after midnight GMT on 17 January 1991 and we're on our way to war.

"Twenty seconds. Fifteen. Five."

"Committing."

There they go. The aircraft vibrates rapidly as our JP233s dispense their loads. There's a pulsing glow from beneath the aircraft. Then suddenly, two massive thumps as the empty canisters are jettisoned. A quick thought: 'So that's what it's like.' Then, alarms sound, the autopilot drops out, we lurch sharply upwards and my heart rate increases to about 400 a second as I fight to get back down to low level. "What are those flashing lights, AJ?"

"AAA, you idiot!"

"Jesus!"

The flashing lights become white stair rods arcing over and around us. Away to the right the sky erupts in orange flames, quickly followed by a curtain of incandescent white lights as more and more AAA (anti-aircraft artillery) fires into the darkness. A hundred fleeting experiences, too rapid to recall in any detail. We rush onward. Homeward. I haven't touched the throttles or moved them from their max dry power setting, but I see we're now doing close to 540 knots as we jink left and right of track to avoid the threats illuminating our radar warning system. Let's try max wing sweep to see if we can get a few more knots out of her. I don't want to use reheat; it lights us up like a beacon, and anyway we can't afford the fuel. Check the rest of my formation in on the r/t. All there, thankfully.

The chart that amused them all during Gulf War One.

Time seems to stand still, and the brown line that marks the international border creeps so slowly down the moving map display. I suppress the irrational desire to laugh as we pass over a printed notice on the map: 'WARNING: Flight in Iraq outside controlled airspace is STRICTLY PROHIBITED.' Then, just as suddenly, we're over the line. We're safe! We're alive! My God, we've done it! Now, where's that tanker?

Whenever I think of the Gulf, these are amongst my most vivid memories. But that is not where it all started. It was in November 1990 that my station commander told me to start getting a new detachment ready to go to the Gulf. We might be going to Bahrain, or it could be Tabuk; or even some other location. There was no firm date for moving, but mid-December looked about right. Such were the times and, in any case, at RAF Brüggen we prided ourselves on our ability to do anything, anywhere – any time. The station already had one detachment at Bahrain and we had plenty of experience to draw on. So we set to work.

The basics were easy. I was to command the detachment, which would comprise twelve aircraft with twenty-four crews and a war establishment of ground crew. The majority of crews were to come from my own 31 Squadron, with the remainder from numbers IX(B), 14 and 17(F) Squadrons, who were even now together as a composite team because their 'other halves' were already in the Gulf. I would take all my ground crew and engineering management, again topped up from other Brüggen units and from elsewhere. Training was the priority, and by now we had the benefit of an Operation Granby work-up syllabus to guide us. The station was marvellous and nothing was too much trouble as we made increasing demands on all sections in our drive to get ready and packed. As mid-December approached with no sign of an order to move, or a destination to move to, we managed to stand most people down for a bit of leave. Four of my officers took the plunge and opted for early weddings, and life seemed to become one long round of ground defence training, night air-to-air refuelling, writing will forms, and ceaseless speculation.

Undoubtedly, the families had the hardest time as plans changed, then changed again. The festive season would serve only to add poignancy to the prospect of six months unaccompanied service in the Middle East, together with the possibility of going to war. Then, just a few days before Christmas, we were told at last. We were off to Dhahran in eastern Saudi Arabia, and our advance party was to move out on 27 December. Not everyone was pleased about the location, especially those who enjoy a tipple, but at least it would give us the opportunity to do things 'our way'; although, with only two weeks to go to the UN deadline, it was going to be very tight.   .

So it proved to be. Through no fault of the RAF, the situation at Dhahran was even less prepared than we had hoped for. Coming so late into theatre we were very definitely at the back of the logistics queue, and our operational accommodation, comprising a rather sorry set of portakabins on what was to become one of the world's busiest airfields, left quite a lot to be desired. But this was no time for carping, and my team set to with a will to make the best of things.

Not least among our new experiences was learning to deal with our host nation. "*Inshallah*" ('if Allah wills it', the translation implying an element of 'we hope, or assume, that it will happen') quickly became one of our stock expressions, but it was surprising how often, just when my SEngO was about to rip out the last of his rather sparse hair covering, that all that had been promised would arrive. Money was the thing that made things move, so it was local purchase to the rescue, and in no time at all we had computers, colour copiers, vehicles and all the paraphernalia necessary to get things going. We started in-theatre flying training on 3 January to familiarise crews with the desert by day and by night and to hone our newly learned air-to-air refuelling skills. Day by day, the detachment grew as new personnel arrived via increasingly exotic routes: from Hannover on a British Airways Jumbo; from Gatwick via Athens and Al Jubayl on the flight deck of a decrepit Boeing 707; or from Frankfurt in the hold of a USAF C-5. But arrive they did and we were pleased to see them, as our intelligence and mission planning organisation blossomed from a bare room with a telephone into the hub of a semi-hardened operations centre with attached chemical-proof air raid shelters. All mod cons and with room for future expansion, all set in a rather fetching car park.

It was just as well that we had some spare capacity, for soon after I arrived I learned that six Tornado GR1A reconnaissance aircraft with nine crews were to be integrated into my detachment. SEngO (by now, totally bald!) took the news rather well I thought, and the reconnaissance intelligence centre (RIC), housed in several mobile containers, certainly filled that annoying space at the back of the car park.

My major concerns as the UN deadline approached were still aircrew training, the spares supply situation and, most importantly if war was to start, the whereabouts of the *Atlantic Conveyor II* which had most of my weapon stocks on board. However, by 14 January, Al Threadgould's II(AC) Squadron recce team had arrived, the ship was off-loading at Al Jubayl and my 'bombers' had completed their in-theatre work-up. Best of all, things seemed to be coming together in all departments, and people were working well together, which was always a concern with aircrew from four stations and seven squadrons (XIII Squadron having now joined, while a crew from 27 Squadron would later), and ground crew and support personnel from a host more. Even the tragic loss of one of my crews in a training accident did little to slow our momentum. Indeed, if anything it steeled our resolve to see this thing through if called upon.

By now a few of us had been briefed on the overall plan and on our specific targets if UN Resolution 678 was to be implemented by force. It didn't take the brains of a rocket scientist to figure out that we would be going against airfields. And, as the deadline ticked past at 0800 hours local on 16 January and we were ordered to cease flying training, load the aircraft and stand at several hours readiness, there was a definite air of tension about the place. Were we ready? Had we done enough training? How would we cope? But time passed quietly, and by 1730 hours it looked as though nothing was going to happen that day. I drove back to the quarters I shared with OC IX Squadron (Wing Commander Ivor Evans) and settled down with one of his cold beers (alcohol-free, of course!) to watch CNN for an update on the political situation. 'Our man in Baghdad' seemed happy enough and, indulging in what now was clearly wishful thinking, I speculated that Saddam was obviously going to start pulling out of Kuwait now that he had faced it out past the deadline. Ivor, however, was less optimistic. Almost as he had finished speaking, the telephone rang and my operations officer told me to come straight to work. He didn't need to tell me why, and I've never doubted Ivor's judgement since.

The drive to the airfield was interesting. I thought there was something wrong with the petrol until I realised that my accelerator foot seemed to have a life of its own. Group Captain Cliff Spink, the RAF detachment commander, met me with a top secret signal which, in very few words, told us to go to war. A quick check of the plan showed that we would have to take off at about 0130 hours local, some time before the official 'off', so that we would reach our target on time. This gave us three or four hours to get everything buttoned up and ready to go. By now the rest of my formation had arrived and, after I had broken the news to them, we busied ourselves with our preparations. We were apprehensive but there was no time to brood about it. We filled the time by briefing ourselves to death: radio procedures; tanking procedures; route details; target details; enemy (for that's what they had now become) defences; friendly forces; escape and evasion; and so on. It was a strange atmosphere because many of those around us didn't know what we were about to go and do – and we couldn't tell anyone who didn't need to know. Thus, there were amusing comments like, "If the boss is going night flying does he want the weapons taken off the aircraft?"

But then it was time to go; predictably, we went to our aircraft far too early and sat there in strained silence waiting for the minutes to tick by to our take-off time. As soon as we were airborne things were a lot better. We were busy and there was no time to worry. We just got on with the job.

The sky was full of aircraft, the AWACS radio channels nearly jammed with mission after mission checking in. This was history in the making and there we were, right in the middle. It was all very exciting and, on top of everything, I think we sensed that, whatever the outcome, things would never be the same again. All too soon it was down to low level, lights off, across the border and ...

We had all hoped, of course, that Saddam would get the message very quickly and that he would soon be scuttling out of Kuwait. After a few hours sleep, I was back at the squadron to see how things were going and to brief the next formations on our experiences. From here on it became a bit of a juggling act to make sure we spread the load evenly amongst the aircrew, getting the missions flown and ensuring that there was sufficient rest for all. The 'reccies' were off to a very good start and found a Scud launcher on their first sortie, which was magnificent, but we were all concerned as Tornado losses started to mount. These were friends and colleagues, and it mattered not which squadron or detachment they came from.

Thankfully, we ourselves were obviously having a lot of luck, and despite a few bullet holes the team kept coming back. We were definitely not amused when SEngO said he was glad that the battle damage repair teams now had something to do! Most of the nights were punctuated by Scud alarms and we all got very good at sleeping with our gas masks on. Our GDT instructors would have been proud of us. We were certainly very proud of Dhahran's resident US Army Patriot batteries, and we all became life members of the Patriot fan club. Perhaps Raytheon could now develop a quiet version that doesn't give you a heart attack every time it's fired.

The Iraqi air force was not taking part in the war so we soon found we could operate more freely than had been expected. After not a little discussion and heart searching it was decided that we should start to move up to medium level, around 20,000 feet. This allowed us to integrate ourselves more closely with the defence-suppression forces and with the available fighter escorts. It was remarkable how easily we all worked together, and on a typical mission we would be supported by two EF-111 Ravens and four F-4 Wild Weasels from the USAF, and by F-14s, F-15s, F-16s or F-18s from the USN, USMC, USAF, Canadians or the Royal Saudi Air Force. On every sortie we were refuelled by RAF TriStar, Victor or VC10K tankers, who quickly established a reputation for reliability and to whom we owed a great debt. Our targets were changing too. Gradually, we moved away from the airfields and started to attack industrial targets such as oil refineries, oil storage facilities and power stations, as well as ammunition dumps.

No one, least of all those who have flown in war, exults in destruction, but it would be true to say that there is some cold satisfaction in seeing a target blow sky high, having beaten the defences to get there. I've always believed that the job of the military is to exhibit a capability to one's potential enemies such that they are deterred and war is avoided. Actually having to fight, although the ultimate expression of our determination, is in some sense a source of deep disappointment. But even with this in mind there was satisfaction from the results we were achieving. We took great heart from General Schwarzkopf's attitude that "if we had to fight we were going to go in hard and decisively". That was the way it seemed to be going, although I don't think anyone at my level was expecting the air war to go on for quite so long. Now, of course, we know that this had to do with the time it was taking for our ground forces to get into position, but then my concerns centred on sustainability. We were using up our bombs at a fair old rate and the aircrew were getting pretty tired. The aircraft were standing up magnificently, but not without a great deal of hard work from our ground crew.

As the war progressed the 'reccies' stayed on night operations but the 'bombers' moved to daylight sorties, carrying out most attacks with laser-guided bombs, designation being performed by the worthy Buccaneers. This addressed the problem of weapons usage; we just didn't need to drop so many to achieve the required accuracy. The rate of sortie tasking had also reduced so that I could introduce a fairly settled routine for the aircrew.

I came to recognise that there were two distinct types of fatigue: the normal, short-term result of physical exhaustion and a longer-term, more insidious tiredness which is perhaps the result of sustained pressure and stress. However, with regular routine this seemed manageable and, certainly, the aircrew could probably have gone on for some time long after it all finished. But no-one was disappointed when the land campaign started and achieved such rapid and spectacular results. It was a very happy wing commander who woke up one morning to find Ivor Evans's note pinned to my door: 'Bush declares cessation of offensive action. Last one back at Brüggen's a sissy!'

A GR1 of 617 Squadron armed with two JP233s on the fuselage stations.

The six weeks of war now blur in the memory. Twenty-one Scud attacks and as many false alarms. The losses. The POWs. The hits and, not too often, the misses. The fatigue, frustration and fear. The exhilaration and excitement. Mission by mission, target by target, we were part of a massive, unstoppable force. Old myths were dispelled and new tactics evolved. Long-held beliefs were dismissed in a moment as the situation changed, like so many sacred cows slaughtered without a thought. All to be replaced by new truths and the fundamental rule that 'if it works and it keeps you alive, it's good'.

Through all the ups and the downs – and there were plenty of both – there was a constant feeling of massive support from home. Hundreds, thousands of letters from the whole spectrum of society. From the USA, Canada, France, Australia, Italy, South America; from all over the world people sent their best wishes and their appreciation for what we were doing. It was very gratifying, not to say humbling, to know that people cared.

So, for us all, a whole host of memories. My own will always include the simple bravery and fortitude of our families back at home. The sheer guts of the 'plumbers' loading bombs as bits of Scud rained down. Watching young, inexperienced aircrew grow quickly into seasoned campaigners. The sheer professionalism of everyone and, most of all, the feeling of immense personal privilege to have shared such company and to have commanded such people. All that and, of course, the fact that AJ, my flight lieutenant navigator, once called me an idiot!

CHAPTER 6

STILL LEARNING AFTER ALL THOSE YEARS

Every pilot who's flown a multi-crew type remembers the first navigator he was crewed with. And although I had flown Phantoms many years earlier, it's my first Tornado nav I remember best. Wally Grout was an extremely pleasant chap with whom to share the cockpit, a calm and reassuring presence, and I like to think we made a good team. He had a good number of GR1 hours behind him by the time I met him and had many Gulf War One missions under his belt, so he had plenty of experience to fall back on. Although reading a couple of the stories he's given us here, it's perhaps as well that I didn't, at the time, know all his history!

It wasn't until many years later that I realised just how much use he thought he'd been to me. The venue was a bar, the occasion a reunion, and the time late at night. Wally was deep in conversation with another nav who'd been on the squadron at the time I'd joined, and I sidled up to join them. Blow me, they were arguing about which of the two of them had taught me more. There was nothing for it but to buy them both a beer.

SQUADRON LEADER WALLY GROUT (RETD)

So there I was, just approaching my 40th birthday and all fired up to participate in my first Red Flag exercise in the States. After just four missions, my pilot and I were tasked as the lead crew for the package on 9 April 1990. I had spent my earlier years on the mighty Vulcan, having been posted from nav school as a navigator radar, and was lucky enough to be one of the first to cross over to the Tornado GR1 in January 1982. Red Flag was, at that time, a distant dream.

I was now on my second Tornado tour; I had 440 hours on type and, together with my pilot, was now to lead the planning and execution of a typically complex mission into the heart of Red Flag territory. I had come a long way.

Our mission was to penetrate the defences and drop two inert 1,000 lb bombs onto an airfield target using a loft manoeuvre. All Red Flag aircraft are fitted with a telemetry pod and, much like Formula One racing cars, are able to transmit information back to the HQ so that supervisors and spectators can watch the progress of the 'war' on a big screen in real time. After much head scratching and liaising, we finally completed the planning and briefing. Everyone within the package appeared happy with their relevant tasks.

We were airborne on time and proceeded to Caliente, our holding point for entry into the Red Flag area. Whilst orbiting, checking maps, timings and aircraft systems we detected a fault; fuel was not feeding from the wings into the fuselage tanks. This problem was not insignificant and, although the checklist gave advice and possible solutions, the fault could lead to serious fuel imbalance and possible mission abort.

We were approximately three minutes from our push time; just sufficient to go through the initial actions from the checklist. But we had no time to see if the problem was cured; the moment had come to enter the exercise area, descend to our operating height of 100 feet and concentrate on the routine of searching for threats, both visual and electronic, maintaining formation, avoiding known defences and staying alive. The aim was to penetrate to the target, get the bombs released and not get 'shot down'.

The ingress went well, with appropriate reactions to the few threats detected. We completed the pre-target checks, found the initial point and performed the attack. Job done, bombs on target, time to recover. Once settled we did a routine op check. As we covered 'fuel' our heart rates increased. We had not cured the fuel transfer problem; both of us having been fully tied up with the mission, we'd not double-checked. It was now clear that we didn't have enough usable fuel to get back to Nellis, even in a straight line.

The next few minutes seemed to last forever. From the map, Tonopah was our nearest diversion, and I gave my pilot the relevant track information. Simultaneously, we transmitted to Red Flag control that we were diverting with an emergency. In fact, with the telemetry pod 'big brother' probably knew already – but that call seemed to set the cat amongst the pigeons. Tonopah at that time was home to the USAF / Lockheed 'skunk works', a highly secret development site for the stealth bomber programme. We all knew about the F-117 but, as yet, it hadn't been officially cleared for public consumption.

You can now imagine the reaction over the radio. "Why do you need to go there? You cannot go there. What exactly is wrong with your aircraft? Why can't you go to Indian Springs?" (a less sensitive diversion airfield). We even had our detachment commander quizzing us. All the time fuel was reducing and we were getting closer to Tonopah. Between us we convinced all and sundry that our only alternative to Tonopah was an ejection over the desert. That shut them up, and we now got a period of relative quiet on the radio while we concentrated on getting our aircraft safely on the ground. We hadn't really thought about what would happen after that.

Tonopah consists of a single, very long runway, numerous hardstandings and taxiways, several large, windowless hangars, and many support buildings. All of this in the middle of the Nevada desert miles from habitation. Unlike most air stations it had no on-base accommodation – which helped keep its secret programmes clear of unnecessary eyes and cameras.

In the usual cloudless blue sky and unlimited visibility we were cleared for landing. After touching down we were instructed to clear the runway, stop and

A 16 Squadron GR1 sports the 'stealth' zap of an F-117, having made a precautionary landing at the top-secret Tonopah Air Force Base.

shut down. We complied, made the seats safe and raised the canopy.

What happened next is the stuff which makes Hollywood great. Several vehicles formed up in front of the aircraft, including one full of armed soldiers. Steps were brought and we climbed out. A USAF major greeted us; he confiscated the film cassettes from the HUD and the data recorder, told us that the aircraft would be looked after, and escorted us under armed guard to the operations centre. Good job that I didn't on this occasion have the 35mm camera I usually carried with me or they really would have thought we were spying! He guided us to a windowless room with blank walls and minimal furniture. We sat down, wondering what would happen next. We both felt reasonably relaxed, apart from the armed guards – after all, we had saved the aircraft and felt justified in our actions.

The major then explained our predicament. Landing at a top-secret establishment in the USA is not an everyday occurrence and we were now going to be questioned – or, as it later turned out, interrogated. To quote Monty Python, "Nobody expects the Spanish Inquisition!" Our interlocutor asked all the standard questions: name; rank; squadron; nationality; why we landed at Tonopah. And some more personal: marital status; family background; and educational qualifications. All the while, two large military personnel armed with carbines stood by the door.

Having finished with his questions the major left the room. We sat, with our guards, wondering what next? I do remember muttering quietly to my pilot: "What the heck is this all about?" (or words to that effect). After a few minutes, another male entered the room, dressed casually in civilian clothing. No introduction, no name given, just more questions. It was almost a repeat of those we had already answered. However, erring on the side of, 'let's not make waves', we both answered them. He was very keen to have our social security numbers, something akin to UK national insurance numbers. We politely told him we did not have those. It took quite a bit to get him to realise that we didn't, in the UK, attach so much significance to those numbers. Instead, we gave him our RAF service numbers, which seemed to satisfy him.

He left and we sat chatting about our situation while the guards remained in the doorway. It was now time for my bladder to complain; a post-flight comfort call was needed. I told the guards I needed the 'john'. The response took me by surprise; a guard would have to escort me – I assume to prevent me from running amok. He duly stood a few paces behind me as I took relief. I was escorted back to the room and we waited some more.

I then recall a further interrogator asking the same questions and getting the same responses. The major returned to tell us that our aircraft was now confiscated and that we would be flown back to Nellis in one of theirs. We would be told when we could have ours back, and we would be the only crew allowed to return to pick it up. He left us to puzzle why.

Soon we heard the sound of aircraft taxiing. We asked a guard if the F-117s were flying this afternoon, to which he shrugged. I said, "I suppose you have to wait until the surveillance satellites are clear before you fly the 117?" His response was standard USAF: "I do not know what you are talking about, sir." Further questions elicited similar responses. We gave up. More aircraft noise from outside; more flying tonight? It was getting late in the afternoon.

Eventually our 'friendly' major returned with news that, for operational reasons, we would not be flying back to Nellis but it would be a road trip instead. We asked if the operational reason was the fact that they were flying the F-117. He gave a non-committal smile.

More waiting, but then we were told that transport was available and asked to get our kit together. The next move stunned us both; we had black cloth bags put over our heads. We were led out of the room and outside; we could hear the sound of jets but thought it better not to ask more questions. We were helped into the rear seats of a vehicle. As the doors closed, our guards in the front seats had a few words for us to digest. "Do not remove your blindfolds, we are live armed." "OK," we said; the understatement of the year.

We drove in silence for what seemed an age. The bags had not been tied under our chins and I made a conscious effort to get a handle on the direction of travel by looking down and using the shadows; it was now getting close to sunset and I estimated that we had been travelling west for the majority of the time. When we finally stopped and the guards told us to remove our blindfolds, I turned round and could just see a tiny speck in the distance, which I assumed was an F-117 in the circuit. We were at the main gate and the aircraft must have been about fifteen miles away. What a main street to an airfield!

For our journey back to Nellis we were given brown paper 'sacks' of sandwiches, crisps, chocolate and fruit juice – courtesy of the Tonopah fire department dinner lady. That was about the only friendly gesture we'd had all afternoon, and boy, was the food welcome.

In muttered conversation between us we wondered what the consequences of our actions might be. Had we got the checks right? Had we analysed the problem correctly? What else could we have done? How deep was the guano going to be? We concluded that there was little else we could have done, but we speculated on what our reception would be on returning to Nellis – and on when we would get our 'toy' back.

The welcome at Nellis was cool but not hostile. It came as rather a surprise to the RAF commander that we would be told when we could have our jet back. We hadn't serviced the aircraft, but NATO air forces regularly exercised on each others' aircraft so we assumed our 'hosts' had a capability. Furthermore, strange as it may seem, there was an RAF pilot on an exchange tour on the F-117 at that time. Indeed, digressing slightly, during the Iraq War an ex-Tornado pilot took an active part in operations, flying an F-117. But did we think we had got away with it?

Next day a telephone message told us to get over to the other side of Nellis airfield, where a USAF Beechcraft was waiting to take us to Tonopah. We were met by a very young USAF pilot; we boarded, made ourselves comfortable while the crew gave us a quick safety brief, and off we went. The pilot wanted to know why and how we had gone to Tonopah, and also asked if we needed anything doing to our aircraft.

As we approached the field the pilot informed us that we would have to be airborne in less than forty minutes after arrival. He couldn't say why, but he let on that there would be jets out for flying. We were not allowed to see them but, as we broke into the circuit, he hinted that if we looked out of the starboard window we would get an extremely good view of two 'invisible' aircraft. Shame that I'd left my camera behind!

He dropped us close to our aircraft and, once again, armed guards watched us; our friendly major was on hand to see us off, repeating that we had forty minutes to get airborne. As we did an inspection we noted that the guys at Tonopah had a sense of humour after all, for the silhouette of a stealth fighter had been stencilled on each side of our tail fin. And in the cockpit, tucked under the windscreen, was a police parking ticket for illegal parking on US military soil. We had with us a couple of squadron prints, one for operations and one for the fire department. As we gave these to our major he presented us with a print of the F-117, even though it didn't officially exist. Last time I had the chance to look, the print was still on the walls of the crewroom at Marham.

That's not quite the end of the story. Having debriefed the engineers about our fuel problem, they did their investigation and found that the transfer valve was indeed not working. Hurrah, at least we got that bit right. However, in hindsight, that well known exact science, we should have monitored the fuel flow more closely and, if necessary, aborted the mission. But you know how it is – leading the pack, adrenaline rush, must complete the task, and all those other excuses for not giving up. All very well in peacetime to press on – but what about real war?

Before actually getting into combat I must mention the 'phoney war', which is what the build-up to Gulf War One seemed like. On 19 September 1990 four Tornado GR1 aircraft took off from RAF Brüggen en route to Muharraq, Bahrain. They had specially modified engines which could cope with the hot and sandy atmosphere of the desert, where the ingestion of fine sand particles combined with the heat of the engine had caused glass to build up on the surface of turbine blades. The cure was to install 'single-crystal blades', and the intention of this mission was to deliver four modified aircraft; the crews would stay overnight and return to Germany the following day with four of the originals. This would be routine business, with air-to-air tanker support.

And indeed the outbound, seven-hour flight was uneventful. The weather was clear; we had wonderful views of the Alps, Mount Etna and the Nile Valley, while the Red Sea was a beautiful shade of turquoise. As we descended into Bahrain at dusk the desert shone in myriad pastel colours. All was well with the world.

We received a warm welcome from the detachment personnel, and following the usual handover of aircraft to the ground crew we looked forward to a beer downtown in our hotel. However, instead of being shown to our transport we were led into an isolated room within the detachment HQ and told to wait. Puzzled looks all round. I should add here that our formation leader was a squadron commander from Brüggen.

The detachment executive officer arrived a few minutes later to explain that there had been a change of plan. We would not be going back tomorrow; we would be staying here for the foreseeable future. Reaction from us was as you would expect. Why? How long? We have no kit with us. Shock, horror – and all that! Before we had time to protest, the detachment commander, a group captain familiar to us from earlier Brüggen times, came in to explain the situation. The current squadron commander had a medical condition; he had effectively gone doolally. We were to stay in Bahrain as an operational formation of four crews while he was returned to Brüggen; the rest of his formation would take the four jets back to base.

You will well imagine the resulting comment, most of which is unprintable. After much protestation, followed by assurances that our personal kit would be flown out and that we would be relieved as soon as possible, we calmed down. But mayhem returned after we'd been left for half an hour with our thoughts. At that point we were told we would not be staying downtown in a luxury hotel; as there had been a change in the security state we would be staying on the airfield in temporary accommodation, and we were quickly shown to a portakabin. It contained cramped and unsavoury dormitories, with assorted old beds and cheap, self-assembly furniture. This palace was in very close proximity to the aircraft hardstandings, and had minimal sound insulation.

The enormity of what was happening was fast becoming a hell on earth, and to say we were not happy bunnies is a gross understatement. All thoughts of that cool beer in the hotel bar had vanished. We must have looked an extremely sad band of brothers as we herded back into the headquarters and contemplated our fate. By this time at least two hours had passed, and we were now resigned to having drawn the short straw by being on this formation. There was no option but to make the best of a bad situation.

The next announcement changed all that. In walked the 'doolally' squadron commander, face wreathed in smiles, followed by one of his pilots, a well-known practical joker. Yes the whole issue had been a spoof – and boy we had fallen for it hook, line and sinker. No, we were not staying in Bahrain; no, no-one had gone mad; yes we would be returning to Germany tomorrow; and yes, we were now going for a beer. Lots of protestations that "We knew all along it was a joke" followed – but our tormentors knew we hadn't. Transport appeared and we were whisked off to a very nice five-star hotel. The order was given that we were to be ready in reception in half an hour for transport to a local restaurant. Just time for a quick shower and change before we headed off to partake of some very welcome and enjoyable beers and some excellent Tex-Mex food at Senòr Paco's in Manama. There were plenty of laughs at our expense, but that sort of thing went with the job at the time. Some might call it childish, but such spoofs often helped to relieve tension. As we always said, "If you can't take a joke you shouldn't have joined!" The next morning, after a splendid breakfast looking out at the pool and the sunny blue sky, we flew back to wintry Germany and handed the jets to the engineers. But that's another story.

Fast forward to January 1991 and to King Abdulaziz air base, also known as Dhahran international airport. We are now in Saudi Arabia and Operation Desert Storm is in full flow. Same squadron, different pilot. The base had two parallel runways separated by approximately half a mile; not unusual, as there is a lot of spare land in Saudi. The western runway was used by civilian traffic and the eastern by the RSAF's Tornados and F-15s – and by the coalition. Dhahran was the hub for re-supply, and a constant stream of both military and civilian aircraft including C-141, C-5A, C-130, DC-8 and Boeing 747 arrived and departed around the clock.

All our war missions involved AAR, normally on the outward leg by Victors based in Bahrain and on return by either VC10 or TriStar. On this occasion, several missions into the war, we'd been operating at night. Our four Tornados had flown within a large package which included SEAD, fighters and EW support aircraft. Not all of those were based at Dhahran, while we were not the only bombers flying that night. The scene was set for an adventure, parts of which should never have happened – and all of which constitutes a salutary lesson for all aviators.

The mission had been successful with AAR as planned, penetration into Iraq without opposition, bombs released on target and little evidence of Iraqi AAA defences. Once we had crossed back into Saudi airspace we successfully located our tanker and took on more (contingency) fuel, following which we set course for home feeling very positive about the outcome of the mission. The medium-level transit back to Dhahran was routine. We were a little heavy for landing so, before we started our recovery, my pilot and I decided to get rid of some of our fuel. Now, over unpopulated territory, was a convenient point to do so, and we dumped to a level we considered safe for landing, with reserves for any subsequent emergencies.

Crucially, we hadn't yet contacted Dhahran ATC, and you will no doubt guess what's coming next. When we switched frequencies to Dhahran, the first message we received was to 'hold off' as the air base was at air raid warning red. Scud missiles were inbound. Our first thought was that maybe we had been a bit hasty with the fuel dump, but it still shouldn't be a problem; fuel consumption was low up at altitude and we still had sufficient to hold off for the duration of the air raid.

The warning was eventually cancelled and we were now in position to get our jets on the ground. But there were, of course, several formations queuing to recover to the military runway. To compound the problem, fog had started to form along the coast and was drifting towards the base. Following instructions from ATC our formation joined the stream and positioned for an ILS approach. All went well initially, but as we descended towards our minimum approach height we were well and truly in thick cloud – the sea mist. We made a missed approach, as did everyone else, and set up for another try.

By now the radio chat was getting tense, with voices becoming somewhat agitated. I was concentrating on our options, with fuel looking perilously tight (shades of Tonopah?!) All aircraft missed their second approaches, and we were debating whether to declare an emergency for a diversion to Muharraq. But our discussions were cut short by the next radio transmission: "I can see the threshold of the western runway." A second later, the voice from ATC changed from Arab-accented English to American and the instruction that will stay with me forever came across: "If you can see a runway you are cleared to land." No call sign, no aircraft type; just a general call to all the aircraft in the circuit.

It now became even busier in our cockpit; I had the western threshold in sight, and my pilot told me to keep it visual and start a commentary on where it was in relation to us while he started visually plotting the aircraft ahead – with the aim of finding a space to position for a visual approach. At the same time I was constantly updating fuel and keeping tabs on where we were in relation to Muharraq, as it was still possible to do a 'dirty dive' there if we had to.

We were now on the downwind leg with the threshold in our ten o'clock position. I was still giving my commentary, and my pilot could see several F-15s lined up on final approach. He saw an opportunity and pushed into that queue of F-15s.

My eyes were on stalks looking for other aircraft, my pilot now concentrating on getting the jet on the ground.

Only the approach lights and threshold were visible, with the rest of the runway completely obscured by thick fog. Now we had no fuel to divert or try again; this was our 'do or eject' moment. As the wheels hit the runway we disappeared into a soup of impenetrable fog, with only the faint glow of runway edge lights visible. We knew there was a stream of aircraft somewhere ahead of us but had no idea how close. We were both praying that they didn't stop too quickly – and that the guy behind didn't stop too slowly. Knowing there was little they could do, ATC stayed silent.

We found an exit and cleared the runway just as the fuel warning light came on; ouch, that was too close for comfort! We hadn't operated from this runway before, so we taxied very cautiously using the Jeppeson plate (a printed diagram of the airfield). Miraculously, we found our parking slot and shut down. As I stepped onto the hardstanding I felt like getting on my knees and kissing terra firma – but, given that there were witnesses, I managed to resist the temptation.

The formation debrief was interesting. We admitted to our predicament but played down its seriousness. We explained that we hadn't declared the problem in flight as there were already enough major factors keeping the formation leader busy. I think we got away with that explanation. Much discussion followed as to what we did, why we did it and the consequences.

Why had we dumped fuel? Had we been thinking of peacetime procedures? Had we been complacent? In hindsight (exact science again?) we should have kept all our fuel. So did we – did we all – learn a lesson? Well, I should say so; on all subsequent missions no fuel was dumped unless the crew was guaranteed a safe recovery and landing, even if that meant dumping on finals. After all, when you fight you have to make sure it's the enemy you destroy, not yourself.

CHAPTER 7

ACHTUNG – ENGLANDER'S BOOTS!

Exchange postings are marvellous things. Intended as a way of improving understanding between NATO's and other allied air forces, they undoubtedly fulfil that remit. But there are additional benefits. Ideas may be poached and brought back to the parent air force; different and exciting aircraft may be flown; and of course there are opportunities for aircrew, plus their wives and families, to enjoy living abroad and to soak up a different culture. Some would say that an exchange tour gets in the way of a high-flying RAF career, and for those who are intent on ascending the slippery promotion ladder as quickly as possible that might be true. But I've known plenty who have still done very well after also having enjoyed an exchange, while in any case one always has the opportunity to say 'no thank you'.

The Tornado programme has evolved over the years. Initially, exchanges were limited by the nuclear role; the UK's national weapon sensitivities hindered inbound exchanges to its strike squadrons. But the strike role disappeared, and now the situation is easier. The term 'wives and families' could need adjusting, too, for at least one RAF Tornado squadron has recently hosted a USAF lady WSO as its exchange officer.

I personally have no regrets about my own tour with the Norwegians, flying the little F-5 Freedom Fighter. I'd better not say that it was a three-year holiday – but it wasn't far off! On return to a Jaguar squadron as a flight commander I met Steve Randles, who was one of a host of extremely lively first tourists who already had their feet well under the table. They were having a lot of fun, were extremely sharp, and we all enjoyed ourselves. Several years later, on taking over my Tornado squadron, I found to my delight that Steve would be my deputy. He had, by then, three tours on the 'Fin' under his belt, as well as experience in the Gulf, so as a new boy on the jet I picked his brains a lot. It is a pleasure for me to renew his friendship by way of this story of his own exchange tour in Bavaria – which certainly sounds enticing.

WING COMMANDER STEVE RANDLES (RETD)

I thought it was the end of my exchange tour before I was even a week into it. I even had a fleeting thought that it might be the end of any RAF career I might have. I was leading four German air force Tornados from Lechfeld on a low-level training mission in southern Germany. The visibility in Bavaria is usually very good, but that day it was a little hazy and forward visibility into the afternoon sun was not great. At the limit of vision I began to discern an airfield – a very big airfield. A quick look at the map display showed nothing. A glance left and behind showed me that the other three aircraft had closed up from tactical formation into what could only be described as a loose gaggle behind me. I asked the WSO if he was happy with the navigation kit and with where we were. He was, and any slight chuckle there might have been in his voice was lost on me as panic started to rise. Another glance forward confirmed that we were closing at 450 knots with something that was starting to look like Heathrow. Two very long, parallel runways, huge parking aprons and a multitude of modern buildings; it was a large international airport. We were now so close that we were inevitably going to overfly at least some part of it. But my WSO, far from being concerned, was encouraging me to go faster and get lower, and the other aircraft weren't holding back either. I was convinced that we were all for the high jump and that I, as the leader, was surely for the highest jump of all.

The runway and approach lights were not illuminated and, as far as I could see, there were no aircraft to be seen either on the ground or in the air – and the moment passed. There were no calls on the emergency radio frequency, the other three moved back into tactical formation, and we continued on our way. When pressed, my WSO admitted that he and the others in the formation had planned my little shock. They had correctly guessed that I was unaware of the construction of Munich's new international airport. Although nearing completion it was not yet marked on any charts. It opened a few months later and I henceforth always gave it a wide berth. This was not to be the last time on my tour that I encountered German humour.

My interest in an exchange had been sparked during my first tour on Jaguars. On 6 Squadron we had had two exchange pilots: a Dutchman and a Frenchman. I struck up a particular friendship with the Frenchman (Bernard Molard, who contributed beautifully to *Jaguar Boys*). From that moment, an exchange tour always featured on my list of preferences for next posting.

But following that tour I was sent to Tornados, joining the newly-formed 16 Squadron at Laarbruch in Germany. Four years later, after continual requests for an exchange, my flight commander, Bob Hudson, told me that the posters were offering a tour with the West German air force flying Tornados at Lechfeld. I should like to say I jumped at the opportunity, but that was not the case. The exchange I really wanted was with the Canadians flying the F-18 or with the USAF on the F-16, both of which were coming up around the time I would finish my tour. Despite having lived in Germany for four years, I couldn't speak much German beyond ordering a meal, some beers and the bill. I also had my wife and two young children to consider. This message was relayed back to my posting officer, who replied that policy was now that only pilots currently flying single-seat aircraft would be considered for single-seat exchanges. It was the Luftwaffe or nothing.

Prior to 16 Squadron, Bob had been on exchange with the Germans at the navigator training school at Fürstenfeldbruck. Another navigator at Laarbruch, Al Sawyer, had flown Luftwaffe F-4Fs at Wittmundhafen. Between them, Bob, Al and their wives provided valuable insights to what would lie ahead. And after a great deal of discussion with my wife, I accepted the posting. Four weeks later, the F-18 and F-16 exchanges were offered to friends of mine on other Tornado squadrons, one of whom had never flown single-seat aircraft. Such is life.

I spent the next six months at the RAF's German language school at Rheindahlen. The assumption was that course members, all destined for posts in Germany, had no German to start with – not far from reality – and instruction was designed to get us to linguist standard. It was hard work; seven hours a day, five days a week for six months. By the end I could speak the language to a very high standard, while my wife received 100 hours of tuition to give her a grounding before being cast adrift in Bavaria. The children received no language instruction at all.

Luftwaffe bases do not have service-provided quarters for personnel; everybody, single or married, lives in private accommodation in a widespread area around the base. Years earlier there had been an RAF exchange pilot at Lechfeld flying the F-104, but during the Luftwaffe's conversion to the Tornado the position had been vacant – so I had no predecessor to help me. I had been allocated a squadron liaison officer, but he resided far from where we wanted to live and couldn't really help with finding accommodation. So my first serious use of my new language skills was in legal discussions about renting houses. Tricky! Especially as the RAF had taught me *Hochdeutsch* – the equivalent of Queen's English – whereas Bavarian seemed to be completely different with a vocabulary all its own. Nevertheless, we found a very nice house in the small town of Kaufering, about twelve miles from Lechfeld.

Being current on the Tornado I went straight to my operational German squadron. The first thing that struck me was the lack of history on display in the headquarters; quite different to an RAF squadron. In fact there was little in the way of 'military' decoration at all. However, there was an old pair of what looked like RAF flying boots nailed to one of the beams. Odd, I thought, but didn't ask. For obvious reasons, there was no reference to events prior to the reinstatement of the Luftwaffe in 1956. Even the squadrons themselves were newly numbered, with only historical air defence units remaining active – for example the Richthofen Wing and the Mölders Wing survived. I was to fly with the 2nd Squadron of Jagdbombergeschwader 32 (JaBoG32 – Fighter-Bomber Wing 32 in English).

In the RAF the basic unit of air strength is the squadron, which has its own aircraft, aircrew and ground crew. In the Luftwaffe, the basic unit was the Wing, and it was the Wing that 'owned' the aircraft and ground crew. Each Wing comprised two squadrons of aircrew, which 'borrowed' aircraft from the Wing on a daily basis. Insignia and emblems on the aircraft were those of the Wing. I was quite thankful for this, as Lechfeld's Wing emblem was quite distinguished, whereas at some point during the formation of the new Luftwaffe, the 2nd Squadron had decided to call themselves the 'flying monsters' and had a badge to match. It's possible this may have been a surreptitious reference to the old Luftwaffe, as I've seen similar insignia in photographs of WWII Messerschmitts.

A major difference to my working life was that the two Lechfeld squadrons, as indeed at all GAF bases, operated a shift system. With insufficient aircraft for two full units, each operated either the *Frühschicht* – early shift – or the *Spätschicht* – late shift. The early squadron came in very early, breakfasted together in the crewroom, flew the aircraft in the morning, had lunch together and then went home. The late squadron came in for lunch, flew in the afternoon and again at night, and then went home. The squadrons alternated on a weekly basis.

Another major difference to come to terms with was the flying order book. In the RAF, the FOB lays down comprehensive boundaries within which one may operate the aircraft. In the GAF, the FOB laid down precisely how most things were to be done with little room or freedom to deviate. There was no opportunity to 'freestyle'.

The pilots and WSOs were all very welcoming and curious at the arrival of their new exchange officer. They had all trained in the USA and spoke excellent English, which was both helpful and a hindrance. Helpful because, if I got stuck with the language, someone would always rescue me. But a hindrance for the same reason; had I not had so much help my language ability would have progressed far more

Steve Randles' first flight with his German squadron is officially marked.

quickly. I was also fortunate in knowing one of the pilots already. 'Ossi' Reinert had been one of my instructors at the TTTE so, having completed the arrival formalities, I was handed over to him for my first Luftwaffe flight.

I had flown German Tornados before, the TTTE having aircraft from all three participating nations. There were minor differences: the take-off flap angle differed slightly, giving different take-off speeds, but as Lechfeld is 1,800 feet above sea-level the speeds were different anyway. And, while the E-scope in the front cockpit of RAF aircraft was purely a TFR display, the German one also repeated the GMR display. That, however, compromised the quality of the TFR picture. Moreover, given that the WSO in the boot was adept at working the radar and was the only one to have the controls to do so, I preferred to concentrate on flying and looking out of the window. This was appreciated by the WSOs I flew with; it seemed that some of the German ex-F-104 pilots got too involved in the WSO's task, irritating them with 'helpful' advice.

It was hard to come to terms with the difference in ethos between the two air forces. In the RAF at that time the squadron was effectively your way of life. You also lived on a married patch, with social life revolving around squadron or station events. But the crews on Luftwaffe squadrons definitely viewed their service simply as a job. At the end of the day they all went their separate ways, having very little mutual social contact outside work. Fortunately, and quite by chance, the road where I had found a house was known locally as the 'uniformed street'. There were perhaps only a dozen houses, but all except one of us went to work in a uniform. We had a policeman one side of us and a Luftwaffe staff sergeant engineer, who worked in a large maintenance bunker in Landsberg, the other side. Opposite was a Luftwaffe helicopter pilot from Penzing and the deputy boss of a Hawk missile battery. We made very good friends with our neighbours, and remain in contact with most of them even now.

I really liked the routine of the early shift, the communal breakfast at the start of the day before getting on with the job of flying, and the lunch together. Most of the aircrew would then go home, but a small core would stay behind and play cards for an hour or so. I watched with great interest their games of *Schafkopf*. It is a very confusing game, and the suits are different, too; but I gradually got to grips with the basics and was, after a time, invited to join in. This cost me a fair amount of money to start with, the game being played for a *pfennig* a point. A newcomer in a card school of Bavarian sharks is easy prey, but by the time I left I was adept, invariably coming away a little in credit.

Daily flying, just as in the RAF, usually comprised two and four aircraft formations carrying out low-level simulated attacks against a variety of targets. But, while the RAF would often assign one aircraft in the formation to act as an aggressor, enabling bombers to practise tactics against air defence fighters, the Luftwaffe didn't do this. When I suggested it might be useful training, the response was that it was not in the

FOB. I pointed out that FOB didn't say that we couldn't do it – but that argument didn't prevail; there was nothing in the FOB to say that we could, therefore we couldn't! Another thing we didn't do in the Luftwaffe was air combat training. On days when the weather was unsuitable for low-level training, an RAF squadron would often carry out medium-level combat. Not so at Lechfeld. We were a fighter-bomber wing and air combat was not in our remit. Consequently, on those days when we couldn't fly at low level we would fly navigation exercises on top of the cloud and carry out simulated attacks using the radar.

One interesting aspect to my German flying was AAR. (At the time I flew Tornados at Laarbruch, only UK-based RAF squadrons practised AAR; it wasn't until the year before the Gulf Conflict that the role was introduced to RAF Germany.) The Luftwaffe did not have any large refuellers such as the Victor or VC10. They would occasionally practise with the USAF using a specially adapted KC-135. This was always exciting, as to convert the aircraft's rigid boom into the probe and drogue system used by the Tornado they simply added a short length of flexible hose and a basket onto the end of their boom. In order to get the fuel to flow following a successful contact you had to position your aircraft to achieve two 90° bends in the hose. With even the slightest twitch whilst in contact, the hose with its double bend would start snaking around and doing double back flips. Under these circumstances, it was easy to wipe off the probe and sensors on the right side of the fuselage. Thankfully, I got away with it on the couple of times I tried it.

But I also became a tanker pilot. For tactical use, the Luftwaffe had a specially adapted fuel tank which could be fitted to one of the shoulder pylons under the Tornado's fuselage. This tank had a hose and drogue unit within it almost identical to those fitted to RAF tankers, allowing the aircraft to act as a small refueller. I was assigned to fly this one day and expected a thorough brief, but none was forthcoming until I asked. Then, it was quite concise: "Not below 1,000 feet, straight and level if you can, but no more than forty-five degrees of bank if you have to." Not enough information really, as the unwary could certainly embarrass themselves; the special tank equipment was an integral part of the Tornado's own fuel system, so there was potential for the 'tanker' to be sucked dry. Anyway, I became a tanker pilot. I also experienced it from the other end of the hose, and I must admit that tanking behind a Tornado at 1,000 feet overland was quite exciting.

I soon found my feet with the squadron, and after about a year I was again leading a four-ship on a simulated attack. One of the older hands, Wolfgang Leuthner, had selected the simulated target, a substantial dam on the fringe of the Alps south of Lechfeld. I expressed my opinion that it was not a very suitable target for the American 500 lb bombs, which were the largest that we had available. This was accepted, but everyone was eager for the plan to go ahead. We had no photograph, so I only had the 1:50,000 scale map to go by. From the map I could see that the dam, with its large lake behind, was in the foothills of the mountains, posing a bit of a problem for the escape route. Nevertheless, I planned what I thought to be a suitable and workable attack and briefed accordingly. I clearly hadn't learned from my earlier experience at Munich airport that the Germans can be quite mischievous. Nor did I pick up the mounting mirth in the planning room.

As we approached the start of the simulated attack run against the dam the terrain did not really look as I expected it to be. For a start, the mountains were a lot higher and a lot closer than I anticipated. The planned attack from my initial point for the start of the attack was about a minute and a half long; about twelve nautical miles at the speed we were flying. As we set off, all looked good. Features came and went as depicted on my map. But about halfway to the target I started to get very twitchy. First, there was a huge mountain in front of me, getting rapidly closer; and second, I couldn't see the large lake and dam at all. We were at 500 feet above the ground and the visibility was limited only by the curvature of the earth, but I still couldn't see it. I gave it a few seconds longer and then gave up. The rapidly rising terrain behind where the dam and lake should have been was now very close and I had to turn away hard to avoid it. I was really annoyed with myself; I very seldom missed a target, especially one that I'd planned personally. There was little sympathy from the back-seater, who did his best to wind me up about missing such a large and obvious target.

Back at base, the other three crews all claimed hits on this easy target, which made me even more grumpy. It was only during the debrief that Wolfgang explained the problem. What I had taken to be a single contour line on the map just in front of the dam was in fact a dozen or more contour lines all superimposed on top of one another – because the dam and lake were actually on top of an 800-foot, near-vertical cliff. At 500 feet above the ground, the dam had actually been 300 feet above me on the attack run rather than well below me as I expected. I'd never even thought to look up in my vain efforts to find the dam. This target fooled other pilots new to the squadron, too. I don't know whether the team tried to catch me out again during the time that I had left at Lechfeld, but if they did I never fell for it.

There were not many air weapons ranges in southern Germany so I didn't drop as many practice bombs as I would have on an RAF squadron. However, we did enjoy the same armaments practice camps at the NATO base at Decimomannu, Sardinia. Now, the Germans take their health and well-being very seriously. In the hot Mediterranean summer we were all issued on arrival in Deci with tubes of what they called 'Afrika Korps cream' (!) – a very effective sun block. The German way of operating in Deci was a pleasant contrast from RAF methods, as they always flew about a forty-minute low-level route to the range at Capo Frasca. It was always the same track, as the Italians only authorised one route, but it was a pleasant change from the RAF's high-intensity dash direct to the range.

Another aspect was that the Luftwaffe carried out night flying at Deci, whereas the RAF would usually be out sampling the delights of the local hostelries as soon as it got dark. Night flying again comprised one authorised route around the island, flown at 1,000 feet using TFR and culminating with a single practice bomb on the range.

It was on one of these night flights that I again fell foul of the dreaded FOB. There had been some discussion about the wind that evening. Because of the lack of full approach lighting on runway one-seven at Deci, night flying was only authorised if runway three-five was to be used and could be guaranteed to be in use for the duration of the night-flying period. On this particular night the wind was forecast to freshen and turn to favour runway one-seven at some point during the evening. The desire to achieve the monthly quota of flying hours got the better of those in charge, and a stream of about twelve aircraft was launched into a very dark night. I was towards the end of the sequence. Just before arriving at Capo Frasca my aircraft developed a problem and we lost the use of one of our hydraulic systems. We consulted the flight reference cards and took appropriate actions to mitigate the failure. However, the problem required us to land into the approach-end cable, which the hook at the rear of the aircraft would catch; we would be decelerated to a gentle, but firm halt.

The Mediterranean sea breeze had set in by now, and there was a good fifteen to twenty knots of tailwind on runway three-five. We hung around waiting for the last of the aircraft to land before making our approach, as the runway would be closed for a time after we took the cable. Everyone landed happily, albeit with a strengthening tailwind. By the time we were allowed to land, the tailwind had put us above the limit to take the cable on runway three-five, so I elected to land on runway one-seven. My WSO said, "Steve, we are not allowed to land on runway one-seven at night". I acknowledged his concern but told him we were going to do it anyway as we would probably rip off the back of the aircraft if we landed at the other end. He went very quiet and said no more.

I don't know what the concern about approach lighting on runway one-seven was all about, as the lights turned out to be far better than on most RAF runways I had flown from at night. We landed quite happily at the right spot on runway one-seven, took the cable and came to a smooth halt. As I shut down the engines I noticed that the reception committee was rather larger than you would normally expect in such circumstances.

I was met by every German officer with anything to do with flight operations, supervision and flight safety. All of them were keen to know why I had landed on runway one-seven when it was specifically forbidden by the FOB. All acknowledged the fact that the tailwind on runway three-five was too great to take the RHAG, but still none seemed to understand my decision. I felt a bit grumpy about the whole thing until I was taken aside by the officer whose decision it had been to continue with night flying despite the forecast. He thanked me for landing on runway one-seven; he would have been held responsible if I'd landed on runway three-five and the aircraft had suffered damage to the back end. This cheered me up no end.

The following year the Wing deployed instead to Beja in Portugal for four weeks in the summer, a new and pleasant experience to me. I had never been to Portugal before, and using the air weapons range just south of Lisbon, having flown a low-level route around the Algarve to get there, was interesting. Only one thing marred it; football's World Cup 'Italia 90' was being played at the time. So each evening's entertainment usually involved watching a football match and drinking a few beers. All was going really well until England met West Germany in the semi-final. I'm not really a football fan, but the squadron felt that I ought to be there to support 'my' team. The score was drawn at full time, and at the end of extra time was still one-all. Then it was on to penalties – and I ended up having to buy a lot of beer!

Towards the end of my tour at Lechfeld the base was to undergo a NATO Taceval. In the RAF this is a big event, invariably involving a number of smaller, internally generated exercises leading up the big one. This was not the case at Lechfeld; it all seemed a little low-key and I was seriously worried about whether the station would be ready for the visit. My concerns were unfounded, though, as the station took all that was thrown at them and performed to a high standard.

The three Taceval days were the busiest period of flying I experienced on the exchange – for an unexpected reason. Non-native English speakers are assessed by NATO on their language skills during the evaluation. The squadron's answer to achieving a high score in this area was to get me to do all the briefings. So from the off I presented the met brief for the day, then planned and briefed the first task we were allocated. After flying that mission I naturally debriefed the crews, before being handed another mission that had been planned by different crew. This I then briefed, flew and debriefed. The same happened again for a third time. Three flights in one day, all under evaluation conditions. They were not particularly long flights, which helped me, but they really should have been; the Germans had not discovered that the longer they could stay airborne during Taceval, the fewer simulated air raids and chemical attacks they would have to endure.

The same happened on each of the remaining days of the evaluation, with the squadron scoring very highly on its language ability. Before the evaluators left, a Canadian praised me for my English. I was wearing a German flying suit and he clearly hadn't noticed my RAF badges of rank, so I thanked him without feeling the need to enlighten him.

Following the Taceval was a flight designed to test our ability to bomb accurately. Crews took off individually, flew a specified route, attacked a simulated target at a specific time, and then dropped a practice bomb at Siegenburg range. Timing at the simulated target was critical and the bomb had to be within 100 feet of the target. As we were taxiiing out, my WSO told me he wasn't happy with the way the navigation system was performing. I assured him that we would cope. Shortly after take-off the system degraded to a tertiary mode, leaving us very little by way of navigation information. I knew where we were and I had confidence that Wolfgang could give me everything we required to get to the target and then to Siegenburg range. It was early morning, and the visibility was not great, with a kind of milky opaqueness about the sky. After ten minutes I wasn't so confident, and asked Wolfgang what he thought our heading was. He replied that it was something like 040 degrees, which agreed with what my HUD was showing. Why, then, was the sun showing dimly through the haze straight ahead? A number of rather quaint German expletives issued forth from the back seat as Wolfgang slewed the heading reference around to the correct datum. By now we were unsure of our position and heading towards the Czech border. I knew we hadn't crossed the Danube, so I suggested that we stay on our current course until we came to the river and then make a decision whether to turn left or right depending on what we saw. The Danube came up and Wolfgang recognised a feature on it from which he could update the remnants of our navigation kit. Satisfied that all was now well, we went in search of our target.

It soon became apparent that, even if we flew direct, we would arrive too late and would earn a black mark for the squadron. He began to lament his lack of attention to the heading reference; however, I had flown with enough wily RAF navigators to know that all was not lost. One of the navigator/WSO's tasks on sparking the nav kit into life was to enter the current time into the computer. So now it was a simple task to work out how long it was going to take us to get to the simulated target and make a small 'adjustment' to the input such that the recording of our time over target would show us to have arrived bang on. Another adjustment post-target, together with a short cut, would see us over Siegenburg on time, too! No black marks for the squadron and two ticks in the well-done column. Wolfgang was in awe of my guile, and spread his new-found wisdom around his colleagues.

I have a great interest in military history and would often try to engage my colleagues in conversation about Luftwaffe history. Most were reluctant, although the local Bavarian *Weissbier* helped a lot in loosening tongues. I took four aircraft and crews to RAF Coltishall one day and we went to the officers' mess for lunch. Afterwards, in the ante-room, I found my boss, Major Unterstaller, looking pensively at one of the paintings on the wall. "Steve," he said, "I have looked at all the paintings in the mess. Why are the Messerschmitts always in front of the Spitfires?" I smiled; it didn't need a reply.

The person I had most response from about Luftwaffe history was Wolfgang Leuthner, he of the tricky dam. After about eighteen months on the squadron Wolfgang took me to a small, almost disused building on the far side of the airfield. Inside was a very interesting display of Lechfeld's history during both world wars. It was sad that such artefacts were not allowed to be on open display. But as a result of my interest in their history, I became known as '*der lezter Kriegsgefangener*' – the 'last prisoner of war', and I was always introduced to visiting German crews as such.

As a family we found living in Bavaria delightful. We were an hour's drive from the Alps, which provided wonderful walking in the summer and skiing in the winter. We were also only an hour from Munich. Kaufering, where we lived, was on the

'*Der lezter Kriegsgefangener*' – the 'last prisoner of war'. Steve Randles at 'Stalag Luft Lechfeld'.

Romantische Straße and had the river Lech running through it. Not five miles away was the pretty town of Landsberg, while the Ammersee and Starnbergersee lakes, both offering lovely walks and lively beer gardens, were on the way to Munich, It was hardly surprising, therefore, that almost everyone we knew came to visit. At some points we had the kids doubled up in one room, every other bedroom full, and visitors in the cellar, too. Fortunately, the cellar was warm and dry.

It wasn't just friends, either. In order to gain and maintain an appropriate security clearance, RAF officers have to undergo a vetting procedure at regular intervals. An acquaintance had nominated me as a reference on one such review. I had acted in such a capacity for several people over the years and had never had to do more than complete a form and return it to the authorities. Not this time though; the official carrying out this review contacted me, saying he felt it important that he see me and carry out an interview. I was puzzled, but didn't know enough about the system to query it. He asked for details of any local hotels that I knew and I offered to put him up as we were 'vacant' that week. The penny dropped when he said that he would be accompanied by his wife, and could she please stay too?

The seemingly endless procession of visitors had clearly not escaped the notice of our neighbours, leading to our being surprised one New Year's eve. A large number of them, all dressed in travelling clothes and carrying suitcases, knocked on the door at midnight and enquired whether we had any vacancies. They placed a large sign by the front gate declaring the property to be 'Randles Guesthouse', with 'vacancies always available'. They also brought several bottles of champagne with which to celebrate the New Year.

I was at Lechfeld throughout the period when things were happening in East Germany, indeed throughout the Soviet Union and the whole Warsaw Pact. The first evidence we saw was the influx of vast numbers of East Germans to our area. Many started moving to the West via Czechoslovakia or through Hungary and Austria into Bavaria. The Berlin Wall came down, but to be quite honest the full impact of that was not immediately apparent. My German colleagues were of mixed opinions on the whole process of reunification. All were excited at the prospect of the two countries becoming one again, but that was offset to a large degree by the realisation that it was going to cost them a great deal in taxes. Bringing the East up to western standards would mean that government spending in the West would be much reduced for many years. After I left, reunification had a great impact on the air force, with opportunities arising to train with and against many Soviet aircraft types. Indeed the Luftwaffe was able to offer training opportunities to the RAF during the run up to Gulf War One. But that would all be for later.

Steve with his German colleagues celebrating his last flight.

My exchange tour finished in 1990. After my final flight with JaBoG32 I was met by the squadron and station hierarchy together with all my new-found friends and colleagues, and we enjoyed a very fine lunch and a few *Weissbiers* together. Throughout my tour I had worn mainly German flying kit, but I found their flying boots, which were made of hard and durable leather, to be very uncomfortable. Consequently it had not been long before I'd started to wear my RAF boots, which were much more comfortable. Now, as I was about to leave the squadron for the last time, I was jumped on and my boots forcibly removed. Then they were nailed to the beam next to the pair I had seen when I'd first arrived. So now I knew; those were my F-104 predecessor's boots, and he'd evidently had the same problem.

I returned to the RAF on 31 Squadron at RAF Brüggen as a flight commander. Saddam Hussein had invaded Kuwait just before I'd left Lechfeld, and a bare few weeks later I found myself leading four crews to Bahrain to join the Brüggen detachment at Muharraq.

My exchange tour was quickly history. It had been completely different to what I imagined it would be. There were sometimes frustrations but, on the whole, I feel very privileged to have been allowed to fly with the Luftwaffe and to experience the way another air force operates. As a family we made very good friends, perhaps not where I expected to find them, but good friends nonetheless. Our lives are richer for our time in Bavaria.

CHAPTER 8

SCUD HUNTING

As well as replacing Vulcans, Buccaneers and strike/attack Jaguars, the Tornado also took over from a recce Jaguar squadron in Germany. For this role a variant of the aircraft known as the GR1A was developed; the type had internal recce sensors, and a second squadron of these specialists was also formed in the UK. Later in the aircraft's life the nature of the tactical recce fit altered, with advanced, podded equipment replacing the original sensors. At the same time the pattern of operations shifted towards an almost continuous series of overseas operational deployments, with the Tornado recce product becoming an integral – and much in demand – part of the overall ISTAR (intelligence, surveillance, target acquisition and reconnaissance) effort. Thus it became necessary for all crews to be able to perform recce tasks – and the new equipment made this possible. So in time the edges of the traditional tac recce role began to be blurred, but not before the original specialist squadrons had what was undoubtedly one of their finest hours – and one which received extensive press coverage; Scud hunting in the Gulf Conflict.

I first knew Alan Threadgould when we were flight commanders flying Jaguars at RAF Coltishall, he on a recce unit, and I on an attack squadron. As is the way with the RAF our paths subsequently diverged, but it's nevertheless been a pleasure to remake his acquaintance in the preparation of this book. Having been in the front line of operations at Dhahran during 1991, he is well placed to tell us how it really was in Scud country.

GROUP CAPTAIN ALAN THREADGOULD (RETD)

"This is bad-land." With those four words Tim Robinson announced that II(AC) Squadron had joined the war against Saddam Hussein for the liberation of Kuwait. He and I had just crossed into Iraq to the west of the diamond-shaped 'neutral zone'; Dick Garwood and John Hill were somewhere out there in the darkness as we headed off on the first of our Scud-hunting missions.

The recce jets had not flown on the first two nights while the bomber boys rained mayhem down on Iraq. In General Norman Schwarzkopf's words, the Tornado was being the 'thunder and lightning of Desert Storm'. On day three, as I came out of the office Dick was clutching the tasking order that would send us on our way. It was a simple task; two parallel strip searches some twenty kilometres long and ten kilometres apart, with the aim of detecting Scud missiles. Scuds were a very important part of the target library. Keeping the Israelis out of the war was a prime concern of the allies, and Saddam knew this; hence his early Scud attacks on Tel Aviv.

Tim and I set off on the navigation and recce planning, while Dick and John set to work on the other important stuff, particularly escape and evasion. Dick's 'cunning plan' of swimming the Euphrates should we be shot down in the north seemed good to guys who had only been in theatre for five days; the river was such a thin line on the map. It was only days later when we saw on CNN the kilometre-wide raging torrent that we realised the folly of that plan. Still, it has provided many a good laugh since.

The standard fuel fit for peacetime ops was two, or sometimes four, 1,500-litre external tanks. For Desert Storm, approval had been given for us to carry the 2,250-litre tanks designed initially for the Tornado F3. We had not flown with them yet, but out at the jet with checklist in one hand and flashlight in the other, we checked these monsters, aware of the alarming, computer-generated images that BAe had sent to us showing the effect of jettisoning them. How something so big could come off the wing, flip over and possibly hit the top of the wing and then the fin was beyond belief; but that was the least of our worries, and I put the images out of my mind – for now.

We launched into the darkness up the 'olive trail' route to the AAR area. We switched to the AWACS channel where the radio chatter was continuous; so much for all the radio-out training we had done in the past. A first was that we had been handed night-vision goggles. An odd time to learn, but a look though them made one realise how many aircraft were in the sky – the coalition launched some 2,800 sorties in the first twenty-four hours. Approaching the tanker I was very disturbed to get locked up by an S-60 AAA radar. This piece of Russian equipment had been widely sold around the world and, old as it was, a hit from one of its 57mm rounds would not be pleasant. But hang on, I thought, we aren't even in enemy territory yet. We had no range on the AAA source, just a steady bearing out at ten o'clock. All through the RV and refuelling the S-60 was there, looking at us. During the descent to low level it never wavered, and even when we were down at 200 feet doing over 500 knots it was still steady – but had moved around closer to nine o'clock. It was therefore not far away. As Tim announced our crossing into Iraq it had gone round to eight o'clock and from then on fell away. It was only several hours later that we found out it belonged to an Egyptian unit; it had been there for weeks and everyone else was well aware of it. Thanks for the briefing, guys!

With the TFR and autopilot engaged at the 200-foot setting, hard-ride, and with the throttles firewalled and every light on the aircraft turned off, we were plonking along in the mid-500 knot range. The TF was magnificent, although Tim was complaining that the sensor imagery was not good; there was nothing we could do about that, though. It was darker than I can remember any other night trip being. The odd Bedouin encampment slipped past the cockpit, so close that you felt they could be touched. So far, so good – but that was to change.

On our northerly heading we had about thirty kilometres to go before the turn south-eastwards for the strip search. As we approached the turn I glanced at the fuel gauges and was horrified; we were using internal fuel, when the externals should have had tons left. That would have to be a problem for after the target, as I had no spare capacity to work it out at this stage. We completed the strip and turned back southwards. I allowed myself a quick radio call to make sure Dick was OK; now for this fuel problem.

My immediate thought was that we would not make the border and that the boss was going to have to eject on the first night of his war (it would have been my third time, by the way). To stand a chance we had to get rid of these tanks; I seemed to remember BAe's recommendation for jettisoning empty 2,250s was 10,000 feet, straight and level, below 250 knots. But ours were almost full, and who knows what was in the 1,500-litre tanks. We had to stay low and fast for tactical reasons and were eating up what fuel we had left very quickly. Well, needs must, and we were at war – so at 580 knots and still at 200 feet we gingerly pressed the jettison button. Success! All four tanks cleared safely. Who needs test pilots?!

We crossed the Saudi border not long after and zoom climbed to get as high as possible to save what fuel we had left. We contacted AWACS and declared an emergency, requesting an immediate diversion to the absolutely nearest suitable airfield. They came back straight away with, "Turn 150 degrees for King Khalid military strip at seventy miles". What music to our ears – but landing a Tornado on a dirt strip? Shows how little I had had time to learn about the area, for out of the dust and haze appeared an airfield looking something akin to Heathrow. Quite a relief; we landed with just 600 kilograms remaining, right in line with normal peacetime regulations. We quickly refuelled with the help of some American ground crew who told us they had been sent to a UK base six months previously to learn about Tornados. Nothing like planning well in advance! We got airborne in the middle of a Scud warning with most of the airfield lights turned off, so our landing light actually became a take-off light. Taxiing in at Dhahran with all four tanks missing was a great way to get the troops to understand that we really were now at war.

It took our engineering guys over two days to find out why those external tanks had stopped feeding. The tiniest capacitor was at fault – and I was presented with it later.

The Tornado recce jet was an adaptation of the standard GR1 mud-mover. The 27mm Mauser cannons were removed and sensors and recording devices fitted in their place. The fit was an infra-red linescanner mounted vertically, with two sideways-looking infra-red sensors looking left and right. Between them they gave just over 180 degrees coverage. The system was conceived towards the end of the Cold War when our concept of operations envisaged high-speed, low-level, day or night, all-weather flying. For this the sensors were excellent and the quality of the IR imagery so good that it was often hard to remember that it was in fact IR. On the down side, resolution fell off dramatically with altitude; even pictures taken at 1,000 feet were hard to interpret. This would become an issue as Desert Storm progressed – but more of that later.

Each of the three sensors was connected to two tape recorders. The primary tapes recorded continuously when selected, giving about forty-five minutes recording time. The navigator tapes could, however, be deselected, rewound and played back to view sections of recorded imagery. Each target on a mission was given a numbered 'event mark'. To save searching a whole tape after flight the system had an edit function whereby it searched all the prime tapes and took target data off each sensor using the event marks as reference and compiling that data onto a tape perhaps only four or five minutes in length.

One of the system specifications was that any tape could be played on any recorder. With twelve aircraft on the squadron each with six recorders, and with an equal number of recorders in the RIC, it's easy to see that this was a demanding specification, and in my time as boss it never fully worked; we ended up playing 'musical tape recorders', matching those which we knew were better than others.

This had been at the root of our problems from 1 January 1989, the day we had formed II Squadron at RAF Laarbruch. For me, it had been like going home; as I had previously flown recce Phantoms there with II Squadron in the 1970s. Anyway, the technical difficulties with the Tornado recce system meant that our first aircraft had no sensors fitted. But as many of our crews, particularly the navigators, had no previous recce experience, it gave us the opportunity to get them into recce ops before they had to worry about operating the sensors. There had been other teething problems, with some elements of the system being renowned for catching fire. One particular box, the framing mirror unit, often did so, and soon became known as 'the flaming mirror unit'.

The recce system was eventually signed off as fit for purpose and the first set of equipment was delivered to Laarbruch by mid-year. After the first mission that we flew with the system installed, Ken McCallum (navigator extraordinaire) handed the edit tape to Andy Pooley, OC RIC, with great excitement – but the subsequent analysis immediately revealed problems. All had seemed to go OK in the air, but playing the edit tape in the RIC revealed it to be a failure, with lots of missing data. Much effort from industry, the RAF test and evaluation teams, and my navigators and engineers would continue over the following six months. But it was not resolved, which was the reason that we didn't deploy to Desert Storm until the very last minute. Some very senior officers had wanted us out there earlier, but my argument was that if we couldn't fix it at Laarbruch with all the experts close by, including a contractor working party, we would certainly not be able to fix it in Saudi Arabia.

It was while all these engineering investigations were going on that we had a NATO exchange with a Greek recce Mirage squadron. As per normal practice, half of us went to their base while half of their squadron came to us at Laarbruch. On the last night of the exchange the Greeks threw a 'hangar party' at Laarbruch in one of our concrete HASs. The Greek C-130 which had flown in to pick them up had also off-loaded some wonderful Greek food and a large quantity of liquid refreshment. All we had to do was supply tables, chairs and the officers' mess crockery. It was an amazing night with lots of 'Zorba the Greek' dancing and way too much imbibing.

The next day was to be a down day – a good decision by the boss. However, that morning I was woken by a telephone call from Wing Commander Dave Wilby, who was standing in for the station commander. Through the haze of very red eyes and the worst headache I had had for a long time, I heard Dave say that Kuwait had been invaded and that II Squadron's recce capability was urgently needed. "Yeah, right – nice one Dave, very funny. I'll see you later."

But something in his voice made me stay on the line and, sure enough, after a few more minutes I was bolt upright in bed realising we could be going into a war zone within forty-eight hours. I needed more information, but a major and equally daunting task was to first pass by the mess and explain to the manager why most of the crockery he had lent us was laying shattered on the HAS floor. "Don't worry – just send me the bill!" It wouldn't be the last time I would say that.

From the mess it was off to the ops room where several of the station executives were gathering. Dave Wilby gave us as much intelligence as he could, and then it was back to the squadron to start planning. Our callout plan worked remarkably well despite the night before, and I was soon able to break the news to my guys. It was very quiet in the room.

Over the next few hours we went through the routine of 'are we going tonight ... or not going tonight ... or not at all ... or maybe tomorrow?' In the end the initial deployment took a very different direction and we were stood down. But over the next several months RAF squadrons deployed and I started losing experienced crews to bolster those units. Andy Pooley, OC RIC, was also deployed to Tabuk, and it was quite a while before I saw him again.

The year quickly came to an end with no real improvement on the technical side of the recce system. Indeed problems would persist throughout my time in command and for a long time afterwards. But we nevertheless intensified our night recce and AAR training. Some restrictions were lifted so we could train with TFR at heights and speeds we'd use for war – and sometimes in cloud. Now, there are many things I have done with an aeroplane over the years that were orgasmic. But night TF in cloud, at 300 feet and 450 knots in the Scottish mountains in a snow storm, is something that goes in the category of 'been there, done that, don't ever want to do it again, I'm too old!' But soon we would be at war and being fired at – and 'Tommy TF' was becoming our best friend.

Unlike many of our colleagues we spent Christmas at home, but it was a very tense time as we stood by to deploy at short notice. The deadline was approaching for Saddam to leave Kuwait and he was showing no signs of doing so. Eventually we got our deployment date of 14 January, and we also learned that some of Glenn Torpy's XIII Squadron would be joining us. This was good news as they had some very experienced Tornado recce guys. We were to fly three of the six II Squadron aircraft to Dhahran in eastern Saudi, with Glenn and his team taking the other three.

The previously mentioned Dick Garwood had arrived at Laarbruch as one of my flight commanders on the day Saddam invaded Kuwait. We had been on recce Jaguars together and had both flown RF-4C recce Phantoms in Texas, so I was glad to see such an experienced man. I remember calling him as he was unpacking the removal van: "Can you remember how to tank a Jaguar, because the Tornado is similar and you need to come to work now." Since then, weather and aircraft availability had conspired so that he hadn't completed the full night tanking syllabus. Fortunately, though, the first prod on our eventual deployment to Saudi would be at about 4am, so I was able to sign him off at 25,000 feet over France and declare him fully operational and ready to go to war. That was, by the way, his first time refuelling from a TriStar, which was more challenging than the Victor and VC10 he'd been used to.

We arrived in Dhahran at dusk and were allocated shelters next to the few Kuwaiti A-4s that had been flown out of Kuwait as Saddam had invaded. Wing Commander Jerry Witts, OC 31 Squadron, and Wing Commander Ivor Evans, OC IX Squadron, and their guys had done a great job in making some old and scruffy buildings look business-like. Torps and his team had recently arrived, so we now had four squadron commanders fighting over the boss's office. Actually it all worked very well, with Jerry being the flying wing commander. Group Captain Cliff Spink, providing top cover, did an outstanding job of being there when we needed him; he didn't try to be over-wise, just let us get on with our jobs.

With just under three days to the deadline the recce crews had a lot of catching up to do on local procedures, and some even managed to get a few area-familiarisation sorties flown. This included flying very low and fast over the British army to make them aware of what sudden air attack would be like. As with several others, though, my first mission in theatre was to go to war in Iraq.

Torps and I spent quite a while poring over the operation order that detailed the planned missions for the first two days, and we were mind-boggled. It was a large, computer printout about two inches thick with row after row of missions. My first thought was that, with so many missions, this would be over on the first night – but as is often the case I was wrong.

On the 16th we heard that the war would start that night. I had sent most of my people back to their quarters by the time the bomber guys started suiting up. Things were getting tense and the last thing we needed was too many people milling about and getting in the way. I shook hands with Jerry and wished him luck as he and his eight-ship left for their aircraft. The squadron building became ominously quiet. Only ten or fifteen people were left behind when the air raid warning sounded. Behind the building were eighteen-wheeler ISO containers, each hardened with thick pieces of steel and sand; inside were inflatable NBC shelters. All were numbered and we had each been allocated to one. Each held about fifteen, but with so few people left, occupancy was down to a maximum of three. I was with one of the 31 Squadron guys in mine. We were casually putting on our NBC kit when four of the loudest bangs I have ever heard rattled the whole structure. I looked across at my companion, and even through his gas mask I could see two huge, startled eyes looking out. I'm sure mine were exactly the same. The speed of dressing dramatically increased! Dhahran was one of the best protected airfields in the world, with squadrons of F-15s, F3 Tornados, AWACS, EW jammers, Patriot missiles, and loads of point-defence AAA guns. And yet some Iraqi aircraft had got through? Morale hit an all-time low, and in the next few minutes my confidence in this being a one or two-week war was shattered.

It was only when we emerged that we realised there was a Patriot battery just the other side of a large wall, and that what we had heard was them launching. We were to hear many more before the war was over, as the eastern part of the kingdom took the brunt of the initial Iraqi attacks. On this occasion, and once our heart rates were nearly normal, I and the last of the recce guys left for our accommodation in Al Khobar. There, we heard on Radio Bahrain that Yugoslavia had come in with a last-minute peace plan. I looked at my watch and thought that they had better be quick; the first strikes would hit in five minutes.

The Dhahran command team during the first Gulf Conflict. From the left: Wing Commander Ivor Evans, OC IX(B) Squadron; Wing Commander Jerry Witts, OC 31 Squadron and the overall commander; Wing Commander Alan Threadgould, OC II(AC) Squadron; Wing Commander Glen Torpy, OC XIII Squadron (later to become chief of the air staff).

And so to the recce war. The mission I described earlier was actually one of the few I flew specifically looking for Scuds. As well as being politically sensitive targets, several bits of them had landed close to us after having been partially destroyed by Patriot missiles. So the incentive for finding them was there, and we did actually locate one on that first mission – although more by luck than anything else. Just as Dick Garwood and John Hill came to the end of their strip search, their autopilot, which had been in the terrain-following mode, kicked out and the aircraft pitched up into a steep climb. Dick took manual control and flew it back down to 200 feet, but in doing so he flew about five kilometres past the end point of the strip – and at that point overflew the Scud. We never worked out why the imagery from the sensors was very bad that night, but it was still possible to see the shape of the transporter-erector-launcher and the tent that sits next to the missile where all the pre-launch calculations are done. Once the news of the sighting hit the newswires, Downing Street asked for a copy of the photograph. I have a feeling they might have been underwhelmed!

A great percentage of the missions we flew were over the terrain where, eventually, Schwarzkopf's now famous 'left hook' would take coalition forces on their way to Kuwait and victory. For us, who did not know that plan, it was disappointing to come back off so many missions and find nothing on the imagery. But of course that was exactly what the planners wanted to see, and when we eventually found that out we felt good at having contributed to that success.

Glenn Torpy had a visit one night from the SAS unit that was billeted close to our squadron building. They came over to see what help we might be able to give them, and Torps subsequently flew some very long missions out west where he actually covered the ingress route that those guys would take later after being ferried out there by some brave aircrew of the special forces C-130s and CH-47s. Not for them the relative safety of 550 knots.

The Iraqi Republican Guard was a much-feared and well-armed force, and for many days we were not tasked into their area. Eventually we were sent in their direction, and Torps flew the first mission. I understand there were great cheers of joy raised in the coalition air operation centre when he returned unscathed. I flew the second mission into the area later that night. Just as Tim and I approached a point where a SAM-8 had previously been recorded, our radar-warning receiver lit up and we got the tell-tale sound in our ears of a radar lock up. I looked down and saw on the screen that it was actually one of the USN's F-18s. OK heart, you can start beating again. The SAM-8 is a particularly nasty piece of kit and was one of the few that really posed a threat to us at the heights and speeds we were flying.

Sadly, losses began to happen and a decision was made for some very good reasons to push the bomber guys up to the relative safety of medium altitude. Unfortunately, the story went out that the losses were the inevitable result of operating at very low altitude, but this was not entirely true. Of the five Tornados that the RAF lost during Desert Storm only one was shot down below 3,500 feet. Two actually flew into the ground – but they were not shot down. More than twenty years on I am still explaining that to USAF friends who have the idea that low level is fun in peacetime but has no place in war.

Part of my explanation to them emphasised that we, the recce team, continued at low level throughout without loss. Of course we had little choice, for the reasons of sensor resolution I explained earlier. But as it turned out our high-speed, low-level flying was fine anyway. Nothing is ever totally simple and there were no doubt many factors involved; perhaps the enemy were now focusing higher up.

As coalition forces on the ground moved north, a directive came that all aircraft had to be above 25,000 feet when crossing a line some 100 miles north of the Iraq

/Saudi border. Well, this was fine for the bomber boys; they were up there anyway. But for us reccies it meant leaving our comfort zone at 200 feet and climbing while still in enemy territory. And it was here that, again, the radar warner lit up and there, over my right shoulder, were AAA tracers. They were out of range, but it made us realise how vulnerable we were in that manoeuvre.

One of the last missions I flew was a route recce down the main road from Baghdad to Basrah. It had been a particularly difficult mission because the autopilot / TFR combination kept kicking out every couple of minutes. Each time we pitched up a few hundred feet, and I'd take manual control and get back to 200 feet. In the end I flew it manually. As we got closer to Basrah the road traffic built up significantly as the Iraqi army tried to escape the leading edge of coalition ground troops. It took longer than maybe it should have done for me to realise that they didn't have small flashing lights on their trucks – it was actually small-arms tracer!

As we approached the now infamous point that became known as Mutla Ridge, where the Apaches and A-10s had destroyed a huge number of enemy vehicles, we noticed what looked like a very low cloud deck. Soon it was down to 250 feet and I began to smell the burning oil. This of course came from the oil fields to the west of us which Saddam had ignited. The next night the stand-down order came for nearly all coalition aircraft. We were put on standby to do recce of the route that would take Stormin' Norman and others to the meeting at which Iraq surrendered, but in the event we were not called upon.

So with the war over we settled down to sunbathing beside an empty pool and eating more curries at BAe's cafeteria, knowing that, as the last to arrive in theatre, we would be among the last to leave. Eventually we got a departure date; Glenn would take three jets back to the UK and I'd take three back to Germany. But I concocted a plan to have the other two of our crews go back a few days earlier and then launch from Laarbruch to rendezvous with us over Germany – so we could arrive as a five-ship for the much-awaited celebrations.

Well, so much for the best-laid plans. I had just refuelled to full over the north coast of Egypt when an oil-pressure light came on showing the right engine was in trouble. I had to shut it down and, with four external fuel tanks and internals full and only one engine running, the Tornado was only going down. So, once again I had again to blow all four tanks; meanwhile, Tim was rapidly plotting our diversion to Crete, where we sat for four days until the aircraft was repaired. "Don't worry – just send me the bill!"

By way of an epilogue I do remember back in 1982 on 41(F) Jaguar Squadron doing a flight check on a young pilot who was eight months into his first tour. It didn't go very well and I made him retake it. In the debrief we discussed the pressure that he had felt and how that might have affected his performance that day. I said, "Pressure? One day I might have to take you to war. That would be pressure." That young Jaguar pilot was Dick Garwood. He rose to be deputy commander of Air Command – and I know he won't mind me telling the story.

CHAPTER 9

KEEPING THE 'FIN' AIRBORNE

It's no exaggeration to say that an RAF squadron stands or falls by its engineering. The number of technical personnel on a fighter-bomber squadron vastly exceeds that of the aircrew, but few of the aircrew got to know (in my time at least) many of the techies well. Yes, there was daily interface while crewing in and out; yes, there were beer calls and Christmas social events; and yes, the aircrew usually saw plenty of the two or three engineering officers. But to a great extent the two tribes lived separate lives.

I never worked with Les Hendry but I meet him socially nowadays, enough to say with certainty that I would have enjoyed working with him. Navigators might not have agreed, though, as he was always stealing their flying – Les must be one of very few engineers who can boast thirty flying hours on the Tornado.

On the other hand I had a working relationship with Peter Gipson which surprised me somewhat. By the time I arrived at the helm of my Tornado squadron I had been in the RAF for many years. But, perhaps for the 'two tribes' reasons I've alluded to, I was unprepared for the relationship between a squadron commander and the unit's senior non-commissioned man. I quickly came to enjoy and value our times sitting and sorting out the world in his little office in the line hut, and I can still clearly hear the sounds of the place and smell its distinct atmosphere. Peter used to ply me with tea so thick you could stand your spoon in it – and I retain to this day my taste for strong tea. Either that or my taste buds were so cauterised by his brew that I need to drink it strong now to taste it! So pour yourselves a cup and enjoy some Tornado engineering stories from the distinctive viewpoints of a SEngO and a 'wobbly' – a squadron warrant officer.

SQUADRON LEADER LES HENDRY (RETD) AND WARRANT OFFICER PETER GIPSON (RETD)

SEngO at home base

My squadron resided in the north-west corner of Brüggen airfield on a HAS site. We were a nuclear response unit with all that that entailed, and in those days we had an establishment of thirteen Tornados. Although I actually had fifteen, as additional 'in-use reserves' were allocated to each front-line squadron.

HAS operations had their ups and downs, sucking up

huge numbers of men during exercise (war) and always being a tricky scenario to manage. During one particular Mineval (an exercise organised and run internally by the station) it happened that I had forty-odd ground crew away for a couple of weeks manning a Tornado turnround facility in Scotland. In a real war situation they would have been recovered; that wasn't going to happen in this case, so I therefore declared before the exercise to all the relevant people that, when we got to the phase where we would enact a mass launch, I would only be able to dispatch six aircraft rather than the ten I had on site. For exercise purposes they could plan and man the ten but, because of my peacetime constraint, they could not all be launched.

But when the time came the order from the operations centre was to launch ten, and I went about my business up to the point where I could get no agreement on which four were staying on the ground. On the contrary, it emerged that I was indeed physically to launch all ten. Various low-flying teddies were dispatched out of the cot to no avail; my boss, Jerry Witts, was airborne and unable to help me. So in the finest tradition I mustered everybody I had, including myself, and we got the aircraft away, but not in as safe a fashion as I would have wished.

After the exercise had finished I sat down and wrote my letter of resignation as SEngO 31 Squadron. Fundamentally it said that if 'they', my superior officers, were not going to listen to me, they could do without me. Jerry had only been in charge of the squadron for a matter of weeks when this letter hit his desk. We sat down and had a chat about the price of fish, and life at the end of the universe – and decided we would continue as is. I would do my best, but if ever I considered we were in overstretch mode I would be listened to. As it happened, Jerry and I developed a very close working relationship which worked well right through the Gulf Conflict and to the end of my tour on the squadron.

Today I am still known as the SEngO who kept resigning, even though it was only one incident. But I had a system of telling my superiors twice if I thought something wasn't going to work and that we should be doing it a different way. I never told them a third time, merely waiting to pick up the pieces when things fell apart. Jerry cottoned onto this and would occasionally ask "Is it the first or second time you have told me this?" A copy of my letter of resignation found its way into the squadron diary and is still there to this day at Marham.

Wobbly at home base

If you look up the synonyms for the simple word 'busy', every one of the explanations offered sums up our squadron's operating period at Brüggen. It was towards the end of the Cold War. We worked hard and, when we could, we played hard. We were there to do a job and it was done well.

My time on 31 Squadron was busy and exciting. I came to the Tornado from 92 (Phantom) Squadron at Wildenrath, halfway through my overseas tour. My trade was engines, and my recent background was on Lightnings and Phantoms. With a spell in the Tornado RB199 engine bay at RAF Laarbruch behind me I knew about the new jet's powerful modular engine, but the rest of this complex machine was a hidden secret – and one I had to unwrap.

It was a steep learning curve and I spent as much time as I could in the HASs, learning as I went. This was only the second time in my RAF career I'd worked with an aircraft that carried bombs, so there was much to learn, and nowhere more so than in the field of 'special weapons'. Shortly after my arrival I was dispatched back to the UK to learn about this aspect of the role. And I soon learned what a very serious business it was.

That was the only course I had ever attended where the students were not given notes of any sort. It had to be learned there and then in the classroom. You arrived with nothing and left with nothing, except what you had managed to pack into those grey cells. And you discussed that knowledge with nobody. When asked on return to Brüggen by a trusting wife what exactly I had learned on the course, she had to believe the story spun!

I was in a supervisory position as the squadron continued to practise loading and unloading these weapons, with myself and others ensuring that procedures were followed to the letter. This was demanding work. Even writing today, I recall the concentration and the constant tension to get it right; the pressure of that responsibility is still palpable.

SEngO and the bomb

When I arrived at Brüggen we were very much a nuclear strike squadron, and as part of the Wing we took our turn as the duty squadron to 'stand Q', with two Tornados sitting fully loaded with nuclear weapons, at X minutes readiness on the QRA site at the western end of the runway. To go with this was a considerable amount of training for our aircrews and ground crews, which was repeated on an extremely demanding basis. The loading of a nuclear weapon also required an officer, commissioned or warrant, to be present to supervise the load and to ensure that all processes and procedures are adhered to.

Early in my tour I had a call from an SNCO in the armament training cell asking me when I would like to book my weapon load supervising officer training. My response to the call was to say, "No thanks". There was some surprise at the other end of the line and I was told that "all the SEngOs have to do it sir, it's part of your role". I repeated my "no thanks". The next day I had a call from the flight lieutenant commanding the training cell and we repeated the conversation I had had with his SNCO the day before.

On the third day I had a call from the squadron leader running the armament squadron and we again repeated the conversation I had had with his flight lieutenant the day before.

The next day I had a call from my boss, Wing Commander Pete Dunlop, saying he wanted to have a chat. I popped over to his office and was greeted with, "OC engineering just called to say you are refusing to do your WLSO training; would you like to tell me why?"

"I have two JEngOs and a warrant who are trained WLSOs, so the question is whether you would like to have your senior engineer stand next to one aircraft for up to two hours watching four fully-trained men load one weapon onto one jet? Or would you prefer me to be managing the ground effort to get all twelve of our jets serviceable for operations?" Pete Dunlop just smiled. The next day I had no calls.

Wobbly on exercise

I had arrived at Brüggen during a 'bolthole'. The word is defined as a place where a person can escape and hide – but in this case there was no escape and nowhere to hide. With the tarmac of the squadron's dispersal being resurfaced, we were operating from a remote site with very limited accommodation for air and ground crews alike. My personal 'bolthole' was a small, cupboard-sized office shared with the JEngO, hidden deep inside a HAS. A place that never saw the light of day, a hidey-hole that saw us sharing the engineering and administration tasks. A couple of hours spent in such a lightless and airless environment was quite enough for any one shift, so I would get out and about, borrowing a Land Rover to do an inspection of progress of work at our home dispersal. I was never satisfied, but in fact the time spent operating in that environment did us no harm and sharpened our deployment skills.

Of course we had to practise. The whole function of the squadron was under constant scrutiny. We never knew when we might be called upon to carry out whatever task was allotted to us. That's what we did, and we strove to get it right. There could be no back sliding. When the Taceval team arrived, usually in the middle of the night, we knew it had to be right. Those intensely deep tests of the many functions of the squadron would be observed by external teams and reported upwards. If we got it wrong we would hear about it in no uncertain manner. The professional pride of the squadron ground crew was then, and still is, so very important on such occasions.

Defending our squadron site against exercise intruders was, surprisingly, entirely our responsibility. It is a long haul for the average RAF tradesman, normally engaged in maintaining a complex aircraft, to act as an armed perimeter guard. The two duties are widely separate, but both need to be carried out with the same degree of fortitude. The strength of the squadron relies on its manpower, all of its manpower, the multi-role engineering ground crew being no exception.

There are natural leaders in this world, and the squadron had no shortage of them. The SNCOs and JNCOs took on vital management tasks as required. I recall with pleasure the speed after the 'alert' at which the entire site would be secured, even denying the testing team access until identities were proven.

SEngO on detachment

Red Flag is a war simulation exercise held at Nellis air base, next to Las Vegas, to where we deployed from time to time. At Nellis the Americans had a system whereby there was a 'red line' around the ramp, and moving aircraft and equipment over this line was seriously controlled. To get permission to take an aircraft off the ramp into a hangar could take hours, and my squadron didn't relate well to that. One aircraft needed to be raised on jacks for a quick undercarriage retraction test. I made the decision to jack it outside and not bother with trying to 'cross the red line'. So the aircraft was turned into wind (it was breezy) and we commenced jacking.

The engineering chain of command at Red Flag was interesting, to say the least. The aircraft were loaned by the European Tornado squadrons to the RAF unit at Goose Bay, Canada, for the summer exercise season – and then flown onwards to Nellis. For Red Flag I was the operational SEngO as usual, but there was also a Goose Bay squadron leader who was responsible for engineering standards of the aircraft at Goose Bay and on Red Flag. For the sake of this story we will call him 'X'. At Nellis there was also a USAF maintenance colonel in overall charge of base engineering standards. So for three weeks in 1990 I was operating my twelve Tornados at 'war' (a scenario which would be repeated for real in the Gulf the following January).

Now, X saw me jacking the aircraft on the line and suggested we should place the aircraft in a hangar because of the wind speed. Based on my response he left the line! A little while later the USAF colonel came onto the line and asked how things were going; he pointed out to me that X was unhappy with the wind speed. I told him that if X could provide the colonel the wind speed limits for jacking I would defer to his judgement. Neither of them came back to me and the job was completed without incident, in far less time than it would have taken to obtain permission to move the aircraft over the red line. The exercise 'war' continued.

Similar improvisation occurred during the real war. We were the lead squadron for the mud-movers based in Dhahran, Saudi Arabia. We had arrived in theatre late to open this third base station and only had a couple of weeks before hostilities commenced. We were a runway denial squadron and, as such, used the JP233. This required the crews to fly straight and level over an airfield at low level to dispense the weapons. It soon became clear that the Iraqi air force was not as much of a threat as expected, and so we only used JP233 on the first day of operations, after which the aircraft were each loaded with eight 1,000 lb dumb (unguided) bombs. This caused issues for the engineers, as twin-store carriers, originally designed for use by Harriers, had to be used. These were not really up to the strain, to the extent that during a very rapid turnround one of the carriers could not be removed from its pylon. Time was tight and I made the decision to make the aircraft armament system live on the ground and explosively eject the carrier from the aircraft. Horsehair matting and anything else that would break the fall was placed under the aircraft. The aircraft survived the incident; the carrier did not.

Jerry Witts and I had devised a system for having spare aircraft available for each wave. We had hard rules regarding which unserviceabilities would leave the aircraft as 'war goers' and which would not. In particular, the ECM system and IFF had to be fully functional before taxi. On one particularly tricky night we had used up all four spare aircraft when I was informed there was to be another crew-out due to a BOZ pod (infra-red decoy and chaff dispenser) failure. There were no more spares, so I quickly decided to ask the crew to sit tight while we replaced the pod. Normally, engineering procedures permit armament electrical systems only to be worked on when a 'no volts' test has been carried out. Clearly, with engines already running and electrical power fully on, this couldn't happen in this situation, and the face of the SNCO armourer who was tasked with changing the pod was a picture! I stood right by the armourers as they replaced the pod, providing 'top cover'. But I was fully aware that, had anything gone wrong, I would probably have been on a Herc straight back to Germany. But this was war; in the event nothing did go wrong and the eight-ship departed on time.

Wobbly on detachment

During my time we had many demanding and satisfying detachments. Heading for Thumrait, in Oman, I flew from Brüggen on a VC10, with our first re-fuelling stop being at Palermo in Sicily. A beautiful volcanic island at the foot of Italy with the master relief valve, Mount Etna, steaming blissfully and silently away to the east of the airfield. We re-boarded and I was invited to the flight deck; engines were started. On requesting taxi, we were told that Mount Etna was erupting; the airfield was closed and there would be no more take-offs that day. After a short, stunned silence the captain exploded, informing the tower that they had better re-open as we had to be in Thumrait before dark. We taxied out and took off, but I don't actually recall that we had clearance. I believe we avoided Sicily on the return leg.

Thumrait is an airfield surrounded by desert. The facilities were good, and our daily dose of quinine went down well. The eggs, I recall, had been 'treated' to prevent decay before shipping; this made them taste somewhat peculiar. Some of my fondest memories are of trips off camp. Several of us would take a Toyota four-by-four and head into the desert to find remote settlements and do some shopping. We went hunting for crystal amongst the sand – and I still have desert finds cluttering up my house. Salalah, the district capital of the Dhofar province of Oman, also provided shopping opportunities. I came away with two prayer mats sold to me by one of the many market traders very happy to take our money, as well as a marvellous CD; of course I later discovered it to be pirated.

Another detachment was to Goose Bay, Labrador. This time I was on the rear party along with a JEngO and a handful of airmen. At RAF Brize Norton we were herded on to our TriStar; the aircraft was in freight mode with enough seats for us only. After take-off the loadmaster came back and asked us how long we were going to be in Bermuda. Had we got on the wrong flight? If so, perhaps this was a good move, for who wouldn't swap Goose Bay for Bermuda?

It transpired that the aircraft was first taking spares to Bermuda for a broken VC10 (the truckies were famed for breaking down in the nicest places!). Having disembarked from the aircraft and wandered around the terminal we didn't really want to get back on board. Anyway, we did and were soon off to Goose, where July temperatures average around twelve degrees Centigrade. And that's the warm time. I remember shopping in Happy Valley for a pair of gloves and a muskrat hat. Trips out were interesting, although being eaten alive by insects wasn't any fun at all (the black bugs and mozzies there were said to be twin-engined versions). But the country is magnificent, with lakes and rocky waterfalls abundant.

One lasting memory was of a sergeant who had somehow found something to do all night and arrived back at the mess in time for breakfast. On being quizzed by us all he apparently had no memory of where he had been or what he had done. But he was hungry and ordered a pair of grilled kippers. These he ate by holding the fish by the tails and munching his way from the head upwards, including bones and all. He'd gone native, apparently!

That Goose Bay detachment was a difficult one; the aircraft were troublesome and spares were in short supply. The lads had worked incredibly hard and the boss had resolved to reward them with a clear three days off on return to base. As you would imagine, that announcement was received with huge delight.

In the departure lounge prior to our return flight the boss pulled me aside. He told me that at 6am that morning he'd been awoken by a phone call from the station commander back at Brüggen. This had brought news that tension in the Gulf was mounting and that, on our return, we were to adopt a short-readiness posture for possible deployment. This would, of course, involve a good deal of preparation: gathering kit; administrative work; arranging shifts; and so on. It was absolutely clear that our planned stand-down would go straight out of the window. Choosing the moment to announce this change of plan would not be easy, and we chewed the issue over. "Don't worry boss," I reassured him; "the lads will be fine." Of course they were. In the event the squadron wasn't required to deploy Gulf-wards for another couple of months.

SEngO at large

I was always a great believer in the fact the SEngO was more than an engineer; he had to understand 'the whole'. Each year RAF stations celebrate the Battle of Britain with a cocktail party held in the officers' mess, inviting local dignitaries. For obvious reasons of sensitivity, at the West German stations the event was renamed the 'annual reception'. The headquarters in Rheindahlen also ran an annual reception.

One particular year the flypast there was flown by a squadron from Laarbruch, which for the sake of protecting dented egos will remain anonymous. They missed the mess by a long way, overflying instead some random building, much to the embarrassment of senior RAF officers attending.

So the following year (I'm being deliberately vague about the date) 31 Squadron was tasked with the flypast for the event, with the brief ending with the message "Don't miss!" This was in pre-GPS days, when we were equipped with GR1s. The IN was known to drift off from time to time but, that said, it was a great aircraft in the hands of a good nav. We had a reputation for cracking difficult tasks and so we added in some belt-and-braces; this comprised two officers near the target, equipped with an Aldiss lamp and a radio as forward air controllers.

In the early days of the Tornado the aircraft was very reliable. Our twelve or thirteen jets were allocated to us and were not part of a central pool. This concept meant we had pride in our 'Delta'-badged aircraft and could achieve much higher serviceability levels than any centralised system. This worked well until some staff engineer changed the aircraft identities to a single series of numbers, with aircraft being allocated randomly to squadrons, effectively devaluing *esprit de corps* amongst the front-line ground crew at the sweep of a pen. Fortunately, that happened long after I had left the service, but it still hugely annoys me.

Anyway, for this high-profile task we easily launched the four-ship and a couple of airborne reserves – which, in the end, were not required. I had time to spare so volunteered to accompany a very young Flying Officer Gav Wells as the second officer on the FAC mission. We arrived at Rheindahlen and our initial recce confirmed that the best place for us would be the roof of the mess. A ladder was found and soon the squadron leader engineer and the flying officer navigator were on top of the roof, much to the amusement of the mess staff, who were very kind in providing Gav and me with nibbles and drinks while we waited for the festivities to start.

Meanwhile the four-ship was airborne with Wing Commander Pete Dunlop and Squadron Leader Stu Peach in the lead aircraft doing racetracks around Mönchengladbach, ready to hit the mess as the national anthem finished. We knew how long it would take the band to play the anthem, and as soon as it started we relayed it to the four-ship.

Everything went into action, the radio call, the Aldiss flashing '31' and Stu Peach beavering away in the back of the lead jet – the formation roared over the centre of the mess, on track on time, at a suitable height and speed. Happy smiles all around from senior officers at the function. Gav and I quietly slid off the roof and headed for our transport back to Brüggen.

There, the squadron officer corps retired to the mess for a late-evening sherbet to be met by Group Captain 'Rocky' Goodall, who informed Pete that he had received a bar to his AFC, and so the party continued into the wee small hours. I don't believe the gong was down to the flypast, more for a very good tour in command – but I'm not really sure what would have happened had he missed

Rheindahlen mess that evening.

Wobbly round and about

Despite my busy life on the squadron, I was asked to take on another responsibility
– that of chairman of the sergeants' mess committee. It was a job I couldn't say no
to, and I would have the chance to learn the ropes as deputy to the current man.
However, he became sick and I was rapidly parachuted into the chair. I never really
found out his problem, although I gathered it might have been some consequence
of the British nuclear tests of the 1950s at Christmas Island, to which he had been
a witness.

Anyway, I had a good team in the mess and an excellent SNCO who ran the place
most professionally. At that time a new mess was being built, which I'd really have
liked to have seen opened before I was tourex, but that was not to be. Incidentally,
RAF people always regarded ambitious projects such as the building of a new hangar
or sergeants' mess with weary cynicism. Inevitably the work seemed to herald the
closure of a station – and so it would prove with Brüggen barely ten years later.

The job was never dull. After receiving one SNCO's complaining letter about a
function I offered him a post on the mess committee. I never heard from him again.
A good policy, and one I recommend. And there were plenty of advantages; how
else could one enjoy the bonhomie of fellow airmen at seven different Christmas
lunches, including a spectacular event in the corporals' club?

The end of my tour was closing in. Immense beer calls and handing out of
squadron pots; poor speeches and many headaches. I knew it would be my last
squadron, the last of five going back to 65 Squadron at Duxford. The boss offered
me a trip in a Tornado but I chickened out – to my everlasting regret. I felt my
swansong should have been to Nellis on Red Flag, but I couldn't wangle that one
so I said my goodbyes in the terminal at Brüggen as the boys boarded their flight.
The squadron went one way and I the other. What memories.

Top: *Second to None*, a pair of II(AC) Squadron's GR1As roll out after landing at Laarbruch in dirty weather. From an oil painting by noted aviation artist Mike Rondot. (Mike Rondot, www.collectair. co.uk/second-to-none)

Above: XV(R) Squadron Tornados queue up to take fuel from a TriStar.

Opposite top: A GR1 of XV Squadron, in its 85th anniversary livery, powers up for take-off.
Opposite below: A GR4 of 41(R) Squadron (the operational evaluation unit) touches down at Liverpool Airport. (Les Hendry, www.leshendry.com)

Top: A GR4 at low level, wings swept forward for manoeuvrability. (Ian Sykes)
Below: Hugging the contours, a GR4 at low level. (Ian Sykes)

Top: GR4 during a firepower demonstration. (Ian Sykes)
Opposite top to bottom: Three lined up for take-off. (Les Hendry, www.leshendry.com);
The business end. (Les Hendry, www.leshendry.com);
Taxiing in at dusk. (Les Hendry, www.leshendry.com)

Top: 'Contact'. Note: the apparent hose distortion is caused by the canopy Perspex. (Photo from www.jet-prints.com by permission of Claus Mayerhofer)
Below: Closing up. (Photo from www.jet-prints.com by permission of Claus Mayerhofer)

Top: The GR4 which was decorated to mark thirty years of RAF Tornados. It carries a
RAPTOR pod under the fuselage. (Les Hendry, www.leshendry.com)
Below: The same aircraft touches down. (Les Hendry, www.leshendry.com)

Opposite top to bottom: On patrol;
The last of the many. Representatives of the four remaining squadrons airborne in October 2015 under the leadership of the aircraft painted in fortieth anniversary colours. (©Crown copyright, MOD)

Top: The squadrons represented are XV(R) Squadron, 12 Squadron, IX(B) Squadron and 31 Squadron. By all accounts, three of the five aircraft were due to be broken up for spares during the week following this flight. (© Crown copyright, MOD)
Below: Armourers labour to load ALARM missiles.

Opposite top to bottom: GR1s of 14 and 31
Squadrons refuel from a VC10, while a further 31
Squadron machine waits its turn. The fin of the 14
Squadron aircraft shows typical staining from the
reverse thrust used routinely on landing;
Deployed ops. GR1s under the sunshades in
Dhahran, Saudi Arabia. The apron is shared with the
French, whose Mirage 2000 aircraft may be seen in
the background;
A GR1 loaded with two JP233 weapons.

Above: The Cold War is over, and thereby came
opportunities none of the Cold War generation had
ever expected. Here, GR1s of 31 Squadron escort
MiG-21s of the Hungarian air force towards Fairford
to participate in the International Air Tattoo.

Top: GR1s with a Gulf Conflict workhorse, a Victor K2.

Below: Post-Gulf War, GR1s with a KC-135. The boom has a short 'donkey dick' hose-drogue adaptor to make it compatible with probe-equipped receivers. The nearer GR1 is in peacetime 17 Squadron markings. The further aircraft remains in 'desert pink', although its 617 Squadron fin flash has been reapplied.

CHAPTER 10

A COLD WAR REFLECTION

Following the Gulf Conflict and the untimely and almost brutal reduction in numbers of Tornado units, John Peters was posted from his recently disbanded XV Squadron to join my own team. He had of course become a celebrity following his shooting down, capture, and infamous parading on Iraqi TV. But he rode all that with aplomb, and was the most natural and pleasant person with whom to work. Just as importantly, to all appearances he had shrugged off his ordeal.

We had loads of fun with JP. His book *Tornado Down*, written with his back-seater John Nichol, had become a bestseller and was now to be adapted as a TV film. The production company descended upon Brüggen and found the perfect setting for the interrogation scenes; the sergeants' mess was, as we've just heard, being revamped, and the raw breeze blocks of the building site offered ideal, cell-like settings. What with the book, the celebrity, and now the film of the book, we all felt that JP owed the crewroom a collective beer.

When I asked John to contribute a chapter to this volume his initial reaction was that the world had already heard quite enough about his POW times. I suggested to him that, twenty-five years on, there might be something to say in a reflective tone, and he agreed to consider it. Knowing him as something of a thinker, I suppose I shouldn't have been surprised when he came up with quite a different piece. But one which is equally relevant to the Tornado story and builds nicely on a couple of allusions made in the previous chapter. The subject is the nuclear deterrent.

Opinions abound on deterrence based upon the threat – and the awfulness – of nuclear obliteration. History will be the judge, but many would point out that the second half of Europe's twentieth century was more peaceful than the first. Whatever your own views, there's no denying that carrying out government policy was the duty of, and a stark reality for, Tornado crews, and it played a huge part in their lives – at least until the easing of tension and the ultimate withdrawal of the weapons from Tornado bases in 1998. John's view on all of this is thought-provoking, so see what you think ...

SQUADRON LEADER JOHN PETERS (RETD)

It was a beautiful spring day ... such an ordinarily, beautiful spring day. White puffs of fair-weather cumulus floating in a pale blue sky and the sun shining, casting shadows over the farm land. Driving here, we had passed a couple of villages and a farmer ploughing a field; now we turned off the main road up a track and walked the final distance up to the wire. Peering through the fence I looked up into the sky. My 'nuke' – or 'bucket of sunshine' as it was euphemistically nicknamed – would have detonated a couple of hundred feet in the air above this spot.

The high explosive surrounding the fissile material ignites. A compressional shock wave begins to move inward. The shock wave moves faster than the speed of sound and creates a large increase in pressure, which impinges simultaneously on all points on the surface of the sphere of fissile material in the bomb core. This starts the compression process. As the core density increases, the mass becomes critical, and then supercritical (where the chain reaction grows exponentially). Now the initiator is released, producing many neutrons, so that early generations are bypassed. The chain reaction continues until the energy generated inside the bomb becomes so great that the internal pressure due to the energy of the fission fragments exceeds the implosion pressure of the shock wave. The energy released in the fission process is transferred to the surroundings with an intensely bright flash, followed by a fireball, which burns everything it touches. The explosion is so powerful that it can be felt miles away in a 'heat blast'. The rising fireball superheats the air; air blasts outward in a 'shock wave'. This is violently strong close to the explosion, travelling at a couple of hundred miles per hour, destroying everything in its path.

Thankfully, this never happened in Europe. I had left the RAF in 2000. Now it was 2008 and I had been asked by BBC2 to contribute to a documentary commemorating the RAF at ninety and my time during the Cold War. I was no longer a Tornado GR1 pilot, the Cold War was over and this was no longer the **Deutsche Demokratische Republik**, part of the 'Eastern Bloc' during the Cold War period. From 1945 until 1990, the USSR had administered the region of Germany which was occupied by Soviet forces at the end of the Second World War. Both sides had faced each other with their nuclear deterrents.

I had played my part, but it was over. The Berlin Wall had fallen. The Warsaw Pact had collapsed. The world had changed. Had this not happened I doubt whether Britain would have responded to Saddam Hussein's invasion of Kuwait on 2 August 1990. XV Squadron would not have deployed to the Gulf; I would not have been involved in Gulf War One or been shot down and held as a prisoner of war. Or, subsequently, found myself visiting my former target at ground zero for a television show.

My target had been a SAM-5 site south-west of Berlin. A robust air defence network existed in the DDR, and Soviet air defence units combined to provide a layered air defence network capable of defending the Warsaw Pact's north-western front. The Soviet presence in the DDR included a number of strategic air defence units, providing coverage for Soviet military facilities, including airfields which were home to Soviet combat aircraft. SAM-5, NATO reporting name Gammon, was a very long-range, medium-to-high altitude SAM system designed in the 1960s to defend large areas from modern, advanced aircraft, including AWACS, jammers and other manned and unmanned aerial vehicles. There were four such sites in the DDR.

Now, as I peered through the fence at this obsolete, overgrown, abandoned SAM site, the final parts were being dismantled by mechanical diggers. The silence and the normality of this perfect spring day were balanced with a visceral sense of its former military intent, mirrored in the brutality of its scale. It was probably half a kilometre square, a bastion of iron and reinforced concrete, with revetments and bunkers spread across the site. A monument to the Cold War. In its time, each such battalion had had six single-rail missile launchers for the 10.8-metre-long missiles, as well as a fire-control radar. As a fighter/bomber pilot, I knew that it would take many, many conventional sorties to negate such a threat, but just one tactical nuke. And now, in 2008, after long years of political and economic evolution, it was being dismantled. The operational world seemed a lifetime ago.

I had joined the Tornado GR1 force in 1989, operating in West Germany, first on XV Squadron at RAF Laarbruch on the Dutch/German border and then on 31 Squadron at Brüggen, near Mönchengladbach. As a young pilot arriving in RAF Germany, as it was called, the experience was surreal, exciting and overwhelming. Compared to the UK bases, there was a heightened sense that this was the front line. It seemed so much more operational, compelling and focused than being in the UK.

When I left Tornado training I was competent to fight the aircraft at a basic level, in that I understood the weapon systems, had dropped practice bombs on the range and had learned basic tactics. Arriving on a squadron, the aim was to become 'combat ready' – to be declared to NATO as fully operational aircrew. The first priority was 'strike', which meant you would qualify on the nuclear deterrent and could be declared a 'nuclear asset'. Then, subsequently, fully combat ready, able to be tasked in whatever role was required for a Tornado crew. This whole process took six months of intensive flying to build the skill-set – and exhaustive book-work. So much to learn: missile systems; weapon systems; tactics; recognition; airspace; nuclear, biological and chemical warfare; air traffic procedures; emergencies – the list is endless. But the most important was strike.

Appropriately, this was taken very seriously. Virtually every piece of information we handled daily was classified secret. But nuclear was covered by a higher security classification – UK Eyes B – which meant that only those who needed the information had access. An exclusive club – but this sounds more glamorous than it was. There were cupboards full of classified books, which one might imagine would be really interesting. But in truth there is absolutely no strain in keeping official secrets secret because they are as boring as hell – nuclear in particular. All very necessary. Very necessary indeed. But boring.

So when the BBC asked me to contribute to this documentary, I could not remember any detail – but now we have the internet. Unbelievable! Back in 1989 our highly classified UK Eyes B information was a set of maps and splodgy black and white imagery stamped boldly with red security classification. Now I could see every detail of my former target on Google maps, with latitude and longitude, pictures, 3-D images – and I could literally complete a virtual walk around my target online. All this through a website listing every single SAM site in the former DDR, with full profiles. With technological hindsight our efforts all seem so amateur and ridiculous – but one has to remember that, at the time, both sides were working off that level of information.

Then, the nuclear scenario was the end game we were trying to avoid. My time was 1989-1992, the twilight of the Cold War. It was the era of CND, Greenham Common, cruise missiles, *Glasnost*, the collapse of the Soviet Union and the emergence of the new world order. The nuclear stand-off between the Warsaw Pact and NATO would have been fought over Europe. And this was rigorously practised.

Periodically, each RAF operational base would be subjected to a Taceval by NATO. A multi-national team would complete an examination of every aspect of the operational, support and survival-to-operate readiness of the base while under enemy attack. Other forces would be mobilised to attack the base, so that everyone on the station, from senior commander to aircrew, ground crew to administrators, were thoroughly tested under simulated real-war scenarios. Four long days and sleepless nights.

The format of Taceval would follow a pretty standard escalation. The 'war' would begin with intelligence reports on initial political posturing, move to deployment of military forces, then through conventional military engagement to first tactical use of nuclear weapons – and then to full nuclear launch. Throughout the later stages of this decline to oblivion, Tornado squadrons would fulfil their role and be tasked to fly tactical missions against simulated targets. That is until the exercise, on the fourth day, 'went nuclear'. Once, the world had 'gone nuclear', each crew was issued with their pre-planned nuclear strike targets. Details were updated with weather, intelligence and threat analysis; then each crew was transported to its HAS under armed guard by armoured vehicles (to negate the possibility of *Spetsnaz* snipers killing the aircrew – they being the softest, most vulnerable part of the machine!)

At the HAS, you request access through an intercom in the steel door. Upon entry, you are faced with your squadron ground crew; you know their names, you work with them each day – but they now have a gun in your face. Once you get inside the door there is a thick white line delineating a small, square enclosure on the floor. Beyond this is the 'no-lone zone'. Step beyond this line and, in reality, they have permission to shoot. This is serious. You are there to 'accept' from them what is now a nuclear-armed Tornado. Each party reads from a script, with the assessors monitoring every single word. It has to be correct, word-perfect, before we can step beyond the painted white line; before the ground crew lower their weapons. No errors.

Once the identification and acceptance have been made, the pilot and navigator go together to the weapon (usually a simulated one in exercise) to ensure the codes are correct following the two-man principle. The two-man rule is a control mechanism designed to achieve a high level of security for especially critical material or operations. All access and actions require the presence of two authorised people at all times to ensure no rogue element. And then you board the aircraft awaiting your clearance codes over the secure communications. And you wait …

Eventually, hours later, they are transmitted. By now, for exercise, the aircraft has been reloaded with a small practice bomb – but the procedures remain 'real'. Each crew member translates the information independently to calculate the required clearances and cross-check for accuracy, again following the two-man principle. Checked. Cross-checked. Double-checked. No room for error. This is the start of the nuclear launch. Every action 'to the second' perfect. Start left engine; start right engine; open left HAS door; open right HAS door; taxi out. All in complete radio silence. All monitored from the command centre. Then, from the isolation of this concrete cocoon, detached from the world, consumed within the scream of jet engines amplified within this reinforced box, the canopy is down and you exit the HAS in the serene unreality of an air-conditioned cockpit. Two aircrew, alone, tentatively nudging the nose of the Tornado out of the HAS, very aware that, if you take off one second outside your window, the whole station fails its evaluation. Very aware that the work of the last four days comes down to you; 5,000 people's efforts and expectations that you will do your job. Taxiing out, you are aware of this pressure and confident in your skills, but with a heightened sense of the intrinsic unreality of practising the unbelievable: dropping a nuclear bomb. The exercise assessors even had a scenario to test the reactions of the station should all that pressure become too much for crews and they could not cope with the responsibility. The LMF crew; the 'lack of moral fibre' crew.

But by and large we're launching the fleet. Sixty nuclear-armed aircraft will take off from their base and fly east, all in radio silence. It's a spectacle. Families come out to watch from behind the wire as the procession of Tornados taxies and lines up sequentially, on either side of the runway, and takes off. Minute upon minute of thunderous engines, the ground vibrating as each twenty-five-ton beast accelerates along the runway in full reheat to complete their reason for being. And then silence.

The macabre impression that remains with me of my 'strike ready' days is that this was just one of the two RAF strike bases we had in Germany. Then there were the two other Tornado bases in the UK while, within NATO, there were the US, French, Dutch and other forces – each with numerous bases with several squadrons, all taking off to launch their strikes. At the height of the Cold War, NATO had upwards of 30,000 nuclear warheads, most in a high-alert status to deter the Soviet Union from executing a disarming first strike. These were deployed in submarines, in silos, on the ground, and on dual-capable aircraft such as the Tornado GR1. More than 7,000 nuclear weapons were, at one time, deployed in Europe. That's an awful lot of nukes. Security guarantees were codified through the declaratory policy of extended deterrence. NATO adopted a flexible response policy, indicating a willingness to use whatever level of force was required to defeat the aggressor. To shore up these guarantees the United States refused to pledge no-first-use of nuclear weapons, implicitly reserving the right to initiate nuclear weapon use should circumstances warrant it. Notwithstanding this, Warsaw Pact aircraft were doing the same but heading west. Given the number of aircraft, I feel sure that there was just not enough airspace in northern Europe. We would have been dodging each other in our race to drop our nukes first!

Even more incredible was the brief we received informing us that, although the planners had de-conflicted and sequenced each of our own strikes, we might (obviously!) observe other nuclear explosions. Whilst we had our anti-dazzle lights in the cockpit – very bright internal lights to illuminate the cockpit so we should still be able to see our instruments in the intense light generated by adjacent flashes, we were advised not to look directly at any explosion as it could blind us. Given that possibility, the brief continued unabashed by advising us that, in the real case, we would be issued with an eye-patch with which we should cover one eye on our way to target so that, if this were blinded, we could revert to the other eye unperturbed and continue to complete our mission!

So, once airborne, post the exercise launch, with the pressure removed we would each go to practise an everyday flight, literally to kill time before receiving the 'end of exercise' recall message. Following the launch of the fleet, we never practised (in my time at least) anything post the launch. We never practised anything beyond nuclear strike. The exercise was predicated on the fact, I assume, that we would be dead, that we had nothing to return to. The world would be charcoal. And everything that we knew up to that point had been vaporised. MAD, literally, mutually assured destruction.

And so upon the recall message it was a race to get back to the bar. All aircraft sequenced to land, debriefed – and then pile to the officers' mess. The tensions of the previous days released; the success of the Taceval, the proof of skill. The war was over – it culminated in a massive piss-up. Squadrons would still be competing to be the best, because it is in their DNA: to be the fastest to get on the apex of the mess roof; to burn pianos; and to win stupid drinking games. This was a throwback to a post-Second World War era, before Gulf War One, when life was more predictable; such a different world to that of today.

Back then there were squadron ops embargoes so that everyone could attend the summer ball or Christmas draw. There were tax-free cars, overseas flights to sunny climes, discounted petrol coupons and overseas allowances. There was cheap booze – gin was cheaper than windscreen wash, so we used it in our cars. It was the thrill of being a fighter/bomber pilot. The lifestyle was relentless fun. All under the umbrella of Armageddon.

It took me back to the very first interview I had when I was seventeen and wanting to become an RAF fighter pilot. Despite all my naivety, expectation and willingness to please, I remember spending three hours sitting on my home cricket pitch trying to come to terms with the seriousness of the first question I knew I would be asked: could I drop a nuclear bomb?

Now I've been a fighter/bomber pilot, flown the Tornado GR1, practised for such an eventuality, been to war, been shot down and spent time as a POW. I still don't know the answer to that question. There are some things in life so big that you would only know at that moment. Could I push the button? One can only hope that, in those moments in life, one would make the right decision. I walked away from this field in the former East Germany with my dilemma unresolved.

CHAPTER 11

ADVANCING THE TRAINING

The second half of the early RAF training pattern was at TWCU, the Tornado Weapons Conversion Unit, and it was on that course that I had perhaps the unhappiest time of my entire RAF career. I had enjoyed the TTTE, whose teaching style could have been described in those days as 'modern' – learning by objectives and all that. I'd felt that I'd got a good grounding on the aircraft and was ready for the advanced phase.

But very soon after arriving at Honington I perceived a rather peculiar ethos. The attitude seemed to be that 'you've wasted enough time at that mamby-pamby TTTE, now we're going to shake you up with some proper RAF training'. An example came in the first week of groundschool when the instructor detected a weakness in the knowledge of a young navigator on my course. He probed more deeply with another question, with my colleague stumbling once more. There would be no respite; the next salvo was posed in terms of: "What does mister silly think might be the answer to this?" The victim, unsurprisingly, crumbled with embarrassment. As we left the classroom I engaged the instructor. "Did you realise," I asked, "that you lost Bloggs after the first ten minutes of the lesson? He took in nothing at all after you'd destroyed him." "Well I can't help that", the man replied. "This is a hard school and if he can't keep up he'll be out." Probably unwisely, I persisted: "Wouldn't it be a good idea to try to bring the best out of weaker students?" "Standards are high here," he said, "if he doesn't make it, that's tough."

Well of course I'd been through tough courses before. When I first flew Hunters it was axiomatic that if you didn't 'catch up, number two' you'd be dead! The RAF was training combat crews; standards were indeed high and weak links in the chain were not required. But I still think that the bullying type of approach was, in 1991, as old fashioned as bi-planes; students learn in different ways and at different rates, and there were smarter ways of realising their potential. Not least, the RAF had invested a lot in its students by the time they'd reached the TWCU stage, so the cost-effective solution was to get people through rather than wash them out.

Oddly, I understand that the Buccaneer OCU at Honington had had a similarly hard-nosed reputation, so perhaps it was the place. But for whatever reason I never really recovered any sort of good working relationship with the TWCU staff and was grateful to escape with a bare pass. Incidentally, the young nav at the centre of the story came to my squadron and became a useful citizen – and in later life transitioned to a second career as an airline pilot.

Anyway, there was no doubt fault on both sides, and the Tornado training machine has produced consistently excellent products. There were also many very good instructors amongst the TWCU staff, so let's hear from one of them, Simon Dobb, whom I met while he was doing a stint at the TTTE. Later, he went on to command XV(R) Squadron, the combined OCU, so he's ideally placed to comment (not necessarily agreeing with the views I've expressed) on Tornado training.

AIR COMMODORE SIMON DOBB (RETD)

In 2012 I attended a dinner night at the RAF College to celebrate the Tornado's thirty years in service. It was a marvellous occasion and a great opportunity to meet up with old friends and colleagues, some of whom I hadn't seen for over two decades. As we reminisced about the early days, the 'war stories' became more exaggerated and louder as the evening progressed. Almost without exception, individuals had a tale to recount of their passage through the training system. That system was a vital and ever-present support to those thirty years of stalwart service; like all training regimes, it can be guaranteed to trigger vivid memories, both good and bad, from those who pass through it.

Tornado training certainly filled a full three tours of my own flying career. Initial conversion aside, those tours ranged from one as a flight lieutenant QWI at Honington in the mid 1980s, through a tour as the boss of one of the squadrons at the TTTE, to command of XV(R) Squadron at Lossiemouth at the turn of the century. Altogether, a period of over twenty years of the aircraft's service, until age and promotion percolated me onward and upward to other things. Here goes, then, with a compendium of personal reflections on those two decades.

The TTTE is discussed elsewhere, but I can't resist a few short lines from my viewpoint. As an endorsement of NATO cooperation and combined training the TTTE was a huge success. However, I don't think anyone would hold it up as an exemplar of demanding or cost-effective training. The bar was not set very high and there was much more that could have been achieved in the thirty-five or so flying hours allocated. Certainly, for pilots who had flown the Buccaneer, Phantom, Harrier, Jaguar or Lightning, the Tornado was a piece of cake to fly, with none of the vicious vices of its predecessors. For the navigators, once they had got to grips with the modern electronic cockpit, the new aircraft's potential was obvious. In saying 'modern' it's sobering to think that early Tornados had an 8K main computer, which seems barely credible as I type e-mails on my 16GB iPhone!

Moving to RAF Honington and the TWCU (later known also as 45[R] Squadron and, later still, XV[R] Squadron) we certainly knew we were back in the RAF. It was not that the unit was overly oppressive, but rather that it offered a stark contrast to the relaxed, relatively undemanding atmosphere prevalent at the TTTE. The usual RAF standards were (re)applied and trainee crews exposed to a steep learning curve to catch up on some of the 'wasted' hours flown beforehand. In a short time we covered laydown, loft and dive bombing, and strafe. Then there was ACT, while throughout there was emphasis on the TF flying that was the heart of the Tornado's low-level, all-weather capability. Needless to say, all this was bread and butter to operational ground-attack crews; however, the student composition was a strange mix. The number of first-tour crews was increasing to meet the rising demand of the expanding force in the UK and Germany, but there were still a good number of crews converting from other aircraft types, including remnants of the V force. All told, a broad spectrum of experience and ability for the instructors to manage, and although the syllabus was designed around the training needs of first-tour crews, pilots and navigators from across the experience spectrum fell by the wayside.

This eclectic crew mix certainly made the early days interesting as trainees compared Tornado's pros and cons with their previous aircraft. Buccaneer crews loved the wonderful navigation and weapon-aiming kit but criticised the lack of legs, while erstwhile Jaguar pilots raved about the increased range but thought the rear cockpit and 'talking ballast' would have been better used for additional fuel. Fast-jet aircrew are not known to be shrinking violets, and many a heated debate was had both in the crewroom and, of course, in the bar at Friday night 'twofers'.

Following a short tour in Germany I returned to the UK as an instructor – poacher turned gamekeeper – on the TWCU; having spent two consecutive tours in Germany a posting back in Blighty was a welcome break. The Cold War was moving towards its denouement in the mid 1980s, although we didn't know it at the time, but during my Germany tours I'd spent the equivalent of a short prison sentence behind the barbed wire and watchtowers in the QRA compound. How distant that all seems today.

Although not an operational squadron, the TWCU was great fun, demanding in its own way and equally rewarding. The staff at the time had a mix of backgrounds, experience and age, reflecting the throughput to the new jet. There was a wealth of talent, confirmed by the many who went on to command their own squadrons, with some attaining air rank. The boss was the marvellous Gordon McRobbie, a hugely popular and great leader who sadly passed away in 2014. I don't think I have ever been on a squadron where the boss was held in such esteem.

Unfortunately, one of the side effects of the Cold War was a stasis in our operating posture, training and thinking. There is no doubt that the operational squadrons were well trained, highly skilled and equally highly motivated, but the scenario in Europe and the expected employment of air power had not changed for many years. This 'operational model' was in turn reflected in the training delivered by the OCUs back in the UK, and I don't recall the TWCU syllabus changing significantly during the three years I was there.

The RAF ground-attack force was committed to attack exclusively at low level. The primary weapons were the venerable 1,000-lb bomb (either free fall or parachute-retarded) and the BL755 cluster bomb. The operational squadrons would also practise delivery profiles for the JP233 runway denial weapon and, very occasionally, with the Paveway II laser-guided bomb, although the Tornado possessed no laser designation capability of its own.

To become a qualified weapons instructor was the aim of pretty well every pilot and navigator, being a recognition of one's skill as an aviator and operator, and I was fortunate to be selected for the QWI course very early in my TWCU tour. At the time the course was run by the wonderfully talented Bob McAlpine. Bob was an unrelenting taskmaster and a great instructor, and I quickly gained an in-depth knowledge of all aspects of the weaponeer's art. This ranged from study of the working of each weapon, to weapons delivery calculations (at that time, if you can believe it, we were still using logarithmic tables!) to cine film debriefing technique (the acme of the QWI's art and, yes, it wasn't a typo; the gunsight camera recorded on wet film which, once developed, was played on less-than-reliable projectors in blacked-out debriefing cubicles). There was endless practice on the bombing range, following which any error in speed, height or technique would be pounced upon mercilessly by Bob during the aforementioned cine debrief. At the end of four months of this ritual self-criticism and analysis, one emerged as a newly fledged QWI, armed with sharply honed weaponeering skills and a deep knowledge ready to eviscerate student crews for any transgression.

Although this training was, without doubt excellent, and a marvellous foundation for a future, operationally focused career, it all reflected the traditional old weapons and tactics of the Cold War. And not once during those four months did I ever fly with a live weapon. Like all front-line fast-jet crews at the time I spent endless hours on the academic bombing ranges dropping practice bombs, and it was not without some truth that the course was dubbed the 'east coast range instructors' course'.

All this changed in 1989 with the fall of the Berlin Wall and the collapse of communism. With the threat from the Soviet bear much diminished, Britain cashed in, rather hastily some might say, on the 'swords to ploughshares' windfall. The 'options for change' and 'defence costs study (front line first)' reviews followed in relatively quick succession, resulting in a dramatic reduction in the Tornado force and a review of our Germany basing policy. In the midst of this, Saddam Hussein invaded Kuwait, thus changing our operational focus and priorities.

Life on a training unit wasn't all routine, though. Following a long, late-1980s summer teaching the tyros, we instructors were ready for a break. Four of us set up a weekend ranger (also known as an overseas training flight). The purpose was to take a couple of aircraft away to some far-flung field to gain experience in operating in a foreign environment and to overcome any difficulties that may arise without

A GR1 of the TWCU, bearing the markings of 45(R) Squadron, during its solo aerobatic display in the mid to late 1980s.

the engineering and spares support available at home. We mulled over the options and decided a weekend in Naples would be just the ticket. Unfortunately, the other pilot and both navigators were squadron leaders, and so, as the only flight lieutenant in this intrepid team, it was left to me to organise the plan, arrange the allowances, liaise with the squadron engineers, book the hotel and sort out the administrative trivia ahead of departure. None of which, to be honest, was particularly onerous, and certainly a small price to pay for some late-season sunshine beside the gorgeous Mediterranean.

Departure day arrived and we jetted off nice and early – to maximise drinking time at the far end. A couple of hours later we were beginning our descent towards the beautiful Bay of Naples, with the city sprawling around the edge of the bay and Vesuvius clearly visible to the south. On the ground at Capodichino airport we parked the jets, performed the requisite refuelling and servicing and headed off to our city hotel in anticipation of a weekend of fun and relaxation in good company. Time dims the memory and I can recall little of the weekend per se, save for the excellent grilled *branzino* (sea bass) eaten at a seafront restaurant – and of course who could visit Naples without sampling a pizza? A trip across the bay to

Capri to visit the Blue Grotto and Gracie Fields's last resting place was partially completed; we made it to Capri easily enough but, as is so often the case on OTFs, any pretence of sightseeing got no further than the first bar/trattoria. Many glasses of *birra*, *vino rosso* and *sambuca* later it was Monday morning and time to crank up the jets and head home – naturally, having allowed the appropriate time between 'bottle and throttle'. Our problems were just starting.

We arrived at our electric jets to discover that the battery on one of them (not mine) was flat. Those familiar with the Tornado will have a pretty good idea why this might have been (a diagnostic panel, which needed to be read after flight, was all too easily left ajar), but to spare my erstwhile flight commander's blushes let's gloss over any potential aircrew servicing oversights. Without a battery the crew couldn't even open the canopy let alone entertain any thoughts of starting the engines. Not to despair, wasn't this one of the reasons we went on OTFs, to use our skill, experience and ingenuity to tackle any difficulties that might arise? We put our heads together, carefully, as they were still quite sore. We considered starting my aircraft and then swapping my battery to the broken aircraft to start that up. However, this would have meant flying one aircraft with a dead, albeit slowly recharging, battery. Common sense and the potential ramifications of an in-flight electrical problem quickly ruled out that solution. Common sense, or lack of it, being somewhat the *leitmotif* of the ensuing escapade – as you will see as the tale unfolds.

Undaunted, we investigated the facilities on the airfield. Perhaps there was a battery-charging bay; after all this was a major civilian airport. But no joy. We remembered that the Italian military operated a squadron of Tornados at Gioia del Colle, an airfield near Bari, some 175 miles to the south east. The Italians were sympathetic but declined our invitation to drive for four hours across the peninsula to bring us a spare battery. I'm not sure what the Italian for 'Bloody Brits' is, but we got the message! Back in the UK, the squadron had been scoping the possibility of sending us a replacement battery. Unfortunately, as such items were classified as dangerous air cargo, none of the commercial carriers who flew from the UK to Naples would touch it with a barge pole. So no joy. By this time it was early afternoon and we were running low on ideas.

Suddenly – an epiphany. The RAF armament practice camp base, where crews would sharpen their weapon-delivery skills during a concentrated period, was at Decimomannu in Sardinia. Although late in the season, a quick check confirmed that there were still some engineers from 14 Squadron at Deci and, more importantly, they had a spare battery – deep joy. My navigator (let's call him Dick) and I would fly across to Deci, swap the duff battery for a serviceable one, fly back to Naples, pop the new battery in the broken jet – and all would be well. With a quick flight plan submitted, we were soon on our way westward to Sardinia.

Turning the clock back a while, Dick and I had, on a couple of occasions, discussed the concept of a 'reverse seat sortie'. On joining the RAF Dick had trained as a pilot and had got quite a way through the system, having even flown the Hunter, before he was suspended and subsequently retrained as a navigator. Now, having flown hundreds of hours in the back seat of a Tornado, Dick was easily one of the most experienced navigators in the force and, as his instructor role necessitated, he had a great understanding and knowledge of the front seat operation. Perhaps, given these circumstances, one can understand why he really fancied a sortie – just the one – in the front. For my part I was an instructor pilot and was used to flying in the back seat while teaching the young pilots converting to type. Trainer versions have a duplicate set of flying controls in the rear cockpit to permit instructor pilots to teach/monitor trainee pilots, but still retain full mission capability. Each front-line squadron has at least one trainer in which to carry out periodic qualification and currency sorties. However, as the dedicated conversion training unit, the TWCU had quite a few, and we had one of them with us in Naples.

Of course it is one thing to fly with a fully qualified pilot, albeit inexperienced on type, in the front seat, but would be quite another to fly a navigator there. That aside it was, quite obviously, against all rules and regulations. However, we were both highly experienced and skilled aviators and, above all, a long way from home; what could possibly go wrong? That was the theory, but of course there was never any realistic expectation of it happening – which, as it would turn out, was just as well. We set off happily across the Tyrrhenian Sea seated in our correct cockpits.

Without looking at a map of the Mediterranean one would be forgiven for thinking that Sardinia was relatively close to the mainland, But Deci is a good hour's flight from Naples. It was, therefore, well into the afternoon before we landed there. True to their word, 14 Squadron's engineers were waiting for us and, joy of joys, had the replacement battery to hand. When I say to hand, actually the battery was cocooned in a bespoke packaging case the size of a chest of drawers. As we climbed out of the jet and shook hands with our saviours the flight sergeant asked us where the duff battery was. "In the spent ammo bay", I replied (this small compartment, accessed by a panel on the underside of the aircraft, is where used shell cases go when the aircraft's 27mm Mauser cannons are fired; it provides pretty well the only storage space for a couple of small weekend bags or, in this case, the flat battery). I opened the panel and out popped – fell, if truth be told – the dead battery. A couple of minutes then passed as we revived the good flight sergeant from his dead faint. Concerned about our rather cavalier approach to engineering safety protocols, he was adamant the replacement battery must be flown back in its protective packaging – although quite obviously there was no way that we could fit the oversized transport chest into any nook or cranny in the Tornado. Following a short negotiation he relented and agreed to load the new battery back into the spent ammo bay, albeit with more packaging wrapped around it than you could shake a stick at and with the proviso that we only flew straight and level during our transit back to Naples. I cannot recall the flight sergeant's name; however, a belated thanks to him for his flexibility.

Returning to our cunning plan, both Dick and I were known to some of the 14 Squadron ground crew, while all the others could easily tell the difference between one officer with pilot's wings and the other with a navigator's brevet. The ramifications of such a jape being rumbled still didn't bear thinking about, reinforcing our sensible decision to continue in our correct roles. We may have been a bit daft but we certainly weren't totally stupid!

A very quick start up ensued as the Italians were keen to close the airfield for the day, and we were soon on the way with our precious cargo. We climbed to 25,000 feet and set course for the hour or so flight back to Naples. As we headed eastwards a couple of things occurred. First, the long hours of trouble-shooting and the longer than expected flight to Deci caught up with us. The bright sunlight slipped away rapidly (what is it about Mediterranean sunsets?) and very soon we were night flying. No problem in itself but then, and of slightly more concern, the cloudless skies of our earlier transit started to fill with some of the most ominous-looking cumulonimbus thunderclouds.

As we neared the Italian mainland we were in thick, pitch-black cloud. Dick, looking ahead on the radar, muttered something along the lines of "Oh, that's not good". "Excellent" I said, "any chance of telling me exactly what's not good?" "There's a huge storm cell right on the nose," replied Dick; "no snags, I'll route us around it." Unfortunately, Roma control had other ideas. Civilian traffic had priority and our ever more insistent requests for a heading change were denied. We plunged headlong into the maelstrom just as we started our descent to Naples. The Tornado is normally a stable platform, but in that storm we were flung around like a cork. The buffeting was so severe that Dick's head was bounced against the inside of the canopy; so much for the flight sergeant's plea for a smooth transit! Lightning was discharging in the cloud all around us; I turned the cockpit lights up fully and we waited for the inevitable strike. Some rescue mission this was turning out to be. As you might imagine it was at about this time that we commented on how fortunate we were each to be sitting in the correct seats.

Roma control passed us over to Naples approach; not surprisingly, we couldn't make out a word the controller was saying in the midst of a huge electrical storm. Unable to communicate with air traffic control, in terminal airspace, in the middle of a lightning storm and wary of descending any further as we approached the mainland, the situation was not looking too rosy. But suddenly, as though we had just stepped through a curtain, we popped out of a solid wall of cloud over a beautifully tranquil Bay of Naples, a couple of miles from the airport and perfectly positioned to fit in downwind for a right-hand circuit to the westerly runway.

An immaculate, if I say so myself, landing followed, and as we rolled down the runway breathing slightly more easily we once again ran into the storm we had so recently escaped and which must have been moving eastwards at quite some speed. The rain was coming down like stair rods as we taxied back to the USN facility that was hosting us. The parking area consisted of a pierced steel planking hardstanding which was, at that moment, home to two aircraft – our sister Tornado and an F-14 Tomcat. The US sailor who was marshalling us in was, self evidently, most put out at having been called from his warm office to stand in the pouring rain to see in some Brits. Presumably accustomed to spotting aircraft on the crowded deck of an aircraft carrier, he eschewed the acres of parking space available and manoeuvred us (very) close to the F-14. Full nosewheel steering and hefty application of left brake finally brought us juddering to a halt with our wingtip about three feet from the F-14's. Job done as far as he was concerned; and with no desire to get any wetter our sailor jumped into his truck and was gone as quickly as he had appeared.

The navigator of our second Tornado had hitched a ride out with the marshaller and was now hiding from the storm under our wing. We sat there for a couple of minutes with the engines running eyeing the tempest outside, but there was no way this storm was about to abate in a hurry. There was nothing else for it; I shut down the engines and opened the canopy, exposing us to the deluge. Of course our impatient sailor hadn't thought to bring us any ladders, and so the pair of us made our way gingerly down the spine of the aircraft and, wary of slipping off to a certain broken ankle, lowered ourselves down carefully off the tailplane. As the two navs compared notes under the wing, yours truly, as both captain of the aircraft and, if you recall, the junior mate, scurried around putting the machine 'to bed' (closing the canopy, putting in the safety pins and ground locks, fitting the protective covers and so on) – and getting jolly wet in the process.

The severity of the storm meant that our sanctuary beneath the wing provided little real protection from the elements and so, as our marshaller had long since driven off in his truck, we were left with no choice but to sprint for the protection of the USN HQ building. Not far, say 100 metres, but running in full safety equipment, in particular the anti-G suit, is no easy or quick matter. Three abreast, we advanced at best speed across the PSP parking area. You'll already have guessed what's coming next – that's right, a lightning strike! Not so close that we feared being struck but close enough (and loud enough) to the PSP to provoke a gravity-defying response of physical impossibility. All three of us, in mid sprint, managed to elevate ourselves in perfect unison several feet into the air. To anyone watching our progress on that dark and stormy night we must have appeared like an ungainly audition for River Dance.

In the protection of the HQ building, soaked to the skin but, despite the day's challenges, otherwise unscathed, we were reunited with our other pilot. While we were flying to Sardinia he had been to the nearby NATO HQ where the UK had a small admin cell and, in an amazing feat of persuasion, had convinced the cashier on duty to give him two million lira for our subsistence that night on the promise that he would, of course, telephone him as soon as he was back in the UK to settle the matter. Good skills!

Reunited once more, all we now had to do was make our way back into Naples for the night. The ensuing taxi ride was probably scarier than our exploits in the air that day. Those of you who have ever driven in southern Europe, and particularly in a Naples rush hour, will know what I mean. We arrived at our hotel having driven the final fifty metres on the pavement, scattering the rightful occupants of that space into doorways and the gutter. We tipped the driver handsomely for the 'entertainment' and checked into the hotel. We stood in reception, three of us steaming gently following our earlier soaking. "Anyone fancy a drink?" said Dick. After the trials and tribulations of a long, long day, what followed was undoubtedly the best gin and tonic ever.

The next morning, order had been restored and the Mediterranean was back to normal. There wasn't a cloud in the sky and the autumn sun was wonderfully warm on our still-damp backs. At the airport we fitted the new battery (which was thankfully undamaged despite the buffeting it must have taken during our flight through the storm) to the broken jet, started up and flew home without a glitch. We arrived at Honington, albeit a day later than planned, feeling pretty pleased with ourselves and with our ingenuity in sorting out our myriad problems. The boss, however, had a different take on matters. Dick was hauled into his office and dragged over the coals. The remaining three of us, perhaps fearful of also being invited in for an 'interview without coffee' never enquired of Dick what was said during his reprimand, and he was too much of a gentleman to discuss it; if only the boss had known the full story! Dick and I never mentioned, at least in public, our cunning plan; we both knew how lucky we had been. If we'd pursued the silly notion of swapping seats, our tussle with the thunderstorm would have been decidedly more exciting, while one can only guess at the disciplinary and career ramifications that would have come our way if knowledge of the deed had reached back home – as it inevitably would have done.

Over twenty-five years have passed since these events and Dick and I are now retired, both of us having made it to air commodore – that rank, I trust, being a reflection of our more usual standards of airmanship and professionalism. Sometimes, as I sit in 'pipe and slippers' comfort and the weather outside is stormy, I reflect on whether either of us would have achieved such lofty rank if we had been cavalier enough to see through our jolly jape. As L.P.Hartley said in his novel *The Go-Between*, "The past is a foreign country: they do things differently there." Indeed it is – and they do.

Rolling the clock forward I returned to XV(R) Squadron, based at RAF Lossiemouth, to a very different training world. I joined the new number one course for my refresher training before taking command of the squadron. Why number one? Well the TTTE experiment had run its course and UK training was being reset. The RAF was about to take delivery of the GR4 version of the Tornado, a national upgrade (and a tremendous increase in the jet's navigational and weapons capabilities) not shared by Germany and Italy. The time had come to part; the split was amicable, with the Germans exporting all their training to Holloman AFB in the US and the

Italians doing their own thing in Italy. While those of us who had passed through the TTTE had fond memories of our time at Cottesmore, no one lamented its passing; it was time to move on. For the UK it enabled a rewrite of the training syllabus to maximise the full training value of each hour, and to reflect the Tornado's new operational commitments and weaponry.

The shift in emphasis and the move to a wholly national OCU was perfect. The staff were all immensely experienced, with operational background ranging from Desert Storm onwards. What more could I ask for as the first boss of the new set up? In theory nothing, but of course this was a change to a government organisation. The new squadron was formed around the existing TWCU and its experienced weapons staff; however, of the twenty-two pilot instructors only three QFIs/IPs were qualified to teach student pilots the basics of how to fly the aircraft. Additionally, of the twenty-eight or so aircraft on the line, about half were ex-Cottesmore jets. These were block one, batch one models and were pretty much good only for initial conversion training. They had no pylons, so could not carry fuel tanks or weapons; they had no guns and an obsolete EW fit. You get the picture.

The RAF quickly realised its error and, in quick time, we addressed or worked around the limitations. By the time I left some three years later, XV Squadron was in transition to being fully GR4 equipped and the students were leaving for their operational squadrons already well on their way to becoming combat ready. The difference from my previous experience ten years earlier was profound. While the students were still taught the basics of weapon delivery with practice bombs, they were now also prepared for the weapons they would be employing soon after their arrival on the front line – and in a much wider range of delivery profiles. The ongoing operational imperative made it necessary for students to graduate from the conversion unit at a higher standard of training and readiness, and the experience of crews returning to XV Squadron as instructors helped reduce the gulf that previously existed between the training unit and the operational squadrons.

My two tours on the TWCU/XV Squadron were immensely enjoyable and rewarding. The former was probably the most enjoyable of my career – lots of varied flying, endless weaponry, a QWI course, and the satisfaction of helping countless young pilots and navigators at the start of their careers. I'd also managed a couple of years as the aerobatic display pilot, which brought the fascinating challenge of displaying a variable wing-sweep aircraft. The latter tour, at Lossiemouth, added some of the best low-level flying in the world. Above all, though, one's flying command tour is always something special.

I began this piece by recalling a party to celebrate the Tornado's thirty years of service (and counting); since I penned those first lines I have attended a dinner to celebrate XV(R) Squadron's centenary. It was good to see the unit in such fine spirits under the fine leadership of Jon Nixon, still delivering new life blood to the front line. That role will gradually wither on the vine over the next couple of years as the Tornado heads towards retirement in 2018/9. I'm sure there'll be a final Tornado party at that time when, once again, we will all look back at our experiences in the Tornado training system. I for one will always have fond memories.

CHAPTER 12

BATTLE DAMAGE ASSESSMENT – BETTER LATE THAN NEVER

Those nuclear weapons alluded to in the last-but-one chapter became history, as far as Tornado was concerned, as the political face of Europe changed. The Berlin Wall came down, while the Warsaw Pact and the Soviet Union collapsed. Perhaps it could be said that the West's implacable deterrent posture had contributed to all this, and if that is so then the Tornado force certainly played its part.

In 1986, nuclear readiness was relaxed from fifteen minutes to twelve hours – effectively putting an end to QRA, while the WE177 weapons were removed from Brüggen in 1998. It cannot be said that many Tornado crews mourned their passing.

But if politicians and public were expecting a more peaceful world and, perhaps more to the point, a peace dividend, they would be disappointed. The Gulf Conflict had signalled the start of a series of conflagrations around the world, in which the Tornado force would become heavily and continually involved.

The majority of contributors to this book joined a Royal Air Force configured for deterrent operations. Although they acknowledged that going to war was always a possibility, it was not a high expectation. So how would they react when the call came? Gordon Niven, whom I met briefly when at TWCU and see now socially, gives us an insight.

WING COMMANDER GORDON NIVEN (RETD)

In August 1998 I took up my new posting as a flight commander on 31 Squadron at RAF Brüggen. This would be my last flying tour, as on its completion I would disappear into the myriad ground tours essential to keep the RAF in the sky. I had previously served at Brüggen during Gulf War One, being dispatched early on to Bahrain on Operation Desert Shield; this was the precursor to the better-known Desert Storm. The RAF had operated a strict three-month rotation policy in the Gulf, so in early January 1991, despite live ops being imminent, off we went back to Germany, being replaced by Laarbruch crews who had only just set foot in the Gulf. One of the most experienced Tornado teams in theatre was on its way home without firing a shot – quite astonishing. The senior RAF officer in theatre is reported to have later commented that it might not have been the best decision he had ever made.

So, while remaining on standby to reinforce any of the Gulf detachments if required, we ended up watching the whole shooting match on TV. At the end of the war, those who had taken part assured us that we had had the best deal. Maybe so, but it was still hard to bear; those four crews from our team were now the only experienced squadron members not tested in combat. We even had some of the 'Gulf veterans' returning to complete their official work-up prior to being formally declared combat ready to NATO at the start of their first operational tours!

I don't believe anyone joins the RAF with a burning desire to drop bombs or shoot down aeroplanes. Without exception, we joined through a love of aviation and the challenge of military flying in particular. However, having trained through the quiet years of the Cold War period it was only natural to want to know whether one had what it takes. Post-Gulf War One I flew many surveillance missions over Iraq. Still an operational theatre, it had the potential for escalation into conflict – tense enough, but not hostile at the time.

But as a bomber navigator I felt that my flying career was somehow incomplete, as I had not yet been put to the ultimate test. So now I was back at Brüggen with some 2,000 hours fast jet under my belt, with the prospect of maybe another 500 during this, my last tour, before flying a desk for the remainder of my career – not having fired a shot. For the Cold War warriors this had been the norm. But with the numerous ops which had popped up post-Gulf, the combat experience of many of my juniors was quite impressive. Would I see some of it before I hung up my flying boots for good? And if so, where?

An early 31 Squadron GR4 (later standard aircraft have grey nose cones) launches from Brüggen during 1999's Kosovo campaign.

So now it was 1999 and international pressure was building towards intervention in the Balkans. Serbia was demonstrating a predilection for ethnic cleansing, this time against the ethnic Albanian population in Kosovo. SACEUR was directed by NATO to mount operations aimed at forcing the Serbs to cease their aggression. And so, on 24 March, an air campaign began, commanded by 5 ATAF from Naples. It was known to NATO as Operation Allied Force, the British element being Op Engadine. The bulk of the RAF attack contribution would come from Brüggen. By this time there were three operational Tornado GR1 squadrons on the base, numbers IX, 14 and 31 – 17 Squadron being in the process of disbanding prior to re-equipping with Typhoons. 14 Squadron was tasked as the lead, with each squadron contributing sufficient crews to fly two six-ships. A pool of eighteen aircraft and associated engineers was assembled from across the Wing. The aim was to have six aircraft plus spares available each night.

The aircraft fit was a TIALD (thermal imaging and laser designator) pod plus a BOZ dispenser and a Skyshadow pod, two AIM-9L Sidewinders and two 2,250-litre fuel tanks. Our attack weaponry would be either Paveway II or Paveway III laser-guided bombs; the dumb bombs of Gulf War One were gone for good. PWII was a standard 1,000-lb bomb with a laser guidance kit and tail fin. But its control and guidance (the bang-bang system) was very crude in that the vanes would deflect fully in one direction until the detected laser spot shot through the centre of the reticule, whereupon they would deflect fully the other way – ad infinitum. The resulting roller-coaster ride was very wasteful of energy, which significantly reduced release range and impact angle. PWIII, on the other hand, was a 2,000-lb bomb with a proportional guidance system. This significantly increased the range from which release could be achieved, provided a wide range of impact profiles and, significantly, increased the energy remaining at impact. Sorted? Not quite; other factors would still affect our ability to prosecute attacks – as we were about to find out.

Three VC10 refuelling tankers were deployed to Brüggen from Brize Norton for the duration of the campaign, and a typical mission would see the VC10s, then the Tornados, launch into German skies just before midnight. A pair of Tornados would shadow each tanker through France and out over the Mediterranean, with refuelling commencing prior to the Italian coast. Once over the Adriatic the VC10s would orbit while awaiting our return.

My first mission was conducted in clear skies. No moon, so completely dark, but not a cloud in sight from Brüggen to Kosovo and back. Our target was a buried fuel depot, our weapon PWIII. My first night nerves proved to be unnecessary as we encountered no resistance whatsoever, no AAA, no SAMs, no fighters. Nothing! However, the mission was almost a complete failure, with no weapons on target from four drops. The first lesson was unfolding, with the Wing's other missions producing the same result. Disappointed and relieved in equal measure, and six or so hours after taking off, we eased our way down through the dawn sky to be met by an anxious station commander. Apart from the all-important attack, all had gone like clockwork.

PWIII had only recently been brought into service, and its wide range of employment options was still being evaluated by the weapons instructors. It now appeared that the release parameters in the Tornado computer were inaccurate. The Wing's lack of success was reflected embarrassingly in a tabloid cartoon, where two crusty old pilots propped up the bar, medals spread across their chests. One was pointing out a medal pinned to his knee saying, "I got this one for Kosovo". Harsh, but fair, and the weapon was temporarily removed from our inventory pending further investigation. I was still to have my combat success.

During debrief of the first night's work the question was raised as to how we would cope if we encountered heavy weather en route, and we didn't have to wait long to find out. Our next target was a radio station on a mountain top – as straightforward as it gets. Shortly after take-off, though, the weather began to deteriorate. Rather than the expected loose formation with our VC10, we had to fly tight to maintain visual contact. Try to imagine driving in very thick fog, your only frame of reference the side of an articulated lorry – and doing it for three hours, with the addition of heavy turbulence. So now the articulated lorry also appears to be on a roller coaster, randomly rising and falling.

As we approached the refuelling bracket the tanker hoses were trailed from the two wing pods. Now, in addition to the tanker's oscillations, we had to contend with a very angry, gyrating fifty-foot python – our refuelling hose and basket. Red

A GR1, equipped with a TIALD pod, refuels from a VC10 en route to Kosovo.

lights turned to green, clear to refuel – gulp, you must be joking! During AAR, the man-in-front is not supposed to look at the basket into which he is aiming to insert the probe. He adopts a set position using various references in his field of view. Any small adjustments of position prior to moving forward are 'recommended' by the man-in-back: "up a smidge", "right a tad", and so on. My man-in-front, Stu Oakes, selected the position, but what with the turbulence and the gyrations of the python it was impossible to adopt anything other than a best guess. Providing any meaningful assistance was impossible, and making contact with the basket was completely in the lap of the gods. We missed; we missed again. Refuelling should have been completed over the sea, but time wore on and the Italian coast was looming. If the turbulence was bad here, what would it be like over the mountains? Eventually we made contact, as had the lead, Simon 'Gilbert' Hulme, on the other wing hose. But it was horrendous, easily the worst conditions I had ever flown in.

Not normally short of cracking the odd witticism whilst airborne, I tried to think of something appropriate to say to take the tension out of things. However, I recognised that this was one time when I should keep shtum and let boy wonder 'do some of that pilot s**t'. Eventually though, I felt we needed to get clear of the tanker. Stu replied that all he was trying to do was avoid hitting it. Looking to my right, it appeared that Gilbert was doing the very same thing. Impact with the tanker would almost certainly have necessitated us 'stepping over the side' and enduring a very uncertain parachute decent. It would also, probably, have resulted in the total loss of the tanker crew – no Martin Baker option for them, poor sods. In the end nature took a hand and both Tornados were unceremoniously dumped off their respective hoses, with no damage done apart from to our nerves and remaining heart beats. We had survived the pummelling, and more importantly had taken on enough fuel to allow us to continue the mission.

In all my 2,000 hours plus in the back seat of Her Majesty's finest, that night's events stand head and shoulders above any other in highlighting my utmost respect for the 'two-winged master race'. A huge hats off to Stu and the other pilots that night. Even though I was doing my man-in-the-back bit it was they, the pilots, who were keeping the whole situation under control; just business as usual!

Thankfully, the weather cleared over the Adriatic, so we reformed into our two three-ship trail and headed off into bad-lands. We made ready for the attack: weapon package selected (two PWII); height channel updated to correct for us flying flight levels on 1,013 millibars; check the laser code being fired matched the one set on the weapons; Skyshadow and BOZ set. We also updated the navigation kit as best we could; from height it was possible to mark radar significant features but not with any great accuracy (plus or minus a few hundred feet at best). Had we been in GR4s (we were in the process of converting), which came with leather seats, alloy wheels and GPS as standard, we'd have been all right, but there were no such luxuries on the GR1. In the interim we had a £70 GPS strapped with Velcro to the top of one of the two shades of green TV displays. At an appropriate moment, the man-in-back would simultaneously select 'fix' on the aircraft system and 'freeze' on the GPS. The position was entered onto the TV tab and an error was displayed which, if sensible, was accepted to update the aircraft position. As Heath Robinson as you like, but effective – and in the best innovative traditions of the RAF.

So fix/attack, stab, TIALD uncaged, let's find that target and get the job done. But nothing happened. Reselect – a few flashes on the screen, but still nothing. In an electric aeroplane, if you have a system fault you can generally recycle back through 'off'. Fix/attack, stab, uncage, a few more flashes, maybe a vague view of the ground, maybe not. It was the same across the formation as we all reported "no drop". Not a single TIALD operational, no weapons released. Three-and-a-half-hours flying through the worst weather most of us had ever experienced, only to be denied by a system that was never designed to be flown at altitude, never mind in icing conditions.

And worst of all, we knew the homeward weather we were to experience again. How we had refuelled on the way south without any major incident is beyond me. I think, to a man, we would have diverted rather than repeat the trauma of that outbound leg. Thankfully though, we were able to take on enough fuel for our return while still over the Adriatic before re-entering the maelstrom of the weather front, and we arrived back on the ground after almost seven hours.

It had become the norm to meet the VC10 crews in the bar for breakfast after an op. This time they undoubtedly knew it had been hairy, but I think they could tell from our drawn faces it was probably much worse than they had imagined. Astonishingly, the guys who had flown in Gulf War One said it had been like that on most nights! But still – two trips, no targets destroyed, no combat mission completed. The biggest threat I had faced to date was not enemy action but the weather.

Conducting an air campaign from home base is not something the RAF has done often in its history. Maybe the only other times since the Second World War were the Suez campaign from Akrotiri and Malta, or insurgent ops in the Far East/Middle East. However, we had soon settled into a set routine: plan night one, fly night two, squadron duties and routine training days three and four, a couple of days off in between. In an attempt to retain some normality, the mess continued with its social calendar. And so there you would be, quaffing a jar of German beer and troughing on bratwurst and chips, with the sound of the night's wave getting airborne. Quite surreal! On those occasions, I would spare a thought for the crews as I headed home from the mess; they would be preparing to engage their targets.

Family life, too, was a little unusual. To permit educational stability while parents were posted around the bazaars, my two eldest were, like many others, at boarding school; as it happened, they were with us for the Easter holidays. With them being away for a large portion of the year, we always made the most of our time together. So it was quite odd to plan and fly a combat mission, then set off with the family to a theme park, or cycle round the station on our way to the pool or bowling alley. After one sortie I joined the family on an early morning riding lesson. Our instructor chivvied me, saying I was riding as if I had been up all night. If only she'd known.

During my earlier deployment to Bahrain on Operation Desert Shield my eldest had been about six years old and, when asked where daddy was, he'd replied 'at the golf'. If only! Now, in his teens, he was well able to comprehend what was going on. Along with a few other families, my wife would take our children through the trees at the edge of the married patch in order to watch dad get airborne. Thus they were able to relate to the news on the TV. Having asked him recently, as I write, his only real recollection of the period was that I seemed to sleep a lot.

The Serbs were proud and determined people, and they weren't taking this lying down. Over the course of the campaign it is estimated they fired around 700 SAMs, albeit, in the main, unguided. They managed to down a few aircraft, including a US stealth fighter, the F-117. They also launched every serviceable aircraft they had, almost all of which were summarily dispatched by US fighters. They had a formidable array of AAA, mostly deployed around Belgrade. Over the common radio frequency we heard a number of US missions aborting owing to the ferocity of the defences around their targets. But for us, to date, nothing. Phew!

Our target for mission three was a factory complex in the middle of a town in southern Kosovo, and we routed through the Former Yugoslav Republic of Macedonia. Well, there was no point in exposing ourselves to risk unnecessarily. Our attack run was down a convenient stretch of land running from the open country to the target in the town centre. We would fly south of the target and box round to the left, ending up on our attack heading roughly south-west. Minimising collateral damage to non-combatant civilians and facilities was always first priority, and this routing gave me the opportunity to sneak a look at the target as we headed east – and there it glowed, right under my TIALD cursor. All looked good and so it transpired; two PWII right through the roof. Relief – I felt I'd finally lost my combat cherry! The RTB was as quiet as the way out; all in all it was rather a strange experience to have delivered 2,000 lbs of death and destruction with no reaction from the ground.

In that respect, I'd read a couple of accounts from guys who had flown in Gulf War One. One or two of them had commented on how emotional the experience had been. What, I'd thought; shedding a tear? Really? Well, on this occasion, after the customary debrief and viewing and validation of the TIALD video, I chose to return home to the family. Not the bar for 'breakfast' that day. My wife could sense something was different. I arrived home quietly, made myself a coffee, and retired alone to the back garden. I sat there for quite some time reflecting on what had just transpired. Tears maybe; moist eyes certainly. It was quite an unexpected reaction. Whatever else was going on down on the ground, they were still human beings. There can't be many other professions on the planet where 'proving you can do the job' results in devastation for your opponents.

Six-hour-plus sorties were excessive for what we were achieving, and much work was going on behind the scenes to find a shorter route; in due course it came. Head east out of Brüggen, through the former East Germany, the Czech Republic and Slovakia, south through Hungary and so into Serbia. The plus side was that it shortened the overall mission length by two to three hours; the down side was that it pointed us straight at Belgrade. It's fair to say that my one sortie in the vicinity of Belgrade exposed me to the most spectacular firework display I will ever witness, with AAA tracer everywhere. SAMs as well, possibly, but so far I didn't see any too close to us. (Stu did later refer to me as 'Blind Pew' when he was dined off the squadron – not quite sure why!) We lined up in trail, the target a storage site. Soon, our leader was calling 'chaff/flare', the action call for defensive measures to be deployed. Then 'tanks'! Again an action call in response to a severe and imminent threat – for the man-in-back to jettison the almost-full fuel tanks and bomb load, shedding a great deal of weight and permitting greater manoeuvre. They were only a few minutes ahead of us, but were getting all the attention; to be honest, I was quite happy with that. You could hear the tension in Gilbert's voice as he made the calls.

Hey, ho. A good look out around us before going heads-in for our attack. We did have number three behind us, whose job was to watch our tail. It was more of a psychological boost, as quite how they would spot a missile heading our way in the gloom is anyone's guess. So we pressed on. Again I had a very good mark on the target, followed by weapon release and 'splash'. Exactly what was stored in those buildings was not known to us. However, there was an almighty explosion, and a fireball that blanked my screen for a time, then a pall of smoke and flame rising rapidly into the air; job done. Time to head home – pronto. As a result of our leader's experience the three-ship behind us chose not to press on with their attack. We weren't in a fight to the death for the freedom of the West, after all, so there was little point in taking excessive risks. The decision was not challenged, but that choice will always be a fine line to walk.

In May the Wing deployed to Corsica in an effort to shorten sortie lengths further. Only two six-ships would go, so I elected to remain behind to get the squadron back onto a normal footing. This phase saw the ALARM (air-launched anti-radiation missile) being deployed in anger for the first time. Neither the missile nor the Tornado was configured in any way remotely close to the capability of the USAF F-16 SEAD units. However, on a number of attacks, SAM radars were observed to cease transmitting at the expected ALARM impact time. PWIII also reappeared, and was used to great effect against underground and hardened facilities. Shortly after the deployment, Milosevic capitulated and his forces withdrew from Kosovo. It must be noted though that, as Serb armoured units left Kosovo, newsreels showed a force almost unscathed, with high morale and ready for a fight. Had a ground war been required it would have been a stiff test for NATO.

It had been quite an experience for us on a variety of levels. Whatever the military value of the targets we hit, the 'war' had been won. Conducting the campaign as a Wing reflected HQ's desire to spread the workload, but it had the effect of stinting the campaign from an individual viewpoint. I'm sure 14 Squadron could have completed the task with a minimum of augmentation, but I'm nevertheless glad that things had been done as they had been. Although I only flew six sorties over a six-week period, I now had the combat experience I had so long felt the need of. Not for the glory of battle, nor any feeling of supremacy or power, but just for the simple human desire to see if I was up to the task. You just have to trust that your political masters had done their homework.

Two footnotes are worthy of mention. My final tour in the RAF was with NATO in Naples. One of my duties was overseeing the conduct of air ops over the Balkans, and part of that involved coordination with the director of Serbian air traffic control. On my first visit to Belgrade, the director proudly took me for a tour of the city and seemed to take great delight in showing me the bombed-out TV station and the ill-fated Chinese Embassy. Not the actions of a cowed and submissive adversary or someone ashamed of his country's actions. I didn't enlighten him about my flying history – but then he was no fool, either.

Finally, just prior to retiring, I embarked on a one-week course to obtain my sailing ticket at the services' centre in Gosport, during which I spent a week floating up and down the Solent calling into the various ports and pubs; marvellous, even though it was November. Over the course of the week our joint-service crew inevitably regaled each other with our recent experiences. The army type mentioned that he had led the first NATO troops across the border from the FYROM into Kosovo and on up to Pristina airport (not Captain James Blunt I hasten to add). He commented that he could see the effects of the bombing campaign all around. There was one scene in particular that had stuck in his mind. It was a small town in the south of the country, untouched by war bar for a factory right in its centre. He said it was amazing to witness; the factory had been totally destroyed without any buildings around it being damaged. I mentioned the name of a town – and it was one and the same. He was even more amazed when I said that it was my sortie that had been responsible. So I got a very satisfactory battle damage assessment – a little late but still very welcome indeed!

CHAPTER 13

BLIND AND DEAF

GROUP CAPTAIN IAN HALL (RETD)

So there it was in black and white. After what seemed like aeons on the ground I had in my hand a posting notice telling me that I was to go back to flying. Six years; it had seemed like a lifetime. I'd been lucky with the ground appointments, which had been stimulating and interesting: a tour as a squadron leader at the department of air warfare; a year at staff college in Canada; and then a post as a wing commander at the MoD. But this long sequence away from the front line had not by any means been my preferred way of doing things. Never mind; at last that coveted piece of paper was in my pocket. I was 'posted to command Number XV Tornado Squadron at RAF Laarbruch in Germany'.

Marvellous. Well, fairly marvellous. My first choice would have been a Jaguar squadron. Not necessarily because the aircraft was particularly special, but I'd flown it before and knew many of its people. A short refresher course would have brought me quickly back up to speed, and the job which would follow would have been nothing but enjoyable. But it was 1991 and Jaguar squadrons were, by then, as rare as rocking horse manure. On the other hand Tornado postings were plentiful, so it was no big surprise when the 'Fin' came out of the hat for me. It would be good; notwithstanding my Jaguar preference, I was excited by the prospect of flying what was becoming something of an icon.

Getting there would involve a long re-training process. There would be six weeks shaking the cobwebs off on the Hawk (I hadn't flown that either!) followed by three months on the TTTE and then another three at the TWCU. Altogether it would be nearly nine months from the time I left my desk until I arrived on my new squadron. Still, I wouldn't be the first in this position and would no doubt not be the last, so I was keen to get on with it. I'd never been to Laarbruch before, but I had served elsewhere in Germany and had enjoyed it. So I had little doubt that our new family home and lifestyle would be pleasant. And the bottom line was that nothing could detract from the pleasure of going back to flying. Could it...?

The months between receiving my posting notice and departing from my ground appointment were occupied by the Gulf Conflict, during which I followed closely the news of Tornado successes and losses. As the ceasefire came it crossed my mind that not only would I be joining a squadron as a new boy on the aircraft but that many of my men would be war heroes. An interesting prospect, without a doubt.

Not to worry though; I had contacted the individual who was to succeed me at the helm of my mahogany bomber in the MoD, had diligently prepared briefs and introductions for him, and had arranged that we'd have a week's handover together. I'd given notice on my London lodgings, bought a second car to facilitate the travelling that the coming courses would entail, and now all was ready. The weekend prior to the handover was filled with pleasant anticipation, both of receiving my escape chit from the office and of my imminent return to flying.

Monday morning dawned and I was at my desk bright and early. My successor and I had agreed that he would arrive at 9 am, and I laid out all the briefings he would require. 9 am came and went. 10 am passed and I called his home; no reply. In those days before mobile phones, he was completely out of touch. I was reluctant to make enquiries which might draw attention to his lateness so I sat it out and drank coffee for a further hour. 11 am. Now I really had to know what was going on, so I made a discreet call to a mate in the HR area. "Wait a moment," he said, "I'll see what's up." A minute later he was back on the line; "I'm putting you through to the desk officer concerned; good luck."

Click went the phone as it transferred. "It seems you haven't heard," came the new voice. "Sorry about that – it's all a bit frantic around here. The fact is that Jones is, at this moment, on his way to Kuwait. We've had to send him out there on one of those mopping-up missions which are arising at the moment. He'll be away for three months."

"OK," said I, trying to sound cheery. "So who's going to take over from me instead?"

"Err ..." came back the voice. Now there was an unmistakeably embarrassed tone to it. "Err ... you obviously haven't heard that, either."

"Heard what?" said I. My heart was sinking to my boots; it was clear that this wasn't going to be good news.

"Well, your posting to XV Squadron is cancelled," he replied. "In fact XV Squadron will soon be no more. You're in the MoD. Haven't you been involved in the 'options for change' discussions?"

Well, I had. Certainly, Tornado squadrons had been mentioned as a possible element in the post-Cold War force reductions the government was looking for but, given the aircraft's capability and relative youth, they'd seemed to us to be an unlikely choice. To my knowledge nothing had been decided – and wasn't likely to be decided, let alone announced, while the squadrons concerned were still in the Gulf in the aftermath of the conflict.

"Yes," continued my tormentor. "XV is disbanding soon along with 16 and 20 Squadrons when Laarbruch is turned over to Harriers. I'm afraid your services there will no longer be required."

"So what about my handover then?"

"Well that's the lucky thing," he said breezily, having apparently recovered his composure. "Given that we don't have a job for you to go to there's no need to replace you. So it's all worked out quite neatly. Just sit tight in your current post as though nothing has happened and we'll be back in touch in due course." Click.

Lucky? Turned out neatly? There was no answer to that, and work was still pouring onto the desk at the accustomed rate. What a mess. But the words and sentiment of Monty Python's 'Always Look on the Bright Side of Life' sprang to mind. So I opened the cupboard, avoiding all the skeletons I thought I'd safely stowed away, and in something of a blur turned to my in-tray.

Give the posters their due; they were indeed back in touch before too long to offer me the command of another Tornado squadron, number 31. My replacement duly returned from Kuwait and, three months later, I was off and running. So it all ended happily for me – and even XV Squadron was later reincarnated as the Tornado conversion unit.

Following that false start I arrived on the front line more than seven years after leaving it. Taking over an operational squadron is a wonderful experience, and my mixture of Gulf veterans and spirited newcomers were a good bunch. But there was a shock to come. Soon after my arrival I went for my annual medical. All went well until it came to the eyesight test. "Good grief," said the doctor, "you're blind as a bat! Go and see the specialists at Wegburg RAF Hospital and come back with some glasses. Then we'll try the test again."

Well! During all those years on the ground I had continued to have the mandatory annual medicals – and had always cruised through. In retrospect, it's true to say that, when I'd gone back to flying, I hadn't spotted many other aircraft in the sky. But that hadn't particularly rung any bells with me, nor had it worried my instructors. Why? Well, as all fast-jet aircrews know, good look-out isn't something that just happens. It's an acquired art which can be taught, practised and improved. I was out of practice, which was exactly what the refresher process was designed to rectify, wasn't it? My look-out skills would return wouldn't them?

They did – with glasses. Suddenly the sky was full of aeroplanes. Before long, rather than being easy meat for the junior pilots in one-v-one combat, I was at the top of the ladder. And, hating that interim stage of needing glasses for some things but not for others – because I inevitably mislaid them from time to time – I soon took to wearing them full-time. And became very comfortable with them.

You might ask whether contact lenses could have fitted the bill. At the time, though, we were led to believe that these weren't an option for aircrew flying ejection-seat-equipped aircraft. As we understood it then, the forces of ejection would rotate the lens around the eyeball, severing the optic nerve. Not to be recommended – thus contacts weren't prescribed.

So if we needed glasses we got them, but there were some aircrew (were – perhaps it's different today) who didn't take to them. Whether through vanity or pride, some preferred not to be seen wearing them. Indeed there is one contributor to this book who was well known for not slipping his glasses on until he reached the end of the runway for take-off – and then making the secret manoeuvre under cover of his dark visor. Everybody was aware of his trick – but the strange thing is that he thought nobody knew!

Actually, the unexpected advent of glasses was wonderful for me in more than one way. Driving immediately became easier, most notably at night. It just goes to show how insidious can be the degradation of our senses. But I remain puzzled to this day about quite how the fading of my eyesight remained undetected for, apparently, so long. Had those medicals not been rigorous enough? Or had there been a sudden deterioration? We'll never know.

Just a few days after I arrived at Brüggen to take command of 31 Squadron there was a mess night to say farewell to the outgoing station commander. The centrepiece was a review performed by mess members, and I have a vivid memory of a section of the cast list as it appeared in the programme. It read: 'OC IX Squadron – played by a Buccaneer pilot; OC 14 Squadron – played by a Jaguar pilot; OC 17 Squadron – played by another Jaguar pilot; OC 31 Squadron, played by – oh no – not another Jaguar pilot?' I could see what the sketch writer was getting at. His prejudice wasn't particularly against Jaguar pilots – although there might have been just the tiniest element of that about it – but reflected the station's view that, ten years after the aircraft's introduction to front-line service, the Tornado force should have been producing its own commanding officers. And also, perhaps, that there should by then have been more navigator bosses about. The episode certainly gave me an insight into how Tornado people were thinking at that time, and I found the sketch very funny. But perhaps it was easier to laugh from, so to speak, my particular side of the fence.

In fact, with Phantom time behind me as well, I was no stranger to flying as part of a crew, but I nevertheless felt throughout my Tornado tour that a single-seat background was never totally forgiven or forgotten by Tornado people. Or perhaps I'm just being hyper-sensitive; after all, characters from all sorts of backgrounds adapted happily to the Tornado. Just think, for example, of the culture change for navs when they were posted from the windowless hole that was the rear cabin of a V bomber to the sunlit uplands of a Tornado cockpit.

Whilst on the subject of crews, though, I must recount one particular oddity during my tour. Following my first deployment with the squadron on Operation Jural – the RAF's commitment during the mid-1990s to policing the southern Iraq no-fly zone – the hierarchy decided that, rather than detach further squadrons on what was looking like becoming a long-drawn-out commitment, they would draw crews from various squadrons and bundle them together into a composite unit. I, being already in place, was selected from a cast of non-volunteers to be the first CO of this bunch, so while my own people returned to Brüggen at the end of the detachment I remained in Dhahran at the head of a mixed and motley crew. The ground crew were from 14 and 17 Squadrons and dubbed themselves '147 Flight', while the aircrew came from everywhere and anywhere. Not surprisingly, the clumsy arrangement was not judged a success and Op Jural reverted thereafter to squadron detachments, but for that period I had the curious privilege of flying with back-seaters from every Tornado squadron except my own.

Ah, Dhahran. A fascinating place and an interesting detachment with 100 missions over Iraq. Air-to-air refuelling from all different types – Victor, VC10, KC-135, KC-10 – of which I rate the 'tens' the easiest because of their exceptional stability. And a diversion to Kuwait City when an engine blew up deep into Iraqi territory – an event which certainly focused the mind.

I earlier mentioned eyesight, but by the time I was running my Tornado squadron I was 45 years old and another sense was also beginning to fade. Pardon? Yes, hearing was the culprit, and I was well known on the squadron for being less than perfect in that respect. To the point that, at the Christmas lunch, my gift-wrapped present from the boys was a plastic 'trumpet, ear, mark one, hearing for the improving of'. Of course they didn't know it all; as many readers will no doubt agree, 'tactical' hearing loss can be useful from time to time.

Anyway, I wasn't alone in being deficient in the hearing department. Many RAF fast-jet aircrew have suffered over the years from high-tone deafness – if not general deafness – because of the appalling levels of cockpit noise. Notwithstanding the marvellously sound-attenuating helmets with which we were provided, the fact that we sat between twin, roaring air intakes for hours on end took its inevitable toll. Ironically, the Tornado wasn't the real problem, because its very thick Perspex made its cockpit environment quite pleasant. But the Jaguar and Harrier were appallingly noisy.

In fact the Tornado was a Rolls-Royce in many other ways – in the smoothness of its ride and in the amazingly seamless way with which reheat power came in. Its thick Perspex also protected against bird strikes which had, with earlier types, often resulted in catastrophe.

Anyway, the subject of deafness leads me by a circuitous route to describing the events of a missile practice camp which occurred during my tour. For whatever reason we had been allocated nine AIM-9G missiles to fire – not enough for one each but far more than usual. We had nothing much else on at that time and, given that I had never fired a missile in my entire 4,500-hour flying career, I opted to lead the small detachment.

I had earlier spent two marvellous summers at Valley in Anglesey: the advanced flying course; and, a year later after holding, a short refresher. So I had very happy memories of the place. For three days of this missile-firing detachment, however, things went badly; Welsh gales together with problems with the targets meant that, although much curry was consumed in Llangefni and Holyhead (why is it that RAF crews on detachment, be it in Scotland, Wales or Saudi Arabia, always eat curry?) the first missile wasn't fired until the Wednesday afternoon. A hit. Although the weather on the Thursday was still challenging, we got seven missiles away – equalling the all-time one-day record for MPCs at Valley. All looked good, and the last weapon was safely fired on the Friday morning to complete a successful week. There was then an anxious month waiting for the official results – which confirmed that all nine missiles had successfully guided and eight had detonated on target.

That MPC result was one of the best ever, and at the time my squadron had high hopes of being awarded the Aberporth Trophy for the year. But it was denied us on the grounds that eligibility for the 'Aberporth' was limited purely to specialist air defence squadrons. Now, I happened to know that at least one ground-attack squadron had won the 'Aberporth' before – for I had been on 54 Phantom Squadron when that had occurred. I also happened to know the deputy C-in-C Strike Command quite well, for I had previously worked for Air Marshal Sir John Allison in the MoD. But my personal appeal was fruitless. A great shame – but I suppose the benighted F3s had to be allowed to win something!

Returning to the subject of the hearing, on the ninth missile shoot I was after the towed flare with the bit between my teeth. The edge of the range was approaching, but there was a determination to get the missile away. Off it went.

Well, on such events post-flight analysis was intense – and the tape doesn't lie. It faithfully recorded the range safety officer calling "stop", followed some two seconds later by my call of "missile away".

At the time I had been certain that I had made my call first, and on the way home I was chewing this over with my nav, Torben Harris. "I distinctly heard the 'stop' call after the missile had gone, Torbs." "No boss," he said. "That was me repeating the RSO's call for the third time!"

According to the MPC staff it was not unusual for crews not to hear transmissions when the pressure's on. Luckily, the 'stop' call had only been made for timing rather than safety. I of course knew this all along (?!) and in any case the missile both guided and hit. A kill's a kill.

A deaf pilot is one thing, but no pilot is quite another. Over the years there have been all sorts of odd instances of aircraft being left without the optimum number of crewmembers. I recall a Phantom navigator ejecting, believing his aircraft to have some kind of terminal unserviceability, only for the fault to rectify itself and for the pilot to return to base solo. Early in the Harrier's life in Germany a pilot suffered a catastrophic power loss following a compressor stall. Try as he might he was unable to clear it, so was left with no option but to eject. As he floated down in his parachute you may imagine his surprise when he saw his Harrier merrily accelerating away. Presumably the rocket efflux from the ejection seat had restored order to the airflow through the engine intake. As soon as he'd returned to earth our sharp cookie phoned base from a nearby farmhouse to inform them that an unmanned aircraft was now powering its way around Germany. As you would imagine this caused consternation; would it crash onto a city? So much so that the authorities considered launching a QRA Lightning to shoot it down. But, given that it was impossible to predict exactly where it would land after being shot down, this option was discarded. Eventually the wretched aircraft ran out of fuel and crashed, happily without any catastrophic consequences. The staff recommendation after this? If pilots have time, they should shut down the engine before ejecting.

The Tornado wasn't exempt from similarly unfortunate events, and a notable occurrence derived from one of the aircraft's foibles. Not for nothing was it known as the 'electric jet', and one of its primary systems was the CSAS – the control stability augmentation system. This was designed to make an airframe that was somewhat unstable into a flyable machine. But when the CSAS failed it was a real handful.

Early in the Tornado's career crews became aware of occasional unexplained control inputs, and after a while and a bit of data analysis these perturbations were pinned down to the CSAS reacting to transmissions from radio masts. So much so that low-flying charts began to sprout avoidance circles around the worst of these – known as HIRTAs – high intensity radio transmission areas.

A chap on my squadron had previously fallen victim to this, in combination with another of the jet's peculiarities – its command ejection system. Pat King, in his piece earlier in the book, alluded to an unfortunate accident when an incapacitated pilot was lost in a disabled Tornado following his navigator's ejection. The Tornado has a system whereby, in just such an eventuality (it was designed primarily with combat damage in mind) the nav may eject both crewmembers. But pilots are a conservative bunch and enabling this system had not, at that time, been standard practice.

Naturally, that event prompted much head scratching, and its aftermath caused a change in procedure, with the command ejection system subsequently being enabled as a matter of routine. But the law of unintended consequences was never more apparent than in my friend's accident. One fine day he was trundling happily down through Germany at low level when he became aware of a USAF A-10 Thunderbolt crossing his nose at fairly short range. Short enough, in fact, to cause him to take evasive action. His trusty back-seater, surprised by this violent manoeuvre, glanced out of the window. Spying a large transmission mast nearby, he assumed that the CSAS was being interfered with and that the jet was out of control. Whereupon he decided that the only way was out, and without further ado he pulled his yellow and black handle.

It now being the standard operating procedure, his command ejection lever had been selected to 'both' – so his pilot followed him out in short order. We may only imagine the front-seater's feelings as, from his parachute, he watched his perfectly serviceable Tornado disappearing over the horizon. Whether or not the A-10 pilot claimed a kill we may only surmise. But the lesson from that accident was obvious; technology is a marvellous thing, but crewmembers still needed to talk to each other.

CHAPTER 14

THE IRAQ WAR – 'GULF WAR TWO'

I was a Cold War warrior and left the RAF, after thirty-two years service, with no campaign medals. I never expected any and never got any. But we've already seen that things became different as the Cold War thawed. Suddenly, conflicts seemed to be occurring thick and fast.

Paddy Teakle was one who also joined up under the old assumptions and who, quite probably, never imagined actually having to go to war. And yet it happened for him – three times (thus far) during his service. He finished up with a chest full of medals – from the Falklands, from Gulf War One, and, most notably, from the Iraq War. In this last he was awarded the DSO for his work in command of the Tornado Wing which contributed most significantly to an efficient and rapid conclusion to the military action. He is currently the deputy commander of the NATO AEW&C force, and I regularly see him socially; it's good to hear from him now.

I acknowledge, by the way, that many have questioned political aspects of the Iraq War – or 'Gulf War Two' as it came to be known – but I hope readers will forgive if we steer clear of that controversy. The military are ordered by the politicians to do their duty, and we shall concentrate on how the Tornado force carried out these orders.

AIR COMMODORE PADDY TEAKLE

A wise philosopher once said that we are all products of our own history. Now, I am no philosopher but I do recognise that my values, beliefs and actions are shaped by my past experiences – good and bad – and by the experiences of others. So as I lead you through the events of spring 2003 I will occasionally refer back to earlier periods and episodes in my career that help explain why I took a particular decision or chose to pursue a particular course of action.

Like every contributor to this book I consider myself incredibly fortunate to have served on the Tornado force. My association was both long and deep, and I watched it grow and develop over the years into, arguably, the most successful force of the modern era – certainly from a British perspective. But that was not always the case. In the mid-1980s when I was posted to RAF Laarbruch in Germany, a posting that was to be the first of many flying the aircraft from mainland Europe, I think most of us recognised that, in the pecking order of aircraft types, Tornado was some way off the top.

Life was good, though. We worked hard and played even harder; all eyes were to the east and we spent long hours preparing for the war that never came. But that changed in 1990 when Saddam Hussein invaded Kuwait. Suddenly we were campaigning, and there is no doubt in my mind that the aircraft came of age in Gulf War One. It was a seminal moment and, from that day onwards, we were committed to, and dominated by, real rather than potential operations.

With that short backdrop, I'll move the story some years down the line. In September 2001 I had the enormous privilege of moving 31 Squadron from its home for many years, RAF Brüggen, to its new base at RAF Marham. This repatriation was conducted with little fanfare and largely passed unnoticed, but it was a special moment in history as, from that day onwards, the RAF would no longer have any of its fast-jet squadrons permanently based overseas. Marham could not have been more welcoming and we quickly settled into our new surroundings, alongside our great rivals IX(B) Squadron and across the airfield from II(AC) and XIII Squadrons. Our new location was on the unhardened side of the station, which meant that we operated from a flight line rather than from HASs.

Throughout the preceding couple of years, poor aircraft availability had meant that the Tornado force had found it very difficult to hit its flying hours target. In January 2002, I introduced a new management practice, and from that moment onwards things turned round. Morale was great – the aircrew were getting all the flying they needed and the ground crew were justifiably proud of their aircraft generation statistics, which were the best across the entire force. Incentivisation was the key. If we hit the weekly target on a Thursday, we would not fly on a Friday unless there was a particularly important tasking. Therefore weekend working became the exception rather than the norm. The troops would select their incentive; they could have a stand-down day, a sports day or something similar; it was up to them. What they chose says more about them than my words ever could. On each and every occasion they chose, without dissention or hesitation, training days. So we went from strength to strength, consolidating at every turn. My ground crew were the jewel in the squadron's crown and I loved them for it.

From mid-2002 onwards we focused on our upcoming operational deployment as part of Operation Resinate, the Iraq air policing mission. The deployment was to be my last hurrah, as I was due to hand over command upon my return. In early January 2003 we deployed to Ali al Salem in Kuwait for what we all expected would be nothing more than a routine three-month policing mission. We were well prepared and enthusiastic, particularly as we would be using the RAPTOR long-range reconnaissance pod for the first time operationally. Of course, we were aware of increasing tensions regarding Iraqi weapons of mass destruction, but could not, at that time, foresee the events which would unfold.

Deploying a squadron on operations is one of the most rewarding experiences for a squadron commander and brings a tangible focus to the entire unit. But we had recently had a change of key engineering personnel, and my ground crew were taking a little time to adjust to the new style. I was naturally keen to ensure that our new-found ability to hit aircraft generation targets at home transferred across into the operational theatre, and when they inherited a 'bag-of-bits' from the outgoing squadron I knew that they would have their work cut out. But they were not giving up their reputation as the best engineers in the force without a fight – and the fleet was restored to tip-top state in double-quick time.

Op Resinate sorties were historically pretty benign affairs, primarily consisting of the reconnaissance of a number of points – and although we generally flew with LGBs, kinetic events were something of a rarity. After a local area and procedures familiarisation sortie, my young pilot and I flew our first operational sortie. Now, I had always believed in the importance of selecting a squadron's crew combinations, not purely on competence and qualification but also on personality. I'd always found it a fascinating exercise in human nature, and I particularly looked forward to meetings where my flight commanders and I would thrash this out. I still remember the meeting where we built our crew partnerships for this deployment, when I'd been paired with the squadron's most junior pilot. Not because he needed special oversight but because my experience was seen to balance his relative inexperience.

It turned out to be an inspired pairing; we'd thoroughly enjoyed flying together during the work-up and had quickly become a crew to be reckoned with. Now on our first op, we had prepared ourselves comprehensively for a pairs reconnaissance mission. So it was something of a surprise when, shortly after getting airborne and whilst still in Kuwaiti airspace, we received a call from AWACS tasking us to attack an Iraqi air defence facility in response to earlier surface-to-air fire. So a mere ten minutes after crossing the Iraqi border on the first operational mission of his life, young Pete Beilby found himself dropping two laser-guided Paveway II bombs onto an Iraqi air defence bunker. Talk about a baptism of fire!

It was soon clear to me that things were beginning to hot up in political and diplomatic circles. The infamous 'intelligence dossier' was placed before Parliament on 3 February and efforts began in the UN to secure a new security council resolution authorising the use of force in response to Saddam Hussein's defiance of the arms inspection regime. The Americans had invited the UK the previous summer to join them in planning for possible action; a UK national contingent commander and a UK air component commander had been appointed in the autumn. Now, in the second week of February, both came to theatre and, at the same time, additional aircraft and personnel began to arrive at Ali al Salem. As we entered March it was patently obvious that the UK would be a major part of the coalition brought together in response to Saddam Hussein's refusal to comply with existing UN resolutions. But whether it would actually come to that, and the potential timing for any action, remained unknown.

My squadron was due to be replaced by another at the end of March, and HQ 1 Group and RAF Marham's station commander still considered that to be the preferred option. I can only surmise that, with no firm date for the start of, and no idea of the duration of, any offensive action, they believed that extending us in theatre beyond the planned three months would be detrimental to morale. That geographically detached viewpoint made absolutely no military sense at all, while pulling us out just as things were getting interesting would have been a massive kick in the teeth to us all.

I knew that I would have limited success in arguing my case with those in the UK, so I would have to convince the UK air component commander (who as luck would have it was also AOC 1 Group) that his best option would be to extend us in theatre indefinitely. My argument was simple: not only did we have the most up-to-date and comprehensive operational knowledge of the theatre but we were also the most current and accomplished operators of RAPTOR – a unique, long-range reconnaissance capability that would be crucial to gaining and retaining operational situational awareness. I knew my case was strong, and Air Vice-Marshal Torpy accepted it completely – and all thoughts of withdrawing the squadron evaporated. As an aside, and to show what a close-run thing it was, I learned many years later that Marham's station commander was only prevented from coming out to Ali al Salem to order us home because the aircraft that he was due to travel on broke down at Brize Norton.

Throughout March more aircraft and personnel arrived; Ali al Salem was growing, and elements of five Tornado units were soon in place. These were numbers II(AC), IX(B), XIII, 31 and 617 Squadrons, the first four from Marham. The Lossiemouth Wing was setting up a second detachment at Al Udeid in Qatar, although 617's Storm Shadow team was to remain with us in Kuwait.

With a mixed team and with two other squadron commanders now in residence, it was vital that we formalised the command and control arrangement to avoid anarchy. I therefore approached the UK air commander for direction and guidance. Clearly, as the resident squadron commander I had control of the Op Resinate mission, but how did he want to play Operation Telic, the combat phase? Once again the cards fell kindly for me, and so it was that I was appointed the *primus inter pares* of the three squadron commanders at Ali al Salem. Although this established some degree of authority, it fell short of formal command status.

I pondered my options. I discounted the 'lead squadron' idea, having experienced how divisive it had proved to be at one of the deployed bases during Gulf War One. An adversarial relationship had been created which, even at the time, I could see was unhealthy. So I was determined to seek an alternative which would place everyone's contribution on an equal footing, while at the same time establishing the necessary degree of authority I needed in my role. In the end I decided that the best option was to establish a single Wing under a combined identity, and I finally settled on the title 'Combat Air Wing'. This approach effectively did away with individual squadron identities for the duration of the campaign. The advantage was that it formed a single team and more easily facilitated the mixing and matching of resources to task. It was not a universally popular approach, indeed one of the other squadron commanders was vehemently opposed, but I knew that I could sell the idea to even the most hardened detractor. In the end, I was delighted that the vast majority of personnel embraced the concept wholeheartedly and that the team spirit and Wing ethos built quickly.

Since Gulf War One the Tornado had developed enormously in capability, equipment and versatility. Stand-off weapons, advanced precision-guided bombs and long-range recce equipment were now within the GR4's inventory; all amounted almost to specialist roles, and would have to be exploited to the maximum extent during the campaign. To deliver the best effect across the entire spectrum of combat capability, I decided to allocate discreet missions and roles to the individual squadron elements. All in all, I had thirty-six combat-ready crews, so packaging roles into specialist cadres made perfect sense. As well as conventional interdiction sorties with precision-guided munitions (PGMs) I knew we would be called upon to employ ballistic weaponry, including cluster munitions, as the campaign progressed. This was the force's bread and butter, and any one of the crews could tackle that task. But we would also employ the Storm Shadow stand-off missile, conduct suppression of enemy air defences using ALARM, fly Scud-hunting missions at low level using the joint reconnaissance pod, and of course continue our vital medium-level reconnaissance task with RAPTOR.

It was clear that the Storm Shadow task was best placed with the 617 Squadron crews; although we had all been trained on the weapon's use, they were the current experts in its employment. The low-level Scud-hunting task was given to the specialist crews from II(AC) and XIII Squadrons who had undertaken mission-specific training prior to deployment. The decision to give the ALARM role to IX(B) Squadron was the one that caused most angst. To me the decision was a 'no-brainer', but to the 31 Squadron aircrew it seemed counter-intuitive; after all we excelled in that particular specialist role. But I knew that, at that moment in time, there was nobody better with RAPTOR, and that we just had to focus in that direction.

I addressed the Wing on 18 March and announced my decision on role allocation. It was not the easiest notion to sell, with one pilot comparing my announcement to the feeling of being the last kid to get picked for playground football. I suspect that my own squadron felt a little cheated at being denied the more glamorous kinetic roles, but their loyalty to me, their understanding of the importance of long-range reconnaissance and the promise of kinetic opportunity later on quickly brought them onside.

But for two individuals the news was even more devastating – they would not

Wing Commander Paddy
Teakle addresses the troops of
the Tornado Combat Air Wing
prior to the commencement of
operations in 2003's Iraq War.

be flying at all. The first of these was a navigator who, despite being an accomplished Tornado GR1 operator, had found the transition to the GR4 a real challenge. The second, and more difficult, decision concerned the 31 Squadron QWI pilot. QWIs are masters of their trade and, as such, naturally expect to be leading war missions. I totally agree with this philosophy, but being at the forefront of operations does not necessarily mean being in the cockpit. So when I was asked by the combined air operations centre to provide a Tornado expert to assist in tasking and targeting, I immediately knew the best man for the job. But that did not make breaking the news to him any easier. His reaction was predictable – he was enraged and I feared, at that moment, that I might have lost his support, respect and trust forever. But in the days following his arrival at the air headquarters the quality of our tasking improved considerably, and this alone more than vindicated my decision. I don't suppose that he will ever fully forgive me for denying him his chance, but in later years he will come to realise that his individual influence over the campaign was immeasurably greater there than it ever would have been at Ali al Salem.

In the build-up to hostilities I had come under some pressure to switch pilots so that I might lead four- and eight-ships into battle. But I resisted; firstly I owed some loyalty to the young man who had been my pilot over the preceding three months and with whom I had built a strong relationship; and secondly, I firmly believed that my role was to lead the Wing as effectively as I could, and that leading individual missions might not allow me to focus on what really mattered. Anyway, we had ample and excellent airborne leaders.

On the ground crew side, I formed mixed shifts of engineers drawn from across the squadrons. I had been approached by one SEngO with the suggestion that the two shifts should each be composed of personnel drawn predominantly from single squadrons, augmented by additional personnel, and that these shifts be encouraged to 'compete' against each other. I thought this would be divisive and would undermine the team ethos I was seeking through the Wing. I valued all of the ground crew equally and I knew that by combining them into two shifts with a single purpose we would be able to achieve an aircraft generation rate far in excess of that which would be possible were the two shifts driven by vested interests. And my approach paid off. My affection and admiration for the engineering team was such that it was to them, and not the aircrew, that I first broke the news that we were going to war. In that one moment the identity of the Combat Air Wing was cemented.

Historians will say that the war officially started at 0234 hours GMT on 20 March 2003, but certain precursor missions were flown in advance against artillery, SAMs and air defence systems in the south of Iraq. Additionally, a leadership target of opportunity was engaged, but this turned out to be a false lead. And of course accurate, detailed reconnaissance had been needed beforehand.

It all felt very different for me this time around. The fear of the unknown, which had been palpable in 1991, was entirely absent; this was familiar territory. However, amongst the team things were a little different. For the vast majority of crews this was their first taste of war, and I could feel the frisson of their excitement and sense their trepidation. In all honesty the nights of 19 and 20 March were a bit of a damp squib – not so much a case of 'shock and awe' but more 'snooze and bore'. All that changed the following night, though, when cruise missiles and PGMs rained down on Baghdad and other target areas. From the slow start on 20 March, the coalition doubled its sortie rate the following night with the Combat Air Wing at the forefront of the RAF's contribution.

From the outset it was clear that the operational tempo would be high and that we would be tasked with multiple roles within any twenty-four-hour period. I felt entirely vindicated in my decision to allot specialist roles to cadres. With astonishing accuracy the 617 Squadron element employed its first Storm Shadow missiles against hardened, strategic targets on the night of 21 March, and at the same time the IX(B) Squadron element was leading our efforts to degrade Iraqi air defence systems. Simultaneously, the low-level recce crews from II(AC) and XIII Squadrons were Scud hunting in western Iraq. Other crews were conducting interdiction missions against high-priority targets.

All the while there was an insatiable appetite for the unique product of the RAPTOR pod. The strength of that system is its ability to provide strategically important imagery through exactly the same tasking process as a tactical reconnaissance asset. RAPTOR allows the aircraft to stand off many miles from its target and yet still provide startlingly high resolution imagery, day and night. Many of the vital points of interest lay within Baghdad itself but, in an effort to deny intelligence and prevent attack from the air, Saddam had erected a potent air defence ring around the city. However, this 'super-MEZ' had no answer to the stand-off RAPTOR, Storm Shadow, Tomahawk, or stealthy USAF B-2 and F-117 bombers.

In similar fashion to 1991, Iraq's SSMs posed a problem for the coalition. In the west of Iraq they were considered to present a significant threat to Israel, and politically it was in no-one's interest for the Israelis to be drawn into the conflict. From eastern Iraq the threat to coalition mounting areas, airfields and key population centres in Kuwait was real. We became familiar with the wail of the air raid sirens and the dash for shelter – familiar yes, complacent never, and we were thankful for the Patriot batteries that had been deployed to counter that particular threat. But those same Patriots would very soon mark the nadir of our campaign.

On 23 March Flight Lieutenants Kev Main and Dave Williams were killed when their GR4 was shot down by a Patriot missile on their recovery to Ali al Salem, within Kuwaiti airspace. This book is not the place to examine the circumstances behind this tragic event or apportion blame, indeed such events highlight the inherent uncertainty of combat – the 'fog of war'. The Combat Air Wing had taken a punch, and rocked back on its heels. In the hours that followed, as I walked amongst the team I encountered shock, disbelief and in some cases anger, but I also saw stoicism and resolve. The Wing stood firm, and we came out fighting. I believe to this day that our 'all one team' ethos allowed everyone to recover more thoroughly and rapidly than would have been possible had we been operating as separate squadrons.

During the first week of the war our operations were focused on attacks on the leadership, command and control nodes, airfields and armoured formations, all supported by a significant reconnaissance effort. But the emphasis was beginning to shift from relatively static units towards mobile targets, particularly those associated with the Republican Guard. In just over a week, the coalition ground forces had moved to within fifty miles of Baghdad and, as predicted, all my crews were now getting a piece of the bombing action. We were now very much in the close air support game, working with the US Army V Corps and the US 1st Marine Expeditionary Force. As well as traditional close air support, where we worked in support of a forward air controller on the ground, we were also using a new procedure whereby we would be directed to a 'kill box' which was known to be free of friendly forces and within which we were able to find, identify and engage our own targets. Clearly, a 'hunter-killer' tactic such as this requires an accurate picture of what is happening on the ground, so our reconnaissance efforts remained as crucial as ever.

On 3 April, coalition forces took control of Baghdad airport. The Republican Guard was taking a hammering, and by early April many units were no longer capable of coherent defence. The tempo of our offensive air operations was on the wane and we were beginning to see preparations for the final assault on Baghdad. There was a marked increase in reconnaissance tasking and a completely different emphasis on the points of interest we were looking at. Our tasking was taking us further and further afield, including reconnaissance sorties in the far north of Iraq. We were no longer primarily collecting intelligence on the Iraqi leadership and military, we were now helping to build the picture of the humanitarian situation on the ground so that aid could be rapidly brought to bear where it was most needed.

According to US records the air campaign ended at 0259 GMT on the morning of 18 April 2003. Reconnaissance and other support missions continued until the end of the month but, to all intents and purposes, offensive air operations ceased

We wuz there! Evidence of the long-standing Tornado detachment at Ali al Salem, Kuwait.

four days after the fall of Baghdad on 14 April.

On 26 April, Pete and I flew our last operational mission, a flight which also turned out to be my penultimate Tornado sortie. My thoughts now turned to our recovery to RAF Marham and to my handover of command which was slated for 23 May. 31 Squadron left Ali al Salem on 28 April; sadly our departure also marked the end of the Combat Air Wing. Despite elements of more than one squadron continuing in theatre, the remaining squadron commander was an advocate of the lead-squadron construct and reverted to this approach the moment our TriStar was airborne. After a night stop in Cyprus, where the amount of steam let-off could have powered the Victorian railway system, we were finally reunited with our loved ones on 29 April 2003.

Few squadron commanders have the privilege of leading their squadron in combat, and even fewer have the chance to lead a composite Wing. 2003 marked the high point of my association with the magnificent Tornado and a truly outstanding force. In hindsight, would I have done anything differently? Quite simply, no. The concept worked and the courage, generosity and loyalty of everybody who took part in that venture were staggering. Although commentators may now question the motivations and legality of the war, when asked to step up and deliver, the Combat Air Wing did it in spades.

CHAPTER 15

ALL AT SEA

Those who flew the Buccaneer in the anti-shipping role loved the aircraft. Its long legs, its ability to fly very low and its comfortable ride all made it a favourite, and its crews were fiercely loyal to the machine. But by the early nineties it was undoubtedly reaching its best-before date, and as Tornados were withdrawn from Germany under the 'options for change' defence review they were the obvious choice to replace the Buccs. Accordingly, in its GR1B version, Tornados formed the maritime attack force until they were withdrawn from the role around the millennium.

2010's UK defence review reassessed the threat (and, perhaps more pertinently, the nation's finances) and resulted in us, today, not only having no fixed-wing anti-surface shipping capability but, with the cancellation of Nimrod MRA4 and the abrupt withdrawal of Nimrod MR2, no dedicated land-based maritime attack or reconnaissance capability at all. Whilst we all understand the financial imperatives, to leave such a capability gap until the anticipated entry into service in 2020 of the Boeing P-8 was taking a huge risk – to say nothing of leading to embarrassment from time to time as we asked NATO allies to cover the gap.

The Marineflieger had operated Tornados in the anti-shipping role from the outset, although that task was turned over to the Luftwaffe in 2005. But whether RAF Tornados were ever particularly successful in their short-lived maritime role I leave you to judge from this chapter by Gordon Robertson. He was a QWI veteran of the Buccaneer era before converting to the Tornado – so if anybody can cast light on this little-known aspect of RAF Tornado ops then he's the man.

WING COMMANDER GORDON ROBERTSON (RETD)

Before starting I need to say that I regard the Tornado as exceptional at what it was designed to do. In bad weather or at night, using TFR it can ingress hostile airspace undetected and drop bombs in a bucket. Its nav kit, its radar and its avionics are unparalleled. However, when you are trying to find 28,000 tons of Kirov class battlecruiser that's doing thirty knots in an unspecified direction from a rough position that's six hours out of date, the ability to find a nail in a fencepost and hit it with a big hammer is not the greatest of your problems. In considering the Tornado's effectiveness in the maritime role, inevitably comparisons have to be drawn with the aircraft it replaced: the Buccaneer. In doing so, we must remember that the Buccaneer was specifically designed for anti-shipping operations and the Tornado was not.

The job of finding and attacking ships, or anti-surface warfare as it is properly known, had long been done by the Nimrods and Buccaneers based at Kinloss and Lossiemouth in the north of Scotland. The 'kipper fleet' role was to locate and track any Soviet surface action group (SAG) poking its nose round Norway's North Cape and consign it to the icy depths of the North Atlantic at the earliest opportunity. Having been brought into service in 1969 as a short-notice gap-filler for the cancelled TSR2 and then F-111K, the Buccaneer had given the RAF sterling service for almost twenty-five years. But despite having the reputation of being as tough as the proverbial brick outhouse, time was catching up with it, and years of abuse had left the aircraft at the end of its fatigue life. It was said that there were upwards of four feet of (carefully managed) cracks on each airframe.

A replacement had to be sourced within a dwindling defence budget. A number of alternatives were considered, with Buccaneer crews offering a wish list to the authorities ranging from new Buccaneers, through F-111s, to F-15Es. Strangely, the MoD was reluctant to give these alternatives any serious consideration, proposing the Tornado GR1 as the only realistic option. And so it was that the Tornado found itself being shoehorned into the maritime role.

Number 12 Squadron was selected as the first maritime Tornado squadron, with 617 Squadron re-roling shortly afterwards. The plan was for 27 Squadron, operating Tornados at RAF Marham, to disband and for its number plate to be immediately passed to a Chinook unit. Number 12 Squadron Buccaneers at Lossiemouth would simultaneously disband and its number would be handed to Marham Tornados, thereby ensuring that neither 12 nor 27 Squadron had breaks in their histories. I arrived at RAF Marham having just completed conversion from the Buccaneer to the Tornado to take on one of the squadron leader posts on 27 Squadron just weeks before the re-numbering and impending move to Lossiemouth. As the new boy on the outfit, and already having a few years service under my belt, it came as no surprise to me that, mysteriously, I was the only aircrew squadron leader available to act as flight commander on the up-coming disbandment parade. It's strange how these things happen and how, at this critical time, every other squadron exec couldn't fit into their dress uniform, had a bad leg, other commitments, or two left feet. So while everyone else was filling their boots with the last of the overland flying I was re-familiarising myself with the finer details of parade and sword drill for the ceremony.

Perhaps the boss felt guilty, for I was rewarded by flying the first official 12 Squadron Tornado sortie. On the last day of September 1993 we positioned a pair of freshly painted 12 Squadron Tornados from Marham to Lossiemouth ready for the designated 'first' on 1 October. Knowing that others back at Marham would be trying to claim the title of the first to fly a 12 Squadron Tornado sortie, the race was on to get airborne. The boss, Wing Commander Cas Capewell, had secured an early take-off slot at Lossie and we slipped the surly bonds at around 0800 hours on a crisp, clear Scottish morning. We did a quick round tour of our new backyard and threw it back on the deck after just twenty minutes, indisputably winning the 'race'.

As Cas and I taxied back in, feeling rather pleased with ourselves, we could see the 'scrambled egg' of a group captain's hat atop the figure waiting for us at the edge of the pan. It was certainly unusual to be met by the station commander, but a nice touch. Cas, however, seemed to have a guilty conscience. "What have you done?" he asked me over the intercom. "Have we dinged anything sensitive?" A born leader, clearly, immediately deflecting any blame onto his subordinate! "What do you mean me? We've only been airborne twenty minutes; even I would be hard pushed to drop us in it in that length of time!" As we got closer it became clear that the figure of authority belonged to Nigel Maddox, out-going OC12 (Buccaneer) Squadron, recently promoted to group captain and, that day, acting as station commander. 'Mad Dog' was known to both Cas and me from our earlier Bucc times, and maybe he was there to shake our hands rather than our throats. After all, few upwardly mobile group captains can resist a photo opportunity, and a squadron with a new aircraft type would ensure coverage in the local rag. Had I anticipated that a photographer from the *RAF News* would also be present that morning I might have chosen a different T-shirt to wear under my flying suit. But the centre-page spread in the next issue was eternal testament to my sartorial ineptitude; I stood proudly in front of the 12 Squadron fox on the Tornado's fin sporting a bright yellow 27 Squadron T-shirt.

The squadron as a whole didn't move to Lossiemouth until 1994, but arrived in some style on 7 January flying a diamond nine across the airfield. Thus began the Tornado's short-lived tenure as the UK's maritime attack force. No 617 Squadron, the Dambusters as they like to be known, or 'six foot seven' (6'7 – get it?) as everybody else calls them, arrived later in the year to complete the maritime Wing. Although the Moray Firth is a wonderful location with a great weather factor, fabulous flying conditions and a safe and clean environment to raise a family, there was some reluctance amongst many of the servicemen and women and their families to make this enforced move. The same had been true ten years previously when Buccaneers had moved from Honington to Lossiemouth. Families were forced to uproot, sell houses, give up jobs, re-locate kids at school and move lock, stock and barrel to the frozen north. As a Scot I'd like to think that things were not as bad as folk imagined, and I think that that is borne out by the number of people who, from both moves, have made their lives in Morayshire and have remained there for decades.

But as well as resistance to the move there was a reluctance to take on the maritime role, which was viewed as boring and undemanding in comparison to its overland equivalent. Again, this mirrored the earlier Buccaneer experience. On both occasions a number of maritime crews had been dropped into the new squadrons to provide relevant experience. Having been part of that maritime core both times I can say that convincing Tornado crews that the maritime role was rewarding was a damned sight harder than it had been with the Bucc mates. To a large extent this was down to the optimisation of the Tornado for the overland role and I'll discuss that shortly. But first, let's look at the tools we were given to do the job.

Integral to the capability was the missile, and the Buccaneer had already been equipped with the BAe Dynamics Sea Eagle for some years when Tornado took over the role. The missile was a development of and a successor to the Martel, which had been used in both its anti-radiation and TV-guided forms on Buccaneers. Sea Eagle employed a Microturbo jet engine for propulsion, giving it a range of around 60 nautical miles in its sea-skimming profile at about 560 knots. It flew at extremely low level, the exact height depending on the sea state, which was assessed by its radar altimeter. The large warhead (230 kilograms) employed a Misznay-Schardin plate, a type of shaped charge which provides a high degree of armour-piercing capability by forming a slug of molten metal without needing a precise stand-off distance or impact angle.

Sea Eagle had an autonomous radar seeker head that could be targeted in a variety of modes to select different targets within the SAG. Sophisticated electronic counter-measures made it extremely resistant to jamming and other electronic protective measures. In the terminal phase the missile reduced its height even further to impact the target just above the waterline. But for all its many excellent features the missile had one weakness. At a short range from the target it popped up to over 100 feet to acquire the target, permitting its J-band radar seeker to see over the radar horizon caused by the curvature of the earth. The range of this manoeuvre and the pop height were calculated assuming a target of zero height. To the best of my recollection, though, there were never any Soviet ships that met this criterion, so the pop manoeuvre was entirely redundant, exposing the missile to unnecessary risk.

When Sea Eagle entered service, the Central Trials and Tactics Organisation commissioned a study to determine the number of missiles required to achieve the loss of the highest-value unit within a nominal SAG comprising a representative number of the most capable capital ships. The study's simulations took into account Sea Eagle missile profiles, ship disposition, surface-to-air missile acquisition, fly-out and reload times and the number of Sea Eagle hits on other ships. When the sea spray settled and all the sums were done, the answer wasn't forty-two (the solution to Douglas Adams' famous *Hitchhiker's Guide* question), but twenty-four. I imagine that it could only have been serendipity that the Buccaneers operated in six-ship formations and were capable of carrying four Sea Eagles each (as well as four 1,000-lb retard bombs in the internal bomb bay, by the way).

The Tornado could also carry four Sea Eagles, but only at the expense of its two large underwing fuel tanks. In order to retain practical range, the normal operational load was just two Sea Eagles plus two 2,250-litre fuel tanks. So a Tornado formation would, to start with, be short of weapons.

In preparation for any maritime attack, crews would plan knowing the ships' latest known location, when that observation was made and what direction the ships were travelling. From this the ships' expected position at the time of the attack could be projected along their mean line of advance, for example if the ships were detected as travelling north at twenty knots six hours before the planned attack time, then the attack should be planned to take place 120 nautical miles north of the detected position. Having just re-read what I've written, the overland guys might have had a point; maybe the maritime game wasn't that demanding after all! But of course those ships were under no obligation to maintain heading and speed while we got our act together, and those sneaky, underhand, naval types regularly changed both course and speed to make our lives difficult.

At some considerable distance from the target the attackers would split into two sections, perform some speed adjustments, and launch their Sea Eagles at forty miles before, as Blackadder had it, returning for tea and medals. The idea of adjusting the speeds before missile launch was to try to get all the missiles to appear over the ships' radar horizon at the same time. While I couldn't disagree with the maths and the rationale, I always regarded this practice as unnecessary. I argued that, whatever the orientation of the SAG, a 90° split tactic would allow the ships to employ both their forward and aft defensive weapon systems, whereas a single axis assault at least gave the attackers a chance that one system would be unable to bring its acquisition and guidance radars or weapons to bear, simply because the ship's superstructure was in the way.

Before maritime software was embodied to twenty-six Tornados (bringing them to GR1B standard), the nav-attack system was also sub-optimal for the role. Maritime attacks rely on each aircraft flying specific splits and timings based on the target position to achieve coordination of the final attack. Before the software update, all the points within the attack geometry were located as fixed latitudes and longitudes. This meant that, although the stored target position could be moved, all the points within the attack remained fixed. The software update fixed this problem by allocating a number of points to an attack and fixing them relative to the target position, so that when the target moved all the attack turning points moved too. This seemed to be a relatively simple modification, but it took an age to come in. You could ask, by the way, why we could not have drawn on existing Marineflieger Tornado experience. Not only was their missile different, though, but by contrast with our 'blue water' scenario they were concerned more with coastal operations.

A Nimrod was essential to a radar-silent attack from beyond the ships' radar horizon, for without an accurate update on the target's location the attacking force would have to find the ships themselves. Having the Nimrod element of the UK's maritime force less than ten miles away from Lossiemouth at Kinloss had allowed for good interaction, and over the years the force had developed co-operative tactics that allowed the Buccaneers to target key elements of a Soviet SAG, firing their Sea Eagles beyond the target's radar horizon. A normal attack would see the Nimrod periodically broadcast an encrypted version of the zulu-zulu (ZZ), the latitude and longitude of the SAG's high-value unit. The attacking aircraft would fly through a pre-arranged position, set as a range and bearing from the ZZ some 120 nautical miles distant. Hopefully, the Nimrod would pick up the attacking aircraft on its radar and provide encrypted updates on the ZZ position.

Similar cooperation worked for Tornado, while in both cases we would revert to autonomous attack if no Nimrod was available. But doing so in the Tornado exposed another of the aircraft's major weaknesses in the role. A good maritime radar can pick up the nice big steel and aluminium radar reflector that is a ship at long range. The Buccaneer's Blue Parrot radar had a maximum range of 240 nautical miles, although 180 was more normally used. The Tornado's radar, although sophisticated, ground-stabilised and multi-mode, had a maximum range of forty nautical miles. So when operating without a Nimrod the Tornado was limited to firing Sea Eagle well inside the missile's normal launch range.

A part of the GR1B upgrade was to paint the aircraft a rather fetching shade of light grey. We were assured that the boffins had done considerable work on selecting the appropriate shade of grey, but with fifty to choose from they could have picked something closer to that found in the North Atlantic. One of the key principles of camouflage is to break up the outline of the object, which is why regular aircraft camouflage used a disruptive pattern and explains the reasoning behind the bizarre dazzle-ship schemes used during World War One. The standard overland disruptive grey and green actually did a good job over the sea. I don't deny that the new, light colour used across the whole aircraft looked good, but we shone like beacons over the North Sea, as well as over land.

My logbook shows that the first maritime sorties we undertook with Tornados were over the period 14-17 September 1993 on Exercise Solid Stance, flying via Lossiemouth and squeezing in a night-stop at Bergen, Norway, to conduct a series of five sorties. Although maritime work gradually increased, for the next year over half of our flying remained overland. This included commitments common to the whole Tornado force, such as Operation Jural, the UK element of the air policing of the southern Iraq no-fly zone in the wake of the Gulf Conflict. We also clung to Exercise Red Flag at Nellis Air Force Base in the States, which I can't let pass without relating the tale of a trip out.

The middle weekend of the exercise was a US national holiday and no flying was planned for the Monday. We had the use of a car, and thought it would be a good idea to drive out to see the Grand Canyon. We gave ourselves a leisurely start on Saturday and set off on our long drive, stopping off at the Hoover Dam to get the tourist tick. We were in no rush, with our plan being to arrive a little before sunset to view the canyon at its most spectacular. It's a lot further than it looks on the map, and we drove for hours, but with Tornado navigational precision we arrived at twenty minutes before sunset.

We soaked up the incredible views, wondering at the play of colours on the canyon walls almost a mile high. Then it got dark; very dark. It does that at night in the desert; it gets very, very dark. You couldn't see your hand in front of your face, far less the bloody canyon. This wasn't the idea, so following a hasty re-plan we decided to drive to Flagstaff, find accommodation there and drive back to the canyon in the morning for the sunrise. Fine plan. But it was a holiday weekend and there was no accommodation available in Flagstaff, in fact there was no accommodation in any of the towns we went through. Before too long we were closer to Vegas than we were to the canyon – so we drove back home. In essence, we'd driven the equivalent of from London to Newcastle and back again to look at a hole in the ground for twenty minutes.

Never mind, every cloud has a silver lining. As we arrived back in Vegas we noticed that tickets were still available for BB King, Doctor John and Little Feat in a triple-header show late that night. I'd like to say how much I enjoyed the gig after the disappointment of our sightseeing trip, but I slept through most of it.

Prior to our operational Gulf deployment we had to endure escape, evasion and resistance-to-interrogation training. So, in preparation for surviving in the desert we were shipped off to Dartmoor for a week in October to find out what it's like to be cold, wet and miserable. For those who don't know or can't imagine – it's cold, wet and miserable. I was paired up with Chris Hazzard, whose enthusiastic, positive and optimistic approach would provide a perfect antidote to our privations. But within an hour of starting our trek across the moors, Chris's sunny disposition was sorely tested after falling in the River Plym and being soaked to the skin. He spent the next few days trying to dry himself out over tiny fires made of damp twigs.

I will freely admit that this episode was not my finest hour. The tone was set in the twilight of the first morning. As the watery sun was creeping up over the horizon, colours were indistinguishable, one from another. When we'd set up camp overnight we had used our parachutes as makeshift bivouacs, being careful to keep the camouflaged sections of the parachute outermost and the orange and white gores to the centre. Chris and I were breaking camp and folding up our parachutes when we glanced down the hill and saw a couple of members of the 'enemy' hunter force approaching. We looked at each other, wondering how we could make our escape, then looked at the twelve feet of parachute we were shaking out between us. In those few moments the sun had finally made its appearance, with the muted colours of the forest now being thrown into stark relief. Stretched between Chris and me was now four yards of vivid orange silk, which we were flapping vigorously like a couple of clowns to rid it of twigs and bugs. If we'd shouted, "Cooee, we're over here, big boys!" we couldn't have been more conspicuous or looked more ridiculous. We spent the next ten minutes face down in the mud, being relieved of our contraband Mars bars and tea bags before being released for another few nights of purgatory.

Things didn't get any better later in the week. Having dug a grave hide I was lying in a pool of stagnant water in a cold, dark, claustrophobic hole in the ground trying to convince myself, as we'd been told, that this misery really was better than being unprepared for the real thing. The roof of the hide was an inch from my nose, and what little kit I had was squeezed round about me. It was impossible to get comfortable, but in an effort to get less uncomfortable I shifted my kit around. As I did so I thought I felt my satellite safety locator beacon switch on. I'd pushed it away out of arm's reach and the only way to retrieve it and check it was to get out of the hide – which would take time. Experience told me that if I got out to check the beacon I'd inevitably find that it was switched off – and I'd have gone to a lot of bother for nothing. I convinced myself that I couldn't have switched it on accidentally and that I should stop fretting. What experience now teaches me is: if you ignore it you will certainly have switched it on and the whole international search and rescue set up will be alerted to a distress beacon being set off in Dartmoor; the entire hunter force will be sent to your precise location to find the twit that switched on his beacon; and that the exercise directing staff will not be best pleased. Ah well, you live and learn! The upside of this training was that I learned, after a few days of dehydration and sleep deprivation during the resistance-to-interrogation phase, that hallucinations are something to look forward to.

In the overland role the best way to get to the target safely was to ingress at low level using terrain masking to avoid enemy radars and missiles. This meant that the aircraft was hidden by the physical terrain or flown in the terrain's radar clutter where enemy radars could not distinguish between the ground and the aircraft. Normally, overland flying training was done at 250 feet, but to practise for wartime flying could be authorised down to 100 feet in remote areas. In the maritime role there was no terrain cover; therefore day-to-day flying was conducted at 100 feet and, with special authorisation, down to fifty feet.

Flying at 100 feet over rough terrain is a hard skill to master, requiring talent and practice (God alone knows why we let pilots do it, then!) Safety margins are small and separation from terrain is achieved visually. The radar altimeter is always there as a back up to provide a warning if things get too close. Over water it's a different story. No matter how rough the sea, the 'terrain' is predominantly flat. Safe separation is still achieved visually but there are fewer visual cues to aid perception, and the radalt becomes a more important aid to flying at the right height. For all its good points, the Tornado's radalt had the unhappy knack of regularly unlocking at under 130 feet, requiring the aircraft to be climbed to re-establish lock before descending again until the next time the radalt unlocked. This made it difficult to stay low in the radar clutter.

Over a relatively cold sea the heat from the jet engines of any maritime attack aircraft stands out like a sore thumb, making a good target for infra-red or heat-seeking missiles. Luckily, at heights below 100 feet these types of missiles are likely to either impact the sea or fuse off it before reaching their target. All in all, as a key defensive measure, operating at very low level was a principal tactic for maritime attack aircraft, so a reliable radalt was essential.

The shift in the geo-political landscape following the collapse of the Berlin Wall meant that there was now perceived to be less of a maritime threat from the Russian Bear, and in a political climate desperate to find the peace dividend expected from the end of the Cold War it was really no surprise that the maritime attack element should come under threat. Sea Eagle integration wasn't included in the GR4 upgrade programme and, although the Tornado remained on maritime work for a while, the role and the missile were axed in a defence review around April 1999.

It's an ill wind that blows nobody any good, and a number of the time-expired Sea Eagles were fired off during Exercise Neptune Warrior. 617 Squadron's then boss, Wing Commander Bambi Thwaites, was allocated two missiles to fire during the exercise (no doubt he was just lucky that his name was drawn from the hat – twice!) On both occasions the aircraft failed to get a firing solution through the main computer. Engineering investigation traced the problem to a wiring fault. The GR1B used the same wiring circuits for Sea Eagle that the standard GR1 used for TIALD. A fleet-wide upgrade in 1998 to make all Tornados TIALD-capable had screwed up the GR1B wiring, and this hadn't become apparent until Bambi's pilot pulled the trigger.

I did three tours on the Buccaneer, achieving some 2,000 hours and gaining a stack of qualifications and specialisations. As a junior officer I had few distractions and was able to concentrate on flying and honing my skills. I felt an affinity with the aircraft and thought that I could operate the kit to maximise the aircraft's effectiveness and that of any formation I was leading.

By contrast, my one tour on the Tornado was as a squadron executive, flying only 250 hours. There were other duties: I was the squadron warlord and managed the outfit from behind the ops desk while we prepared for our first NATO Taceval; at the same time, as a flight commander, a stack of annual reports had to be written. At least I now know what symptoms I should look for to indicate that I am stressed!

I never felt that I came anywhere near achieving the level of proficiency that I did on the Buccaneer. Despite the Tornado's wonderful nav/attack system I always felt that we were asked to fiddle with it too much – don't get me started on the wisdom of conducting radar fixes based on an Ordnance Survey map position – and I never felt truly comfortable operating the aircraft. I always felt that I was either fighting the kit or feeding the beast.

All the same, I have tried to give an objective assessment of the effectiveness of the Tornado in the maritime role. As I said at the start it was not designed for that; it was pressed into service in a role for which it was ill-equipped. But as in everything else the aircraft was asked to do over its lengthy and impressive service history it did it well, or in the maritime case well enough.

It is probably very clear where my sympathies lie. I loved the Buccaneer and had great fun operating it. Regrettably, I cannot say the same for the Tornado, but that is not the fault of the aircraft. Nevertheless, its relatively fragile engines notwithstanding, if I had to go to war I think I'd prefer to do it in a Tornado. For a navigator, there is a comfort in knowing where you are and knowing that the kit is going to get you to the target and deliver your weapons accurately – at least it would do if you were over land.

CHAPTER 16

LEADING FROM THE FRONT

Now another story from Kosovo, that extraordinary episode when Tornados flew combat missions many hours in duration through European airspace teeming with civilian air traffic. This particular sortie was flown by an air commodore, which is a curiosity in itself. He was station commander at RAF Brüggen at the time; without having done exhaustive research in the area, I am fairly confident in saying that war missions flown by RAF officers of one-star rank must be numbered in single figures.

And that, rather than the details of the Kosovo sortie, is why I wanted to include this chapter – which goes on to offer a perspective on other higher-command aspects of Tornado operations. The writer is my friend Iain McNicoll, whom I first met in 1993. While I was at the helm of 31 Squadron, the four Brüggen squadrons spent a good deal of time on quite long detachments in the Middle East. During one of those periods when I was away, command of 17(F) Squadron changed, and the new man had already been in the chair for a couple of months by the time I returned and met him for the first time. It was a Friday evening at happy hour, I recall, when this tall, imposing figure came up to me with outstretched hand. "Ah, at last I get to meet the fourth," said Iain. I took the proffered hand, while pointing out that, being the newcomer, it was in fact he who was the fourth.

Having sorted that out we became firm friends, and with children of similar ages our wives and families got on famously, too. We never served together after Brüggen, but I had no trouble keeping track of him during subsequent years as he rose through the ranks, eventually to retire following a spell as deputy commander-in-chief of Air Command. He was perching on that lofty pinnacle during the time another Tornado milestone occurred – when the force was deployed to Afghanistan in the army support role. Contrary to many people's expectations, that employment was outstandingly successful; perhaps, above all others, it crystallised the aircraft's marvellous versatility. All in all, therefore, Iain is well placed to offer a fascinating perspective on aspects of the Tornado era which we don't often consider.

AIR MARSHAL IAIN McNICOLL (RETD)

My first flight in the Tornado was on 7 December 1981 with Major Klaus Kropf, German air force, from RAF Cottesmore on the snappily titled 'transition-1' sortie. I had come from the Buccaneer and this was space-age rather than steam-age stuff. After conversion to type, I became a weapons instructor on the TWCU at RAF Honington. Subsequently I served on 17(F) Squadron, 16 Squadron as flight commander, and 17(F) Squadron again, this time as squadron commander.

I later arrived at RAF Brüggen as (acting) air commodore station commander in December 1998 for my fifth tour on the Tornado and, coincidentally, my fifth in Germany – the rule seemed to be that if you had not been before you could not go again! The rank, rather than the normal group captain for station commander, was because Brüggen was by then the last remaining RAF Germany station, so I was the senior RAF officer in Germany. This added somewhat to my task, with links to the embassy, but the rank was also designed to maintain some influence with the army in Rheindahlen, who otherwise might possibly have forgotten about the needs of their light-blue neighbours. For example, I sat on the British Forces Germany health board, under the able chairmanship of Major General Christopher Elliott, who became a friend as well as a colleague. I also got to know Sir Mike Jackson, commander of the Allied Rapid Reaction Corps, and renewed my acquaintance with Major General Andrew Ridgway, Mike Jackson's chief of staff, for whom I had worked in the MoD.

As I was getting to grips with the quirks of my position, and in the light of the UN Resolution on Kosovo and subsequent NATO decisions of 23/24 September 1998 and a 'false start' to operations in the October, I did not imagine that the station would soon be on active operations. However, I did maintain a watching brief on events through regular intelligence updates. And when NATO operations started on 24 March 1999 I knew that there was a strong possibility of RAF Brüggen participation. I expected that a squadron or squadrons might be deployed and asked the wing commanders to think – discreetly, since no instructions had yet come from the UK – about the practicalities.

RAF Harriers deployed, along with most of NATO, into Italy, and there was no space in southern Europe for us. But the military ratcheting up of pressure and the desire of the UK Government to do more led to Strike Command and Number 1 Group instructing us to prepare for operations on Operation Engadine (the UK code name) from our home base. The station swung rapidly into gear, and long days, with morning and evening executive meetings, organised us for war, took stock, and sorted out any glitches.

I had to decide who would be the lead squadron commander and found myself spoilt for choice. I opted for Timo Anderson, OC 14 Squadron, as 14 were the lead TIALD operators on the station. Greg Bagwell, OC IX(B) Squadron, and Robbie Low, OC 31 Squadron, acted in support. Regrettably, 17(F) Squadron, under Chris Coulls, was in the process of drawdown, being disbanded on 1 April prior to re-equipping with the Typhoon; little fanfare accompanied this as, with operations pending, major social events did not seem appropriate.

Three VC10s of 101 Squadron arrived as our dedicated tanker support and were placed under my tactical control. Initially, I was fully engaged in leading and managing the station – and in hosting the inevitable stream of high-profile visitors. Whilst these were genuinely welcome and very supportive, not least for the families, they were time-consuming. In the space of a few weeks we hosted: the Duke of York; the prime minister, Tony Blair; the secretary of state for defence, George Robertson; the chief of the air staff, Air Chief Marshal Sir Richard (Dick) Johns; and of course the AOC, Air Vice-Marshal John Thompson. The prime minister, very relaxed and natural away from the cameras, had an emotional moment meeting the newly born twins of one of the pilots. George Robertson starred; after being taken slightly to task by a wife for referring to the 'pilots' rather than to 'pilots and navigators', he revealed that his father had been an RAF navigator. The next weekend he wrote a newspaper article about his day and referred to the 'pilots and navigators' of RAF Brüggen. And I spent a bit of time with Mike Jackson and Andrew Ridgway as they flew in and out on their mission to prepare for potential ground operations.

But I itched to do more. So I started to get myself ready to participate and flew the necessary training missions and simulator sorties. Then on the night of 10/11 May 1999 I flew a mission as number two in a six-ship – two formations of three aircraft. My navigator was Pete 'Rocky' Rochelle, the 14 Squadron weapons leader and very much at the absolute pinnacle of his game – no point in me having anybody but the best to keep me out of trouble! Our call signs were the somewhat American-sounding Mustang 81-83 and the rather Japanese Honda 91-93, and we flew with two 101 Squadron VC10 tankers, each tanker supporting its own three-ship. Cast off over the Adriatic, we continued to southern Serbia – the bit between Kosovo and Bulgaria – where Rocky put a couple of Paveway II LGBs on the target. Then back to the tanker, with no relaxing, as the night trail and AAR brackets, often in cloud, were not easy. And so after seven hours airborne overnight we got back home for the debrief and then a well-earned breakfast. The mess staff were stars and breakfast covered a multitude of eating and drinking options. The rapport and banter between tanker and Tornado crews was brilliant, with our aircrew acknowledging just how the tanker made the transit, drop-off for the mission and subsequent pick-up appear completely seamless. But, although I joined the team for breakfast, I went without the alcoholic refreshment and, after a shower and change, headed for the office, too buzzing to go to bed.

I did clear my participation with AOC 1 Group – although, to be fair to him, that telephone call might possibly have occurred retrospectively! He was content, but he subsequently felt he should get further cover from the commander-in-chief, who was the recently-in-post Sir Peter Squire. Sir Peter then put a stop to me flying on operations. I knew him pretty well – and he me – from his time as senior air staff officer at Strike Command, when I had been PSO to the deputy C-in-C (I was in his office most days on HQ business) and also from his time in the MoD when I had been on the staff of the chief of the defence staff. I held, and still hold, him in the highest regard and he was, as ever, an absolute gentleman about his no-fly decision. We exchanged letters and spoke on the topic. He listened carefully and respected my view – but inevitably his own view prevailed. His reasoning was that I had a different and, in his view, all-consuming task, which was to lead the whole station in supporting those on operations. I said that I had not flown initially in order to focus on establishing the station on a war footing. This it now was, and working very well – and with brilliant commitment from all at Brüggen. In my view I could, therefore, both do that task and fly. As an aside, it was an absolute privilege to see how well the whole station pulled together, helped by a really good team of execs.

Sir Peter said that I had nothing to prove to my team. I did not at that time think this was my reason for flying, though the perspective of the passing years makes me wonder whether I wished, even subconsciously, to prove something to myself. I had flown over Iraq, but only during a relatively quiet period in 1993/1994, so this was my first war mission. In any event, at that time I felt very strongly that I needed the experience in order to make better decisions and to ensure support for the operation was absolutely tuned to the need.

Sir Peter also suggested that, because I was only allocated ten hours flying per month, I could not be fully current and/or competent for combat missions – or, if I was, I would undermine the rationale for establishing a higher minimum number hours for other crews. I demurred along the following lines. First, in order to achieve combat-ready pairs-lead status (the minimum to fly sensibly in squadron training sorties), I had just gone through the full work-up. From January to March 1999 I had over-flown the ten hours per month by a bit – thirty-eight hours in three months. Secondly, I had the great benefit of 2,500 hours on type as instructor, including rear seat, weapons leader, flight commander and squadron commander – and had had relatively brief periods off between flying tours (three years on each of two

occasions). It was therefore credible that I could be current on a good deal less flying than would be required by a more junior and less experienced pilot.

It is interesting that he did not use the argument, which others subsequently did, that were I to be shot down it would be bad for station/RAF/NATO morale (it would clearly not have been great for my morale, either!) This was and is, as Sir Peter no doubt recognised, a specious argument; everybody is equally important and it is no worse – or better – to have an air commodore shot down than a flight lieutenant. There is a small argument that says the propaganda value of downing a more senior officer is

During the Kosovo campaign, Brüggen's station commander Air Commodore Iain McNicoll meets the chief of the air staff, Air Chief Marshal Sir Peter Squire.

greater, but I think we (the rest of you I mean!) could have lived with that. I did later fly as supernumerary crew in a VC10 on another operational mission (there was no restriction on being on this flight) on a 'short' route through central Europe rather than over France and Italy. That mission sparked my love of the VC10, later consummated, if I might use that expression, when I did a senior officer conversion before taking over as AOC 2 Group. At that time I did a full multi-engine crossover course at Cranwell on the King Air and then undertook mini conversions on VC10, TriStar, C-130J, HS125 and BAe146. I flew a good few times in the left seat of the VC10, always with an instructor, including AAR flights and a passenger-carrying sortie to Akrotiri and back. It was a wonderful aircraft, handling like a big Hunter and so easy to land smoothly – or perhaps the wheels were so far beneath and behind me that the crunch was not transmitted to the cockpit.

Returning to the thread, the station continued on operations and then deployed elements of IX(B) and 31 Squadrons to Solenzara in Corsica, where space had been found. But the operation came to a close on 10 June with the team there having flown very few operational missions. I flew to Solenzara on 18 June to see everybody, which turned into a most enjoyable social call.

Whilst acknowledging the debate that continues to this day over what caused Milosevic to cave in, the operations from Brüggen were a major success. Foremost, despite some of our aircraft being shot at by, and evading, surface-to-air missiles and anti-aircraft fire, everybody returned safely. We had mounted complex and demanding, long-range night missions from our home base and the station had performed exceptionally, and been extraordinarily well-supported by the whole community, both on-base and off.

Subsequently, I was delighted to be able to tell some of the participants that their contribution had been formally recognised: Timo Anderson with a DSO for his outstanding operational leadership; and Rocky Rochelle with a DFC for his outstanding performance as lead TIALD operator (not for flying with me!). In addition, through a bit of effective staff work and, crucially, Dick Johns's help after the initial criteria were too restrictive, the NATO medal was awarded to everybody who had flown on the operation.

My tour at Brüggen continued, fortunately less eventfully, but no less enjoyably, until it was abbreviated by substantive promotion and a posting to the MoD in September 2000. But my involvement with the Tornado had not completely ended.

As deputy commander-in-chief operations at Air Command from 2007 to 2010, I found myself in the forefront of the debate about replacing the Harriers in Afghanistan with Tornados. There were only three Harrier squadrons and the continual support of Operation Herrick had resulted in the near loss of their aircraft carrier deployment capability; at the time there was only one pilot night qualified on the carrier. In addition, whilst the Harrier squadrons could undoubtedly have continued, and wished to do so, a large number of their personnel were breaching the agreed harmony guidelines by being deployed on operations for over one fifth of the time. I gained consensus in the RAF for a change, but the politicians, civil servants and other services needed considerable cajoling. The transition would be relatively expensive, since some modifications would be needed to the GR4 and new infrastructure would be required at Kandahar, so it was vital to get all of the MoD on message before tackling the Treasury (as the additional money would come from its reserve).

After a number of more or less acrimonious debates, not least with PJHQ, both with Lieutenant General Nick Houghton, as commander joint operations, and his lead civil servant, whose ignorance of military matters did not constrain her views, the secretary of state was finally persuaded of the merits of the case. It was now up to us to deliver. Fortunately, James Linter and the 12 Squadron team led the field and performed brilliantly – a standard met by each succeeding Tornado squadron from 2009 until the end of operations in 2014.

Some within the Royal Navy, when the Harrier was withdrawn from service in 2010, thought that the RAF had known that this was the likely outcome and had manoeuvred for it to ensure the Tornado continued in numbers and that carrier air power was targeted by the cuts. Nothing could be further from the truth; it was, and still remains a disaster that the Harrier was removed by the so-called 'strategic defence and security review' of 2010 and that Tornado numbers were also reduced. We can only hope for a better – in numbers and in every other way – F-35 and Typhoon future.

As a postscript to the 'senior officers flying on operations' debate, I should note that in my last two tours, as AOC and then deputy commander, I – and others – started and/or continued our encouragement of station commanders taking part in operational flying, and many did so over Iraq and Afghanistan. I always emphasised that they should only fly on operations if fully qualified and competent in every respect – and that I would be very unhappy if there was a hint that they were not both these things. It is notable that the USAF has never had any difficulty with senior commanders flying on operations and certainly many did so, and probably still do so, at least up to two-star level.

My long and happy relationship with the Tornado came to an end with my last GR4 sortie, accompanied by a brave and/or foolhardy navigator, Flight Lieutenant Borrow, on 24 November 2009 from RAF Lossiemouth, making nearly twenty-eight years on type. The sortie included a spot of practice bombing at Tain range; I seem to recall a direct hit, but my memory may be faulty. I did do some further service flying after that: in a VC10, on 26 November on a North Sea AAR towline; and finally in a Chipmunk, solo, on 23 March 2010 from the BBMF at Coningsby. That neatly bookended, after more than thirty-eight years, my RAF flying that started on 12 January 1972 – in a Chipmunk from RAF Turnhouse.

CHAPTER 17

STORM SHADOW

We saw some time ago that JP233 didn't get much use in Gulf War One. Its successor as Tornado's primary heavy weapon was Storm Shadow, a stand-off missile. It offered more than stand-off, though; accuracies had come on in leaps and bounds in the meantime, and the idea of countering the opposition's air effort by cratering his runways had long been superseded. Storm Shadow had the precision to strike more surgically, along with a penetrating warhead to deal with seriously hardened targets.

The weapon is still in front-line service, so readers will appreciate that we may not go into detail on its employment, but the story of its baptism of fire is nevertheless fascinating. To tell it I have called on David Robertson, who was the weapons leader on my squadron when I joined. In fact he is the second member of the pair mentioned earlier who I caught in a bar arguing over which of them taught me more about Tornado operations. David was taken prematurely from my squadron to look after Wing standardisation; although I acknowledged that the Wing needed the best, I was sorry to lose him. But I was delighted to see later that he was selected to command his own squadron, the famous 617 'Dambusters'.

To complete the connection, it was 617 that led on introducing Storm Shadow into service. We've already heard one take on Gulf War Two, but now let's join David for another slant. In it he majors on Storm Shadow's fascinating part – as an immature and unproven system – in that campaign.

GROUP CAPTAIN DAVID ROBERTSON (RETD)

The introduction of Tornado GR4 in 2000 brought a whole range of new capabilities, with a plethora of new weapons systems able to be integrated into the aircraft. It was therefore decided that individual squadrons would be lead on assisting the introduction of nominated systems. 617 Squadron was charged with leading on Storm Shadow, a conventionally-armed stand-off missile born out of staff requirement 1236. For the first two years of our task, the squadron's involvement was minimal, flight trials being conducted in the USA and warhead trials at Pendine Sands in Wales. 617's responsibility was limited to developing standard operating procedures once information became available. I should emphasise right away that the missile wasn't due to enter service with the RAF for at least another couple of years.

At the point in 2002 when it became clear that military action in Iraq was on the horizon, the squadron was in Kuwait on Operation Resinate South, policing the no-fly zone in southern Iraq. We returned to Lossiemouth at the end of September, leaving construction to begin at Ali al Salem of a hardened missile-storage area. Simultaneously a handful of our engineers were seconded to the Air Warfare Centre to assist with flight trials; this gave them valuable experience of loading and handling the weapon.

In the run-up to Christmas we received at Lossiemouth a new software load, together with two drill rounds, that would provide us with loading/unloading, ground and flight carriage training opportunities. We were told to train six aircrews and sufficient engineers to deploy a capability if required. Squadron Leader Andy Myers, our weapons leader, and Flight Lieutenants Andy 'Turkey' Turk and Bob Chevli, the squadron's QWIs, set to work and, in short time, developed SOPs for weapon ground, flight and firing procedures. Chief Technician Paul Brown developed similar procedures for the engineers for ground handling, loading and unloading. All this was conducted in direct liaison with the AWC and with MBDA's weapons and planning experts.

Storm Shadow was a joint RAF/French air force project, the French version being called 'Scalp'. Turkey and Bob were shown the planning system that MBDA had developed, and immediately spotted a problem. In FAF planning systems the aircraft turns ahead of a waypoint, with the aircraft setting off from the point on planned track. In RAF planning systems, the aircraft reaches a waypoint and then makes a turn onto its outbound track. If it were needed, this provided confirmation of why it makes sense for front-line users to be directly involved with manufacturers at an early development stage.

Squadron air and ground crews continued to train in all the disciplines that would be required if deployed. Unfortunately, different GR4 software loads were required for different weapons, plus aircraft had to be removed from the line to be converted to 'operational standard'. This limited the training opportunities. However, we managed to get six crews trained up by the end of the first week in February, which was our initially scheduled deployment date. Subsequently, though, the UK air commander informed us that he wanted a demonstrated Storm Shadow capability by 15 February. Cutting it fine, we deployed on the fourteenth. The rest of our air and ground crews deployed a week or so later to Al Udeid, Qatar, as part of the Lossiemouth Tornado detachment there.

The MoD had not announced that Storm Shadow would be used, so everything needed to be kept as 'need to know'. We were also informed that the media would record the missile at every opportunity; after the first wave, therefore, and provided that it had gone well, the UK would tell the world what had been achieved. Communication security proved a problem in the first few weeks, with a number of transmissions made over hand-held radios referring openly to the movement of Storm Shadow. Consequently, the weapons became referred to first as 'RAPTOR 2' and then as 'combat marrows'.

Armourers work at Ali al Salem in Kuwait to prepare Storm Shadow for action in the Iraq Conflict. (Photo by permission of David Robertson)

The engineers, led by Warrant Officer Ian Winters, were well-versed in the Kuwait environment and settled in quickly, although as normal operations and training continued the team was split between the two-shift patterns that the resident engineers had running. This arrangement created a headache for Ian when missile loading or tasking was required, and needed copious amounts of his tact, subtlety, man-management and organisational skills to maintain a harmonious atmosphere amongst the engineering teams.

The Tornado GR4 used an advanced mission-planning aid to plan sorties and weapon profiles, although the Storm Shadow part of the system was still very immature. Consequently, it was agreed that missile mission planning (from target backwards to weapon release point) would be conducted at PJHQ, and that this information would be transmitted in a data file over satellite to our base. The data file with the missile release point would then be the start point for the aircraft mission plan, which would be from take-off to release point and return to base. This limited our flexibility to amend target data or timing of missions, but it was the only solution that provided an operational capability for a missile – remember this was still long before planned service entry.

I informed the chief of staff at air headquarters, Group Captain Bob McAlpine, that the squadron had demonstrated a capability up to a point, but that we were concerned that a live missile had not even been loaded to a Tornado GR4, let alone flown or fired from one. I also outlined the potential risks to the missiles from reverse thrust (they were not, of course, intended to be brought back for a landing), but suggested that, once authorisation to fly with the missile and software combined was issued, we should load two missiles and fly them up to a simulated 'power on' point. This would provide us with greater confidence in our procedures. He agreed, and I was pleased with his forward-leaning attitude. We necessarily involved PJHQ in the plan.

So on 25 February the authorisation arrived, two data files were received from PJHQ and two live missiles were loaded and checked by the engineers and QWIs. Squadron Leader 'Noddy' Knowles and Turkey planned and flew a simulated live sortie within Kuwait, and whilst all was good with the loading and ground operations, when the launch sequence was initiated only the left-hand weapon responded. The right-hand missile eventually came good – but it would have been too late for real.

Extensive debriefing and discussion took place over the following days to establish the reason for failure. There were two possible explanations; a loose connection or a pylon switch in the wrong position. The latter would have affected the missile loading, so I favoured the loose connection. As this was 617 Squadron's most important task during my tenure in command, I wanted to make sure that the system would work on 'night one', and therefore asked for and received McAlps's approval to fly the missiles again. This time, we loaded the same missiles, containing the same mission files, to the same aircraft, but on opposite pylons. The ground crew double and triple-checked all connections and switches and Andy and I got airborne. We flew two representative sortie profiles and initiated two simulated missile attacks, on each occasion with no problems. We now felt that we had done as much as we could to provide an operational capability.

On 14 March, details of our likely contribution to the first night indicated that four Tornado GR4s each loaded with two missiles would be required on the first wave, with another two aircraft on the second wave. This would continue for the first three nights. We planned to operate in pairs, with Andy Myers and me leading Noddy and Turkey in the first pair, Bob Chevli and Flight Lieutenant Andy 'Ray' Reardon leading Lieutenant (RN) Phil 'Flea' Lee and Squadron Leader Mike 'Old Bloke' Wood in the second pair, with Flight Lieutenants Kev Gambold and Toby Warren leading Flight Lieutenants Bobby Bethell and Al Reid in the third pair.

We had a mix of missiles deployed in Kuwait; initial operating capability and full operating capability; the latter were more capable, so it was critical that missiles were allocated to appropriate targets. Therefore not only were we challenged if an aircraft became unserviceable, but when planning missions we also had a missile loser plot to consider.

The first planned mission our pair was due to fly concerned me greatly, as to reach the missile release point, which itself was within a SAM-3 MEZ, we would need to pass very close to two active fighter airfields. I emailed McAlps to let him know of my concern, and the following day received a response informing me that we would be accompanied by F-16CJ, EA-6B and F-15C aircraft, which made me feel much more comfortable.

On 17 March the detachment commander, Group Captain Simon Dobb, informed the squadron commanders and warlords at Ali al Salem that the first air offensive of the Iraq War would take place on the twenty-first – which just happened to coincide with the 60th anniversary of the formation of 617 Squadron. Propitious?

Only two days before the first launch we received a message from MBDA informing us that, at the UK missile storage facility, they had discovered safety pins still in place on missiles received from the French part of the company. If this were also the case on one of ours, it would mean that the wings would not deploy post-release and the missile would fall into the desert. These 'safety pins' turned out to be small grub screws that could be detected without having to dismantle the missile, so once each weapon had been taken out of its storage crate it would only take about fifteen minutes to conduct the check. Fortunately, all of 'our' grub screws had been removed.

The day before our first missions, Kuwait suffered its first attack when two SSMs were launched from Iraq. Patriot SAMs could be heard launching against them as we dashed for the bunker, which was a reinforced sewage drain. The 'hostiles clear' call came but, just as we had got out of our NBC suits and packed everything away, another attack was made and we reconvened inside the same drain, although this stay was shorter-lived. Eventually back in operations, we continued with our mission planning – and then PJHQ asked urgently whether we could bring our attack forward by twelve hours. This was not really possible, as we didn't have the facility to make amendments to the missile data files.

An hour later another attack came in and we again ran for the shelter and threw on our NBC kit. Eventually, we finished our planning and went back to the mess for dinner. I had just picked up my plate when another air raid was called. Now the shelter was 400 yards away; running with a mask on was a big mistake, as the flow of air into the mask is not great. By the time I reached the shelter I was close to suffocating, but managed to control my breathing and eventually got dressed; I learned a good lesson from that.

21 March was memorable. Missile attacks on Kuwait continued and we ran to shelters at midnight, 1 am, 2.30 am, 3 am and 7.30 am. Consequently, there was little sleep, although I managed a couple of hours between the last two air raids and then two hours after the breakfast alarm. Most of the night was spent in NBC suits. We managed to have lunch before another shelter run at 1 pm. On the final raid, Patriots intercepted a missile overhead the base, with three detonations visible.

Once in the ops building we received another bombshell, as Andy and I were informed that we were overall mission commanders for that night. This was not ideal, not because of the extra pressure involved but because we didn't have the communications available at Ali al Salem for communicating with all participants, in particular those on the aircraft carriers. Nevertheless, Andy worked hard at coordination issues with the participants whilst I worked with the combined air operations centre resolving a couple of issues regarding time on target. In the end the whole thing turned out to be a mistake; the real mission commander was an F-16 pilot. We didn't find this out until he spoke to us half an hour before the mission briefing, so a lot of our time had been wasted.

Eventually, we briefed and walked for our first war mission. At the 'outbrief' we were informed that the second pair's targets were a critical pre-requisite to USAF B-2s going downtown Baghdad – it was a bit late to find this out, but fortunately we had already allocated priority to those. Andy and I led Noddy and Turkey in the first pair on the northerly route with Bob and Ray leading Flea and Old Bloke in the second pair on the southerly route. The third pair, Kev and Toby plus Bobby and Al, planned to launch early the following morning.

On crew-in Andy had problems synchronising the Have Quick jam-resistant radio, but we took off on time, avoided the TLAM/cruise missile lane and climbed towards Iraq. A cabin-conditioning caption illuminated, while the Skyshadow ECM pod failed to a reversionary mode. Both of these systems needed to be working properly for the mission; eventually they reset. Although we didn't realise it at the time, Noddy had also lost his Have Quick and was only able to communicate on clear frequencies. Poor communications, a feature of the Tornado GR4 in 2003, was energy-sapping and extremely frustrating.

En route to the target, both aircraft in our pair were tracked and locked by radar systems on several occasions, although no missiles or AAA were directed at us. There were quite a lot of detonations visible on the ground – disconcerting, as it wasn't clear whether they were part of the land battle or something coming for us. About halfway to target, Noddy and Turkey defended against a missile fired at them, which necessitated their jettisoning underwing tanks. As these still contained fuel they were now short and were forced to climb to height and route directly to the target. Andy and I no longer had visual cross cover, and Noddy and Turkey were now going to be ahead of us. They calculated that they had just enough fuel to get to the target, fire their missiles and then get home.

The AAA visible around every town was amplified by night-vision goggles, and as we approached Baghdad the sky seemed to be alight with explosions, AAA and missiles. Just prior to the start of the attack run, Andy spotted what he believed to be a SAM-2 missile launched at us. It must have been a ballistic launch, as there had been no radar-warner indications; we evaded its trajectory and headed for the target. As we had lost speed, Andy selected reheat, whereupon an engine surged. The sound, and the tail appearing to be on fire, suggested a missile strike – but the 'fire' proved only to be the reheat glow.

Approximately a minute out from our firing point Turkey called to say that his missile had shut down just prior to release but that he was pressing on to fire the other missile at his second target. All this way, all this effort, all this training, all this expectation – all for the missile not to work. What would happen to ours? We were committed and we would soon see.

Our run to the target went uneventfully and we released the first missile about twenty seconds before the planned release point, in case being too close had caused Noddy's missile to shut down. The first launch was successful, to much relief, and we continued towards the second release point and fired the missile successfully.

Noddy and Turkey, tight on fuel already and now with a missile retained and causing extra drag, were in trouble. The 'hung' missile still indicated that it was OK, so once Andy and I were out of the release area they had another go at firing it – but without success. Now there was no way they could get back to base, so they headed off to find a tanker on an AAR towline, with the nearest approximately 200 miles south. They did locate a tanker but were unable to join it in time so, with fuel approaching the minimum, they diverted to a Saudi Arabian station. After refuelling, they were back at base some two hours later.

Our trip home was uneventful, although seeming to take ages, and about 100 miles from the Kuwaiti border we started to see our own troops, miles and miles of vehicles illuminated to NVGs by IR lights on top of each vehicle. Seeing so much firepower on its way north-westwards was quite something.

The other pair had a relatively quiet time, although Bob saw a SAM launch; it passed above their canopy but was no real threat. Back at Ali al Salem we were met by Ian Winters and his engineers, who were as keyed up for this as the aircrew were. At operations we spoke with the third formation, who were about to fly their mission, debriefed our sortie and then headed for the bunker again as another attack was inbound. We were able to watch TV pictures from Baghdad and it looked horrendous, much worse than it had appeared from the air. Mind you, at the time it had seemed that there was as much coming up at us as there was raining down on them.

The small entry hole belies the damage done down below by a Storm Shadow attack. (Crown Copyright)

The following day brought news of the loss of two RN Sea King helicopters, with seven lives lost. We looked at the battle damage assessment from the previous night. All designated points of impact had small holes (the warhead was designed not to detonate until deep inside) exactly or very close to where planned. Noddy then briefed us on what he expected for the night's sortie. We would launch four aircraft, the first pair each with two missiles to fire and the second pair each to fire one, with one each available as backup.

This second mission was as different as chalk and cheese from the first. Communications were good, no threats were encountered and everything in our pair ran on rails. It wasn't quite the same for the other pair. After power had been applied on the ground to Old Bloke's weapons, the left one failed. He could fire his second missile at the target, which was not a problem, although it meant that we had another 'failed' missile. Then when Ray in the second aircraft initiated his missile launch, the air intake cover blew off as planned but the missile's engine failed to light, so the weapon was not released. Although they could have fired their second missile, the crew weren't positive that this would have been a good option and rightly decided not to. So, we returned that night having launched five of the planned six and brought back two 'bad' missiles.

Just as I was leaving to go back to my accommodation, Derek Watson, OC IX Squadron, radioed that a SAM had been launched at them in northern Kuwait. On waking up the following morning, I heard on the radio news that a US missile had shot down an RAF aircraft in a 'friendly fire' incident. I rushed down the corridor to find out whether we were all accounted for, to be told that Flight Lieutenants Kev Main and Dave Williams had not returned. It was a heck of a shock. The missile launch that OC IX Squadron had reported the previous night had been a US Patriot inbound to his wingman. Kev had left the Dambusters only two months earlier and my air and ground crews were all most terribly shocked and upset at the loss of this popular man – although none of us let the tragedy interfere with our task.

When we went in to plan our third mission, there turned out to be no suitable targets available. For the next few days, therefore, we switched to conventional attack tasking. Generally we'd be loaded with LGBs, with tasking received once airborne. On my first no-fly day I was asked to telephone the chief of the air staff, Air Chief Marshal Sir Peter Squire, back in the UK. As I waited for him to respond to my call, the defence secretary was on TV saying how impressive our Storm Shadow results had been. The chief was also really pleased with our efforts and asked me to pass on his congratulations and thanks to all my team for their hard work and effort, particularly while under air attack, and in the light of the Wing's tragic loss. He went on to say that he recalled his time commanding Number 1 Squadron during the Falklands Conflict, when he and his pilots had felt invincible until they'd lost the first Harrier. I could certainly identify with his sentiment. He also mentioned that firing the first Storm Shadow was a great way to mark our sixtieth anniversary. We still had eight missiles and expected three more that week; I asked him to find some additional targets for us.

More targets requiring Storm Shadow's weapon effects soon appeared, and we launched a pair to fire three missiles. That left us with six, sufficient for a four-ship, and this mission went off uneventfully. Now, having fired twenty-four of our twenty-seven Storm Shadows, we awaited a further three to arrive over the next few days. If we could 'repair' the three that had failed, we'd be able to up our 'fired' total to thirty.

In the event we got three missiles airborne on 4 April for our last Storm Shadow mission, albeit one weapon had to be moved to the other shoulder pylon having initially failed its checks. The sortie was relatively uneventful, although Patriot systems were now covering most of southern Iraq and were constantly illuminating and locking us up electronically, which was somewhat disconcerting. We took appropriate action in the cockpit to let them know who we were, but we couldn't help but see the Patriots now as our greatest threat – and one to which we had no counter.

This was our first Storm Shadow mission in daylight and, as soon as we could after missile launch, Andy rolled the aircraft over to have a look at our 'bird'. It was a fantastic sight, its wings fully deployed, turning away from the aircraft and diving on towards its initial navigation point to begin its target attack. A surreal experience, and I remember being surprised at how fast it flew.

So we had now run out of serviceable missiles, having successfully fired twenty-seven. Three missile failures out of thirty – very creditable for a system given its operational baptism before the beginning of its service life. We had demonstrated that the Tornado GR4 force now had an operational Storm Shadow capability – one which would be developed and would next be employed during 2011's Libya campaign.

CHAPTER 18

DESERT TORNADOS

Like most Tornado operators between 1991 and the end of the century, I saw a good deal of Saudi Arabia. It all kicked off with the Gulf Conflict. Then, while Saddam Hussein continued to harass the Kurds and Marsh Arabs as well as defying the UN over weapons inspections, there was air policing of both the southern and northern Iraq no-fly zones. By the time this came to a head with the Iraq War of 2003, the Tornado detachment had moved to Kuwait. Later it redeployed to Qatar, and the commitment didn't finally end until 2009.

During the earlier days of the Saudi mounting bases, I myself twice led the Tornado air policing detachment based at Dhahran during the early 1990s, followed by a stint as commander British Forces Jural based in Riyadh. During those duties I found the country a fascinating place – although by the end of my third unaccompanied detachment, and with ten months in the kingdom under my belt in less than four years, the novelty was beginning to wear off. What I learned in dealing with my Saudi colleagues, however, was to respect their ways, to acknowledge our differences and to ride with them. There was never going to be complete harmony between us, either culturally or professionally. The trick was to recognise each other's strengths and to find a common way forward rather than to seek a total agreement which would never be there.

One group of people who learned, far more than I did, how to work with the Saudis were the people associated with the BAE Systems (formerly BAe) *Al Yamamah* contract. The follow-on continues today, with the RSAF now acquiring Typhoons. For a taste of how our people found it to fly and operate with the RSAF I turn to one of my old flight commanders, Rob McCarthy. I flew with him many times at Brüggen and he is, above all, an international man. Having operated with the USMC on an exchange tour, he married an American lady who was one of the USMC's 'pen pals' during the Gulf Conflict – and subsequently emigrated to the States. But in between his RAF and American lives he enjoyed a fascinating period in Saudi Arabia, which he recounts here.

SQUADRON LEADER ROB McCARTHY (RETD)

The Kingdom of Saudi Arabia is the largest country, by area, in the Middle East, and the world's largest producer of oil. It is also home to the two holiest places in Islam, *Masjid al*

Haram (in Mecca), and *Al-Masjid an-Nabawi* (in Medina). Approximately ninety percent of the population (about twenty-eight million) are Sunni Muslims. Defence spending by Saudi Arabia, particularly on modern weapons systems, has increased significantly since 1980, with the RSAF acquiring large numbers of modern combat aircraft (F-15, Tornado and Typhoon) from both the USA and the UK. Saudi Arabia currently ranks fourth in the global defence spending table, behind only the USA, Russia and China. Politically, I believe that the Saudis see much more likelihood of military conflict with its Shia Muslim neighbours (Iran and Yemen) than it does with non-Muslim Middle Eastern countries like Israel.

Saudi Arabia became the fourth country to operate the Tornado following the *Al Yamamah 1* arms deal, signed between the British and Saudi governments in 1985. Under this contract, the RSAF would receive forty-eight Tornado IDS aircraft (twenty-eight GR1s, six GR1As, fourteen dual-control trainers), twenty-four Tornado ADVs, thirty Hawk trainers, thirty Pilatus PC-9 trainers, a range of weapons, radar and spares, and an aircrew training programme. In return, the British government was to receive crude oil. BAe, who had been involved in Saudi Arabia since the mid-1960s, was assigned to be the prime contractor. A second phase, *Al Yamamah 2*, was signed in 1988 for the delivery of a further forty-eight Tornado IDS types.

The IDS aircraft were divided between RSAF Wing 5 at King Khalid Air Base, near Khamis Mushait in the south-west corner of the country and RSAF Wing 11 at King Abdulaziz Air Base, near Dhahran, in the east of the country on the Persian Gulf coast. 7 Squadron in Dhahran acted as the training unit, with 66, 75 and 83 Squadrons as the front-line squadrons.

My involvement with Saudi Arabia began in late 1997. I was serving on the staff of the RAF's Air Warfare Centre, responsible for helping establish the combined elements of the RAF's and the RN's QWI training for the Tornado, Jaguar, Harrier, Sea Harrier and Hawk. This was my first ground tour after six tours in the cockpit (one on the Buccaneer, one on the Dominie as a navigation instructor, one on exchange flying A-6s for the USMC and three on the Tornado). I had tried hard to remain airborne for as long as possible but now, at age forty-two, my future seemed to offer a series of staff jobs of unknown type and location.

So I had pretty much decided to retire from the RAF and move to the US to try my hand at something different. But I had stayed in touch with Mark Allan, who had been with me on 31 Squadron at Brüggen in the mid-1990s and was currently serving on secondment to the RSAF for three years at Dhahran, and he suggested that this might be something I should consider. I talked it over with my wife, Adrienne, and we decided to look into it. BAE Systems invited me for an interview; they seemed to be in need of Tornado QWIs, and the fact that I was not in current flying practice and was likely to retire from the RAF in a year and a half didn't seem to put them off. So after a four-month attachment to Operation Northern Watch in Turkey, and some negotiation between the RAF and the company, I was seconded as an instructor WSO on 75 Squadron RSAF. My tour in Saudi Arabia would be preceded by an abbreviated Tornado refresher course of four sorties on the TTTE and eight on XV(R) Squadron.

It was good to get back in the cockpit after two and a half years on the ground, and after some initial rustiness I once again felt comfortable in my back seat 'office'. We moved out of our married quarter and sent our belongings to America, where we had recently bought a house as our 'base', only to find that the Saudis had put a temporary hold on new moves into the country. I was in limbo for several weeks while the administrative wheels slowly turned. Finally the word came in September 1998 that I could start in Saudi; I packed my wife and daughter off to the USA and flew to Dhahran.

The Middle East in general and Dhahran in particular were not totally unfamiliar to me. While serving on exchange with the USMC flying the A-6 Intruder I had spent seven months at Sheikh Isa Airfield, Bahrain during Operations Desert Shield and Desert Storm, culminating in thirty-night combat missions over southern Iraq and Kuwait. On the first of these, on 17 January 1991, the strike package included both A-6s and RAF Tornado GR1s attacking a variety of targets in southern Iraq. All the A-6s returned safely to base, but a Tornado from 27 Squadron, which I had recently left, was lost, hitting the ground while exiting the target area. In 1994, like virtually all Germany-based Tornado aircrews up to 1996, I had spent time at Dhahran on Operation Jural, the RAF's contribution to Operation Southern Watch (patrolling the southern Iraq no-fly zone). Most of that time was spent as the RAF's operations coordinator, better known as the 'warlord', but I did manage four operational sorties. Following the bombing of coalition accommodation at Khobar Towers in 1996, by the way, Operation Southern Watch was moved on safety and security grounds to Prince Sultan Air Base (Al Kharj) near Riyadh in the centre of the country.

The base at Dhahran is a huge one. When I arrived it was shared with the civilian airport; however, following the opening of King Fahd International, some twenty-five miles north-west of Dhahran, in November 1999, civilian operations moved there.

On joining 75 Squadron I increased the number of expatriate aircrew to six; two instructor pilots, two IWSOs and two mission-planning officers who provided ground support and instruction. The expats were a mix of secondees on loan from the RAF and ex-military people contracted to BAE Systems. The IPs were QFIs while the IWSOs were QWIs, all with considerable Tornado experience. The Saudi squadrons had additional IPs and IWSOs among their own senior aircrew.

The aircraft were virtually identical to RAF GR1s, although with a beefed-up environmental control system to deal better with operations in a hot climate. There were also differences in targeting equipment and weaponry. Instead of the TIALD pod to provide self or cooperative laser target designation, the RSAF used a Thomson pod, which had either TV or IR capabilities depending on the head fitted. For conventional attack, the RSAF used American weapons, typically Mark 82 500-lb bombs, to provide commonality with the weapons carried on their F-15S aircraft.

After a frustratingly slow acceptance period I settled into routine operations. Most sorties made use of the training areas to the south-west of Dhahran and the local air weapons range at Fahad. In my time there, all sorties took off from and landed back at Dhahran. About half of my flying involved work-up training sorties for either new Saudi aircrew, for those moving up to become pairs or four-ship leaders, or for training on other equipment such as ALARM.

The working day was driven by the climate; to avoid the worst of the heat, days would start early (5.30 am in the summer) and finish by 2.30 pm. Summer temperatures were oppressive, with an average high in August of 46°C. So the first wave would crew-in in the cool, pre-dawn light and get airborne shortly after dawn. Tornado operations were not allowed above 50°C; although we made 49°C on several occasions, I never saw that magic fifty. The aircraft were kept in a row of sun shelters in front of the squadron operations building, but even so the temperature out on the concrete ramp could take your breath away.

There were rules on how long we could be out in an unconditioned environment (from leaving the squadron building to having an engine running and the canopy closed with the ECS running). In practice this meant that, unless any pre-start problem could quickly be resolved, it was often impossible to move to a spare aircraft. Summer temperatures at night would only get down to the low thirties and, being so close to the Gulf, humidity was very high. Some fancy domestic compounds had chillers on their pools to make them usable throughout the summer – but not the company's areas, so our compound pool became uncomfortably hot and unpleasant in mid-summer. In town there was much reduced activity during the heat of the afternoon, similar to Mediterranean siesta time, with shops and restaurants coming to life again in the evening. Many of the wives and children would return to the UK during the summer school break to avoid the most unpleasant period.

On one training sortie our aircraft suffered an air-conditioning failure when we were operating out in the training areas to the south-west of Dhahran. Repeated attempts to reset the system were unsuccessful, forcing us to transit slowly to Dhahran with no cabin cooling. You can get some feeling of what it was like if you can imagine parking your car out in the desert under a scorching sun with the windows closed and no ventilation. About halfway back my Saudi pilot radioed to squadron operations requesting that we be met with ice cream. On opening the canopy after landing safely it was like being hit in the face with a blast of cold air – even though that air was probably close to 50°C.

Another major weather factor affecting our lives was the *shamal*, a strong north-westerly wind blowing from the desert. It would occur a couple of times per year, bringing dust and sand in from the desert and causing poor visibility. During the worst of a *shamal*, flying operations were impractical, and even once the wind died down the amount of fine dust in the atmosphere could form a layer up to 10,000 feet. Then, as it settled out of the atmosphere, a very fine film of dust would coat everything in its path.

The flying routine was also built around the requirements and calendar of the Islamic faith. It is impossible to understate the importance of religion in Saudi Arabia; it is not just part of people's lives but drives everything that happens in the country. The routine working week was from Saturday to Wednesday; Friday is the Islamic Sabbath, with the weekend comprising Thursday and Friday. Even on working days, activity is scheduled around the five daily mandatory prayer times, *Fajr* (pre-dawn), *Dhuhr* (midday), *Asr* (afternoon), *Maghrib* (sunset) and *Isha* (night). The times vary from day to day according to the position of the sun, and are between twenty and forty minutes long depending on which prayer it is. Aircrew have a royal waiver to allow them to fly during prayer time, but all non-essential ground activity stops while the crews pray. They would often head for the mosque, but we westerners grew used to sometimes arriving at a jet for a sortie to find the ground crew praying on mats underneath the aircraft. Domestically, one always drove with a prayer schedule in the car to avoid getting to a shop or restaurant and finding it closed for prayers.

On an annual basis, Ramadan and *Hajj* significantly affect squadron operations. Ramadan is the ninth month of the Islamic calendar, the month of fasting. The start of Ramadan and its duration, twenty-nine or thirty days, are based on visual sightings of the crescent moon. Fasting by adults, to include food, drink and smoking, is practised from dawn until sunset. Expatriate aircrew would normally be assigned a room where we could get a cup of coffee without being seen by Saudi colleagues. But during Ramadan, Saudi aircrew have a royal waiver to permit them, also, to minimally break their fast so that they are able to fly very simple sorties to maintain currency. These would comprise a TF route, which would require the pilot to take off, engage the TFR and autopilot, monitor the system for the duration of the route, and then resume manual control for a straight-in approach to land. For the holiday of *Eid al-Fitr* that immediately follows Ramadan, flight operations would be suspended, with expatriate aircrew being encouraged to take vacation out of the country.

Hajj is the second of the two annual religious events affecting squadron operations. The *Hajj* is the annual Islamic pilgrimage to Mecca and occurs from the eighth to the twelfth day of the last month of the Islamic calendar. The calendar being based on the lunar year, *Hajj*, like Ramadan, moves forward each year by about eleven days on the Gregorian calendar used in the west. As with *Eid al-Fitr*, operations ceased during *Hajj* and expatriate aircrew generally took vacation.

Flying training was more prescriptive than one would find on an RAF front-line squadron, with most training sorties following a 'route of the day' through the training areas. This came partly from a desire to avoid conflictions at low level; at home we tended to rely more on 'see and be seen' principles.

Of course the predominantly flat and empty desert didn't help to add variety or interest to the sorties. Realistic targets on which to run practice attacks were few and far between. The major oilfield areas, with their associated infrastructure, would have offered ideal simulated targets – but understandably they were off limits. Quality and accuracy of the mapping available to us was dubious, making target and attack offset selection difficult. It was not uncommon to miss a practice target simply because it was not where it was shown to be on the map. The Tornado navigation system was extremely accurate, but if the mapping wasn't even good enough to get the aircraft within radar range, things were difficult.

Some variety to the normal training routine was provided every couple of months by composite sorties involving multiple aircraft types from Dhahran's two flying Wings. These would typically include Tornados in the attack and/or SEAD role, supported by F-15S aircraft in a fighter sweep and/or attack role, with the opposition comprising F-15C fighters. Both sides would be supported by E-3 AWACS aircraft based near Riyadh. Less frequent were long-range sorties with other RSAF bases as targets, Khamis Mushait, Tabuk, etc. These sorties required AAR support which, in the RSAF, is provided by KC-130s. This is basically a standard C-130 fitted with two underwing refuelling pods similar to those used on RAF tankers. Because of the KC-130's performance, AAR was conducted much lower (8,000 to 15,000 feet) and slower (210 knots) than is normal with a jet tanker like a VC10. The slow

Contract personnel join Rob McCarthy (second from right) following his last trip with the RSAF.

speed meant that the Tornado had to be configured with mid flap; additionally, the low altitude could put us in more turbulent air making smooth contact with the refuelling basket more difficult on occasions.

RSAF aircrews began their training with schooling in both English and technical subjects at the King Faisal Air Academy near Riyadh, before moving to flight training. Pilots trained initially on a basic trainer before moving onto the Pilatus PC-9 and Hawk. WSOs went to the USA where they were trained at NAS Pensacola in Florida, which handled training for USAF and USN back-seaters destined for tactical aircraft as well as for a variety of foreign air forces. Saudi WSOs destined for Tornado IDS continued their training at Dhahran on a Jetstream equipped with Tornado avionics. Pilots and WSO training then converged on 7 Squadron at Dhahran, where they underwent Tornado conversion before joining a front-line squadron. In the early days of RSAF Tornado operations, experienced pilots from other aircraft types, like the F-5, had been converted onto the Tornado in the UK at the TWCU. Indeed, my squadron commander when I arrived, Colonel Sofyani, remembered me from his training at RAF Honington, which coincided with my time on the QWI course. At that time I'd been way too busy to take much interest in the Saudi pilots, and in any case they'd largely kept themselves to themselves.

Training on a complex aircraft like the Tornado, when English is not your first language, is difficult. As instructors, we needed to try to break things down into more digestible pieces. Expecting them to understand the aircrew manual to the same level or depth as someone in the RAF was not realistic. It follows that it made sense to deal with in-flight procedures or emergencies more slowly than back home; the pedantic approach was, in the circumstances, the most effective and the safest. Fairly naturally, with a western instructor on board, the Saudi crew member would tend to let him handle most things and to give direction. All in all, then, while flying with the Saudis was certainly different, I wouldn't attempt to make any comparison with western standards. Differences in language, training, culture, experience and so on were so great that it simply wouldn't be fair.

During my time there, few of the aircrew had any operational experience. The squadron commander and his deputy were the only crewmembers who had been flying the Tornado long enough to have been involved in Desert Storm, and it was not something they discussed. They were both pilots, which leads me to mention that the relationship between Saudi pilots and WSOs was a little different to that found in the RAF. At home, back and front-seaters are essentially viewed as being equal, with an RAF squadron commander just as likely to be a navigator as a pilot. I did not see this in the RSAF, where virtually all of the squadron's senior people were pilots.

Saudi combat operations have never been a part of the expat crewmember's job specification. And as westerners, we were not expected to mix socially with the Saudi aircrew, so our social life revolved around the BAE Systems people and facilities. Western aircrew would sometimes be invited to lunch with their Saudi colleagues, when we'd sit on the floor and eat meat and rice using the right hand only – it's considered unclean to use the left hand. One exception was the wedding reception of one of the squadron pilots. There were actually two receptions, one for the men and one for the women, as mixing of the sexes is not allowed. The men's reception was fairly staid and unremarkable, but what surprised me was that the wives reported the girls' reception to be lively, going on long into the night.

Domestically, the Eastern Province, where Dhahran is located, was not a bad place to live. As the centre of the oil industry it was probably the most western-friendly area of Saudi Arabia. Western men and women were both required to dress conservatively in public, but this didn't mean that the girls had to completely cover up or wear a veil. The activities of the *mutawwah*, the religious police, seemed to be relatively unobtrusive compared to those in some other areas of the country, and I cannot recall any problems with them.

The fact that we had a very predictable working schedule, would be home every night, and were free from the usual tempo of frequent and extended operational deployments, made a pleasant change for both me and my family, though I did miss the variety and challenges of life on a front-line RAF squadron. BAE Systems personnel were, and still are, housed in compounds, mostly in the town of Al Khobar. Those compounds are surrounded by high walls and may only be entered through a single security entrance. They have up to a hundred 'villas', along with central administrative and recreational facilities – pool, gym, and so on. Within the compound walls, western rules apply in terms of dress code and customs. This 'controlled' situation seemed to suit all parties, including the host nation and the company, quite well, and we were careful to respect the territorial limits of the compound. For if you were caught taking the 'wrong' western habits outside the walls you were on your own and could not expect any help from the company. Along with the facilities on the compound, the company had access to a beach facility on Half Moon Bay, a few miles to the south of the base, for swimming and sailing.

Families were allowed to join us after about three months, and after some initial worries about differences from life at home, seemed to settle well into the life. Wives, bar some small jobs helping to run facilities on the compound, were not able to work, and therefore had more leisure time than is often the case at home. As expats, we were expected to employ a houseboy. These individuals, as with other manual workers in Saudi Arabia, were typically third world nationals from Pakistan, Indonesia, or the like, who were trying to earn enough money to support their families at home. These houseboys performed a variety of domestic tasks at very reasonable rates. I suspect that my wife was typical in enjoying having the mundane housework done by someone else; she wishes, I'm sure, that such an affordable luxury was available back home today!

Personal security, especially where families were concerned, was always in the back of your mind when living in Saudi Arabia. To a large extent we felt safe living there; the housing compounds offered a degree of security, while we felt comfortable in the shops and restaurants in town. Indeed Adrienne felt safer browsing the shops in Al Khobar in the evening than she does doing the same thing in the small town in the USA in which we now live. Most of the locals were friendly and were happy to see a western family with a young daughter out in the town. However, there was always the knowledge that there were a few 'crazies' out there. Nothing unpleasant happened during my three years in the country, but some years after we left there was a terrorist attack on a residential compound in Al Khobar in which twenty-two people, mostly third world manual workers, were killed. It was close to a company residential compound, one we had visited during our stay.

A year into my tour, my time in the RAF came to an end and I changed from being seconded to BAE Systems to being a contract officer. This made no effective difference, even my pay and allowances remaining unchanged. My wife and I had always planned to do three years in Saudi and then to move to her home town in the USA to live, so in mid-July 2001 I flew my last sortie, not only for this tour of duty, but also my last sortie in the Tornado and the last sortie of my career. I flew with one of the more senior pilots on the squadron, leading a four-ship around the local training areas and through Fahad range for some academic weaponry.

Since my departure, the Saudis have continued to operate their Tornados and have engaged in an upgrade programme for the seventy-five or so aircraft that remain in service. The 'Tornado sustainment programme' is intended to keep the aircraft in service until 2020 and to bring the fleet up to a standard similar to the current RAF GR4. With all Tornados now based at Dhahran, the Khamis Mushait operation has been handed over to the F-15S. The Sea Eagle anti-ship missile and the ALARM anti-radiation missile have been withdrawn from service, and contracts signed for new weapons systems such as the short-range air-to-air IRIS-T missile, Paveway IV bombs with dual GPS and laser guidance, Brimstone and Storm Shadow. The original laser designation pod has been replaced by the French Damocles targeting pod.

Having flown 650 missions during Operation Desert Storm, RSAF Tornados went on to participate in 2009 in operations against the Shia insurgency in Yemen. More recently, I think it likely that the aircraft have been in action, again in Yemen, in 2015. I feel privileged to have spent time flying what I consider to be a great aircraft, with some great people, in a variety of training and operational environments. My Saudi experience was a fascinating time, and my last Tornado sortie was a sad day for me. Even nearly fourteen years later, I still miss the aircraft.

CHAPTER 19

AFGHAN OPS

A century ago when the RAF (or more correctly, the RFC) began to patrol India's wild and rugged north-west frontier, the mix of people on a station was very different from today's. Women were few and far between; one had to be twenty-six before being allowed to be married (thirty for officers) while the few eligible daughters who would visit from Britain during the holidays were known, because of the suspicion that they were looking for husbands, as the 'fishing fleet'. Women in uniform were unheard of. The same wasn't necessarily true of the 'opposition', the fierce tribespeople of the frontier whom the British were attempting to contain. Even Rudyard Kipling, in his poems, identified their womenfolk as fearsome creatures.

Times have changed, and British forces now have many women serving amongst their number. Not least, Tornado aircrew. Several press articles on the subject have appeared over recent years, and I confess to often having been dissatisfied after reading them; most didn't manage to get past the stage of 'what a strange job for a woman – but she's quite normal really – she gossips about handbags and boyfriends'. Of course one could argue that, in uniform, there's no difference at all between the sexes – but self evidently that's not true. There's a difference, but not in every sense. In the background has been the army's agonising over whether or not they should employ women in front-line roles. All in all the female aspect is well worth exploring. Extraordinarily, too, British forces have been back on (or at least very near to) the north-west frontier, so it is particularly apt that we are able to combine these two subject areas in one chapter.

I've known Sasha Sheard for several years and always enjoyed both working and socialising with her. When I spoke to her about doing this chapter we discussed all the issues I've mentioned, and I hope you'll agree that her account of recent Tornado work in that most unlikely of twenty-first century theatres, Afghanistan, fits the bill perfectly – from all angles. She is, by the way, currently serving as a QFI.

FLIGHT LIEUTENANT SASHA SHEARD

The final part of the journey to Afghanistan was in a C-17 Globemaster. Wedged in the cargo bay along with the rest of the advance party I wondered what was in store for us over our upcoming deployment. To pass the time I tried to drift off to sleep, a tricky thing to do given how close we were sat to each other, but was disturbed by an announcement that we were approaching the border and that we must put on our body armour. I wrestled in the confined space with lots of other troops in the same situation, and once we were complete the lights were turned off for the approach. This was when the reality of the situation started to hit.

Sat in the back of the C-17, with no windows, I could feel the aircraft commence its final descent, but with no way to gauge how close we were to the ground the landing was inevitably unexpected. We stepped down onto the ramp at Camp Bastion and the heat hit me; despite it being very late in the evening it was still over 25°C. I could hear helicopters departing on a task as we walked to the holding area, and, from this point, we collected our bags before being dropped off at our transit accommodation. I sneaked into the tented room I had been allocated, using my torch to find a spare bed. After quietly storing my kit to avoid waking others I climbed into my sleeping bag, and as soon as my head hit my jacket, acting as a make-shift pillow, I was asleep.

The next morning brought an early start to commence our in-theatre arrival training, which would consist of various briefs, lessons and practical demonstrations to provide us with a refresh of what we had learnt in our pre-deployment training, as well as specific advice pertinent now that we were in theatre. Wearing all our kit in the desert heat was quite something, given that the temperature got to 51°C that day; I had a camelback on, full of water which I drank constantly, but it felt like a one-to-one ratio of drinking to sweating. My respect for our troops on the ground, which had already been high, soared even higher. As I struggled with walking from open tent to open tent for the different lessons, I thought of our troops operating in these conditions every day, with a lot more kit on, and not in the relative safety of being 'behind the wire'.

The Tornado detachment was based at Kandahar airfield; we travelled from Camp Bastion by Hercules, again arriving in the middle of the night, to be greeted by the outgoing squadron and taken to our accommodation. This, comparatively, was nice; shared rooms with showers down the corridor, and again we knew how lucky we were compared to our compatriots out in the field. Over the next couple of days we learnt about our surroundings; the gym, coffee shop, and dining facility. We also 'read in' to the in-theatre documents, an expansion on what we had covered during our preparations back in the UK; and then we were ready for our first sortie. Because we were the advance party, we paired up in formation with the squadron already there. My inexperience in theatre was countered by my navigator, Alex, who had previously completed a tour in Afghanistan and whose experience was invaluable.

I recall the build-up to that first sortie, a nervous anticipation about what was to come. Pre-flight I briefed, 'sanitised' my kit (dispensed with any high-security, sensitive or personal items), collected last-minute information that I needed, put on final items of flying kit, loaded my pistol, and out-briefed; so much to do before even walking to the jet. Then to the aircraft, which was sheltered from the sun.

With temperatures in the high forties I was suddenly very glad I had taken advice and brought an extra water bottle. Once at the jet I was back in familiar territory and started to feel more at ease; I knew what I was doing. Before commencing the walk-round check of the aircraft pre-flight, I put my kit down on the steps. Not on the ground, for I had heard many scare stories of people putting kit down and returning to find a snake or camel spider making its home inside. I didn't want to be one of those stories! I had heard a lot about those camel spiders, large hairy beasts which run after you to stay in your shadow (as they don't like to be in the sun). There are certainly many myths and false tales surrounding them, but I still didn't fancy having to remove one from my kit – or worse, find one in the cockpit. Actually, I only saw two during both of my tours of Afghanistan. On the first occasion the spider was sauntering its way down the corridor in the squadron building, quickly dividing those who were fascinated and those who were trying to get away. Another time I was sat underneath the aircraft checking the weapons when I saw something flit past me out of the corner of my eye and run under the wing. I walked over to investigate; even though it was only a baby spider, it wasn't a pleasant feeling.

I clearly remember my first take-off in theatre; as I rotated, or tried to, I felt I had to pull the aircraft away from the ground. Our acceleration was so slow that I kept looking in at the engine instruments, fully expecting to see that one of the engines had failed, such was the feeling of lethargy from the aircraft. But the engines were fine – and we were off and flying in Afghan skies.

The first time I deployed to Afghanistan was in summer 2011; at that time I'd served on 31 Squadron for a year and a half. That sluggish first take-off wasn't a surprise, as the work-up for the deployment had been well structured and had covered all the different elements we would need to operate in theatre. The flying preparation made sure that every single pilot and navigator was fully competent at all they would be required to do. This involved exams, both written and verbal, a whole host of documents to read, and regular briefs, usually last thing on a Friday as that was the only time all the aircrew would be available. The work-up was partially airborne, but also utilised the simulator; the latter involved having a QWI on the console while the crew dealt with a host of scenarios and emergency handling. Previous exercises to the deserts of North America had provided an introduction to hot and high operations, and the simulator played a crucial part in replicating how sluggish and under-powered the aircraft feels in such conditions. Indeed we had trained in the simulator for all eventualities, so I was already used to the feeling of that first take-off, and another crew was certainly thankful for the training when they lost one engine while airborne. We were thoroughly prepared.

The pre-deployment work-up had covered more than just flying aspects. We attended training courses to ensure that our military skills were not only fully up-to-date but also specific to where we would be operating. We had to receive training in and pass a weapons-handling test; for me it was my first time learning how to fire a pistol, the weapon that we would carry when flying. There were heat acclimatisation sessions in the gym, medicals, including relevant jabs, and kit issues to focus us on where we would be for the next few months. A families day was held prior to departure so that our loved ones would gain an understanding of what we would be doing. The squadron and station offered a great deal of support to the families, both in the lead up and whilst we were away, which certainly helped all of us, as we knew they would receive support while we were not physically there to offer it.

Departure day arrived. Considering what I needed to take was actually quite minimal, I had spent an inordinate time checking and re-checking that I had everything. After a relaxing day spent with my family I changed into my combat uniform and loaded my bags; holdalls, rucksack, body armour and hardened box full of flying kit. I said my farewells and met the rest of my colleagues at RAF Brize Norton. A very long journey had begun – and that's where this chapter started.

Following that first sortie I felt more confident in my surroundings, which was a good thing given the events of my second mission. As we arrived at the ops desk for the out-brief, a phone call came in for the duty authoriser. The mood in the room shifted; there was a 'troops in contact' situation (troops on the ground were being fired on) and we were to launch immediately to support them. Running to the aircraft I could feel the adrenalin flowing, rapidly prioritising in my head what I would need to do. We quickly strapped in and started the right engine; as I ran through my checks I could hear my nav acknowledging as the various systems got up and running. While the left engine was starting up we were also typing information into the kit. I focused on readying the aircraft to get airborne, while Alex brought all the navigation equipment on line, checked the weapons and set up mission information. I heard our leader call for check-in over the radio and responded, before following him through each radio frequency. We taxied forward out of our shelter and stopped to make the ejection seats live, confirming this visually with our ground crew; our leader ahead of us was doing the same. Completing our pre-take-off checks swiftly but thoroughly, we lined up beside him and checked his aircraft over. He started to roll whilst I waited, allowing separation. As I selected reheat ('engine one with a kick, two with a kick') and released the brakes, we started to roll down the runway. On rotate I picked up our leader visually, and Alex also locked him on with the radar as I cut the corner to catch up with him.

We received further details about the situation and location over the radio and Alex typed the coordinates into the kit. Approaching the designated airspace and checking in with the joint terminal attack controller on the ground, we were briefed that a convoy had come under fire while in a valley and were stuck there, still taking fire. They had requested a 'show of force', a response where we would fly as low and fast over a position as we could, at speeds of up to 500 knots and down to 100 feet, creating a deafening sound and an assurance to those who we were flying over that we were present. Despite the name, the idea was to assist the army unit by using no force at all – deterring or frightening away the opposition was the aim. Our leader directed us: "I'll sort the airspace, number two the show of force is yours" – meaning that he would organise deconflictions from any other aircraft in the area while I answered the army's request.

Alex typed the location into the kit and I could clearly see on my moving map, in my HUD and indeed visually, the position that we needed to fly over. We ran through the checklist as we were descending and confirmed everything was set up correctly for the show of force. I had practised this many times during our training in the UK, now it was up to me to do the best job I could. As we dropped down into the valley I noted how different the landscape was to the leafy green of the UK. I parked the throttles forward to get as much speed as I could. 'Beep beep beep', the radalt pinged. The terrain was so featureless that I had allowed myself to get suckered into flying too low – and the kit was warning me. "Damn!" I made an immediate correction and took a mental note not to repeat the error. We continued down the valley, located the briefed position and flew over it before quickly climbing out from low level to rejoin our lead aircraft in the overhead.

Once in our sanctuary block it was time for us to go and refuel so we could be sure of having sufficient to return to the task – or cover any subsequent one. Our leader would remain on task in the meantime. My tanking experience was relatively low at that point; I had completed the prerequisite training, but not much more. I was confident that I could do it, with my only worry being the form of tanking I hadn't practised before, the boom drogue adaptor (BDA). This was attached to the KC-135 Stratotanker and I secretly hoped that today was not going to be the day I had to master this new skill.

However, that wish was not to be granted; when we were given the tanker details my adrenalin levels increased further as I recognised the call sign as one belonging to a KC-135. We needed to return to the task as soon as possible, so this would have to be a quick introduction to this new skill. As we rolled out behind and below the tanker and received clearance to join, I could see the piece of equipment that would be both my friend (giving me fuel) and foe (making it hard to do so). As I selected the probe out and positioned behind the hose I could see the boom operator sitting facing me in the back of the aircraft. This was it!

The BDA is easier to connect to than a standard hose basket but, once connected, the Tornado must be manoeuvred forward and to the side to allow the hose to bend around to start the fuel flow. This was hard. I was concentrating so much, my breathing rate increased and my hand started to cramp as I was holding the control column so tightly. Gentle movements forward and backwards to maintain position were exacerbated due to the proximity of the ironmongery (closer than other forms of tanking) and I got myself into a pilot-induced oscillation and fell out of the BDA. "Get back in" was all I could think about; "Then stay in." I reconnected, and with Alex offering words of guidance about positioning and giving regular calls on the intake of fuel, I fully concentrated on trying not to move out of position – still breathing heavily. Finally I heard the eagerly awaited words "we are full", and I disconnected.

After bidding goodbye to the tanker crew we headed immediately back as fast as we could to get an update of the situation from the leader. The show of force had been deemed successful and our mission at that location was complete. We received instructions to proceed to another area of airspace where we were required, and set off as a pair. An eventful baptism for my second operational mission.

The Tornado GR4 first operated in Afghanistan in 2009, taking over from the very successful Harrier operation, and completed the mission at the end of 2014. The role of the Tornado in Afghanistan was twofold; to provide tactical reconnaissance and close air support. The first role utilised the RAPTOR pod, from which information was analysed by intelligence and used for a variety of purposes, including counter IED ops, route planning, and reconnoitring/selecting helicopter landing sites. Close air support is, in short, doing everything that we possibly could do to help and support our troops on the ground. We provided over-watch: in two-way communications with the JTAC for route patrols; in surveillance of requested areas; by monitoring suspicious activity; and in utilising an escalatory response should our troops come into contact. To aid us we carried the Litening III targeting pod, which provided visual to both cockpits. We also carried Paveway IV precision-guided bombs, the Dual Mode Seeker Brimstone ground-attack missile and the 27mm Mauser cannon, all of which we were trained to operate with both as crew and within a formation. We had a response to any situation. We flew routine planned missions and also, at times, held ground alert – kitted up and with the jets prepared to scramble at very short notice to service any task we were called to.

Operations in Afghanistan were 24/7, and as aircrew we alternated our shifts throughout the five-month deployment. Having never tried to synchronise my body clock to work a night shift I wasn't sure how I would cope, but on a shift change we would all help each other to stay up later and 'push through'. I surprised myself by becoming very used to going to bed at half ten in the morning and getting up at about nine in the evening. For night flying we would wear night-vision goggles, which were attached to our flying helmets so that they could quickly be flicked up and down as required. They are excellent pieces of kit, although somewhat heavy, so after a little bit of time an aching neck was inevitable. Night AAR still used the same basic principles but often seemed harder. Finding the tanker was usually easier, as the aircraft showed up well in the NVGs (although so did all other aircraft in that direction, so we had to be careful to cross check with the kit to avoid joining the wrong tanker!) Once close to the tanker we would turn off our NVGs to tank visually.

Tornado capability was the same day or night, including shows of force. I remember doing one at night in the mountains utilising the TFR (a wonderful piece of kit). We used it to fly low and fast, lights off – and the element of surprise certainly gave the desired effect.

Returning to Afghanistan for a second tour was similar in terms of our role but slightly different in respect to how I felt there. I settled in a lot faster as I was familiar with my surroundings, and was also able to take on the role of a more experienced pilot, bringing previous operational knowledge to the squadron deployment. The sorties that we flew could vary dramatically in length, although we were always airborne for several hours. Unsurprisingly, the ejection seat wasn't very comfortable long term; I used to find myself wiggling around to ease the numbness in my back and legs caused by sitting still for so long. We could eat whilst airborne; nothing too exotic of course, and something you could take a bite of and not leave little bits everywhere. On long sorties we always tried to make sure we stayed hydrated by taking bottles of water in the cockpit; toilet breaks were thus inevitable, but I won't delve into that any further!

This book is sub-titled 'thrilling tales from the men and women who have operated this indomitable modern-day bomber'. As a youngster I had only one dream, which was to become an RAF pilot. It was such a different career path at that time for a girl to choose that my junior school teachers still remember me as 'the pilot girl'. To join the RAF was a goal which I passionately pursued throughout my teenage years, and I feel very privileged now to have the job I aspired to. The response when I tell someone that "I'm a fast-jet pilot" is varied; the most common reply is a slightly surprised "really?" followed by "I didn't mean to sound surprised, it's just that ... well ... uh ... you know ..." I have often had "do they actually let women do that?" and even been accused of lying! I can half understand those reactions, as there aren't many of us, but women have been involved in aviation for a long time – across the world since the early 20th century, and flying fast jets in UK front-line forces for over twenty years.

Over time female aircrew have achieved a string of notable firsts across the full range of aircraft, with female pilots and navigators flying operationally in various theatres. But let me focus for now on the achievements of the Tornado GR1 and GR4 ladies. There have been many 'firsts' by talented individuals; notable milestones include Flight Lieutenant Jo Salter becoming the first operational fast-jet pilot in 1994, Flight Lieutenant (now Squadron Leader) Kirsty Stewart being the first female Red Arrows pilot in 2009, and Wing Commander Nikki Thomas becoming the first female commanding officer of a fast-jet unit (12 Squadron) in 2015. These achievements are testament to the hard work and dedication put in by these individuals, the same hard work and dedication displayed by the talented men who achieved similar successes when they started flying. Modern-day culture highlights and focuses on these female achievements, not just for aircrew but across all walks of women's lives.

I alluded to the surprised responses which I occasionally receive; this actually comes more from people outside the RAF than from those within it, where the

reaction is usually negligible and no one makes an issue out of it. In the earlier days
the big battles that women faced involved the lack of kit – they had to make do with
the often much larger (and differently shaped!) men's kit. Squadrons didn't usually
have toilets for the ladies, separation came from a sign placed on the door. Quite a
few women experienced the squadron 'preparing' for them, in short making sure
there wasn't anything lying around that a lady would be offended by. However, time
has progressed and now female aircrew, though very low in numbers, are more the
norm, with facilities and kit to suit.

I have had the privilege of speaking to a number of successful female aircrew
whilst researching this chapter, and all are of a similar mind set. They are rightly
proud of their achievements and just want to get on with their jobs, be the best
that they can be, improve as professionals and not make a big thing of being
female. I don't get treated any differently from the men, which is exactly what
I have always wanted, and I don't expect it to be an issue. Women go through
exactly the same selection, training and qualification process and reach the same
standards, proving to ourselves as much as to our male counterparts that we can
do it. The male-dominated environment doesn't really exist when airborne. Our
role on the front line is obviously the same; without reading the introduction you
could have read this chapter not knowing what sex the author is. Outside of the
airborne environment, one of the best pieces of advice I have received and stuck
to is to maintain my femininity; just because women can match the men in the air
doesn't mean we have to in all aspects on the ground.

I have flown with male and female navigators, with no difference bar the
obviously higher voice. On my second tour of Afghanistan I was paired up with a
wonderful female navigator, both in talent and personality. We flew together not
least because it made sense practically; we were sharing a room and were crewed up
so that our shifts coincided. We were not the first all-female crew; in 2009 the then
Squadron Leader Nikki Thomas noted in an interview about flying operationally
with Flight Lieutenant Jules Fleming that: "The only difference comes from other
people. When you are air-to-air refuelling they are a lot chattier with us compared
to the guys, and the guys on the ground recognise your voice very quickly."

I'm not pretending that men and women are the same. Despite performing the
same role on a professional level there are obvious differences (not least physically!)
but women in any sector of society can bring a healthy change in dynamic to a
social group, and that's no less true on a squadron. I'm also not trying to generalise
and say that all female aircrew are the same – any more than the men are. Despite
individual personality traits, both male and female in the military seem to have a
similar mindset, which is tested through the training system so that those involved
appreciate the demands that will be made upon them and can be confident that
the lifestyle will indeed be for them.

There are of course times when people's reactions have created some amusing
stories. I have held a debrief phone call with someone who repeatedly asked to be

put on to the pilot. I've had a chuckle when "birds on the final approach" was called when flying circuits with a female navigator – a call made by ATC to indicate a flock of geese nearby – but that point was somewhat lost. On exercise my formation all found it amusing when my navigator and I successfully shot down (simulated) an American F-15; we never got a chance to debrief them as they didn't make contact after the sortie. We weren't sure whether that was because a girl or a mud mover had shot them down! On a squadron, as in the military in general, morale depends to a great extent on ribbing, and as Wing Commander Thomas noted: "The banter is always there. To be honest you will always get banter for something in the RAF, so being a girl is great because you know what it is going to be."

I thoroughly enjoyed my time on the Tornado GR4, from flying and operating the aircraft, to overseas exercises, to doing the role which we spent years training for, in Afghanistan. Working so closely with a navigator brought the notion of crew cooperation to a whole new level. Two people working independently yet together gave me an enormous sense of satisfaction about how much we could achieve. It also gave me the incentive to be the best pilot I could be so that the navigators could do their job to the highest level. Afghanistan was stressful and hard in being away from loved ones for so long, but being on a squadron was fantastic as there was an immediate support network there; the term 'military family' rings true. Everyone played their vital role in the operation; engineers, intelligence, squippers, ops, admin and aircrew all combining together, each element an essential cog in the squadron machine. It was challenging work, being prepared for anything and dealing with urgent situations, but we spent a long time training to deploy, preparation that was fundamental in permitting us to give the best possible support to the troops on the ground. A fantastic aircraft, supportive squadron and varied roles made my entire three-and-a-half-year tour on the front line an incredibly memorable and rewarding one.

CHAPTER 20

THE LONG AND WINDING ROAD
IAN HALL

Today's Tornado GR4 has extraordinary capabilities, undreamed of when the GR1 entered service in 1982. Given that this volume has covered virtually all of the aircraft's thirty-five-year service life I would like to have included at least one chapter in which we could look in detail at the marvellous new suite of weapons with which the aircraft now operates. But readers will appreciate, I have no doubt, the sensitivities surrounding currently in-service systems. Notwithstanding that much information is already available in open sources, today's 'Tornado Boys' are, quite rightly, keen not to betray confidences.

But the long and winding road to the current state is nevertheless curious in many ways, and I was able to follow much of it from the differing perspectives of my three ground tours. The progress of various projects as staffs struggled to get them into service was extraordinarily convoluted and elongated. As always in life, chance played a part along the way.

I first began to be aware of all this when, as a squadron leader in 1985, I was posted to lecture in the Department of Air Warfare at Cranwell. I was to be the 'attack weapons specialist' and it was a fascinating time for weapons development. And indeed a demanding time for a new lecturer; I remember on day one having to deliver a session to the aerosystems course on anti-radiation missiles – a breed of creatures (the missiles, as well as the course members) I had never met in my life. But there is no quicker way to learn than becoming an instructor, and I was soon happily lecturing to the weapons employment and air warfare courses. It was a great life, with many course visits to defence industry sites – whose locations, for inexplicable reasons, always seemed to be adjacent either to breweries or Soho.

The hot topic at the time was the weapons planned to replace the elderly equipment that still armed the ground-attack force. Many recent aircraft types had staggered into service only half ready for combat, equipped with weapons already a couple of generations old. The Phantom, in its early ground-attack days, had used the Canberra's (Lancaster's?) iron bombs, a fixed weapon-aiming system, and the Hunter's SNEB rockets. The Jaguar, which had succeeded it, inherited those 'dumb' bombs, although gaining an improved aiming system. Additionally, unguided rockets were superseded by the (still unguided) BL755 cluster bomb unit. The latter's advantage was that it could be delivered from ultra-low level, but the fact that each weapon scattered 147 sub-munitions in a huge pattern gave away the fact that aiming inaccuracies were still considerable.

One of the coming technologies in the anti-armour area was recognition of targets by 'intelligent' gizmos mounted in weapons; they would image the vehicles in their view, compare those pictures with a stored data bank, and steer the weapon towards the recognised 'enemy' target. The imaging would be performed either by millimetric wave radar or imaging infra-red seekers.

This all seemed to me at the time to be somewhat pie in the sky, although the project was being pursued for real by the MoD (in fact they had been doing so since about 1982) in the form of air staff targets (ASTs) 1238 and 1241; the former was for a short-range weapon, the latter for a powered, stand-off system. But a measure of how far this sort of thing was from maturity was that I was able to complete that tour, disappear for a while on a staff college course, and re-emerge in 1988 as a wing commander in a new ground tour in the MoD – to find them still years from service entry. In that MoD post I was concerned with the future equipment programme, and I was relieved, and perhaps slightly surprised, that 1238 and 1241 remained in the plan. I also had the reassurance that the projects had been firmed up into 'requirements' (ASRs) rather than ASTs.

I was the department's Harrier and Jaguar man, a part of the team constructing the ten-year forward financial programme that would, year on year, neatly accommodate the phased expenditure on coming projects. It was a tri-service business, with army, navy and RAF competing for funds and all three having plenty to say about each other's projects. For example when it came to airborne anti-submarine warfare, the RN, unsurprisingly, would champion frigate-mounted systems and helicopters, while the RAF would advocate the merits of Nimrod. Oddly, though, given the subject, the army would be allowed to throw in their two-penn'th as well, mainly it seemed in a bid to upset the (metaphorical) boat.

Similarly, with the two anti-armour projects we've been discussing, I had to be prepared to deal with the army's views on their competing systems, while still having to watch out for the navy's salvoes from left field. It was a good game, keeping us all extremely busy.

In fact killing tanks leads me to mention that during the time I was in the job the army was signing up to buying the Apache helicopter. With its Hellfire missile it was a formidable system, I had to agree, but as it proceeded through the funding, approval and procurement process, the army did find themselves fighting one unexpected rearguard action. Apache was so good that its imminent introduction put a spoke in the wheels of their case for new main battle tanks.

Money (lack of) was the recurring problem, with ways having to be found to cope with escalating costs. One source of difficulty was the regular under-estimation of bills when new projects were inserted into the programme. This was partly, perhaps understandably, because of initial lack of appreciation of the full complexity of new systems. But there also appeared to be a tactical tendency for services and industry to deliberately underestimate costs in deference to the 'foot-in-the-door' principle;

if the true price were revealed straight away, pet projects would never have found their way into the programme at all.

One of the solutions to the continual pressure to finance the programme was to 'move projects to the right' – in other words to shift expenditure out of one fiscal year and into the next. This could occur at the MoD's request, although there were obvious downsides when much-needed new equipment was delayed. Apart from the capability loss there were usually costs involved in the necessary running on of old equipment to compensate; moreover, there would inevitably be a price increase when the buyer caused the rescheduling. But delays were often because the manufacturer couldn't achieve the planned into-service date, usually because technology which had been optimistically promised was proving harder than expected to put into production form.

As an aside, I mentioned earlier the 'EFA introduction to service plan' with which I was involved during that MoD tour. It defined how Jaguar and Phantom squadrons would progressively be replaced by EFA from 1996 onwards. As we know now, the Phantoms disappeared in 1992 (without being replaced), while EFA progressively became Eurofighter, Eurofighter 2000, and then Typhoon, eventually beginning in 2003 to replace Tornado F3 and the few remaining Jaguars. Truly, one needed to be flexible when dealing with defence planning and procurement!

All that was then, of course, and we are assured that 'smart procurement' now eradicates many of the old problems. Just as importantly, the vast 'black hole' in funding is, apparently, being addressed, with the defence programme being made affordable. We can only hope that all this is so.

Anyway, I forget what the specific problems were at the time with my projects 1238 and 1241, but for whatever reason they didn't seem to be much further on when I left the MoD in 1991 than they had been when I first met them in 1985.

During those two and a half years in Whitehall I shared an office with my Tornado oppo, and for all that time he was beavering away at ASR1236, the CASOM – or conventionally armed stand-off missile. I knew very few details at the time of that aspiration, but I was conscious that he seemed to be having about as much success with it as I was with 1238 and 1241. Time would show, though, how our respective projects would cross each other's paths.

We've spent a while discussing anti-armour, and although the Tornado was to be capable of carrying those new weapons, killing tanks was not the aircraft's primary role. And although Tornado did indeed employ iron bombs in its early days, it had broken the mould by entering service equipped with JP233, a brand-new weapon designed specifically for its primary role – which was offensive counter air.

OCA was designed to reduce, or preferably neutralise, the enemy's air effort so that our own aircraft could operate freely and, just as importantly, our troops could operate free from enemy air interference. In the early 1980s when Tornado was approaching service entry there were reckoned to be several methods of contributing to this objective.

The first was to attack enemy radars and surface-to-air missile sites, a dangerous business but potentially achievable with dumb bombs. Secondly, one could engage enemy fighters whilst airborne and shoot them down. This was the job of our own fighter boys – always assuming they had the spare capacity over and above last-ditch defence of the home base.

The third method would be to attack and destroy enemy aircraft on the ground. Given that the opposition, like ourselves, had opted to house their aircraft in hardened aircraft shelters, this had become something of a long shot. Granted, a direct hit on a HAS would likely put it, and probably the aircraft inside, out of action – always assuming that the weapon impacted squarely on the exterior surface rather than glancing off. But given the accuracies of the dumb bombs available, the chances weren't good. At that time, by the way, it was not reckoned that PGMs could be employed effectively against heavily defended airfields in the envisaged conflict area, central Europe.

Finally one could degrade the enemy's operating surfaces such that he couldn't take off. The Warsaw Pact (for this was whom the Tornado was designed to engage) had not adopted the dispersed, Harrier-style concept, nor the autobahn-operating idea of the Swedes, so bombing their runways/dispersals seemed a good option. Not crudely, with dumb bombs which might ricochet off, but surgically, with many, specifically designed cratering submunitions.

Such was the concept of JP233. Because the weapon contained many submunitions (airfield operating surfaces were huge) each couldn't be all that large, so the possibility remained that the opposition could fill in the holes relatively quickly and resume operations. But JP233's designers had thought of that, adding a complementary dispenser full of mines to deter repair teams. The aim was to keep the enemy base out of action for, perhaps, twenty-four hours, with JP233 re-attacks scheduled as necessary to keep the base closed.

That was the theory, but how about the results? The weapon's only operational use was during the Gulf Conflict, and I don't recall seeing any definitive battle damage assessments. But word has it that the cratering was not as effective as expected – possibly affected by the sandy sub-strata. At any event, in that war it didn't really matter, as the Iraqi air force had opted not to fight.

By the time I finished that MoD tour, Gulf War One had come and gone. I departed to fly my own Tornado, enjoying a couple of years running a squadron on ops. CBUs, dumb bombs and JP233 were still in the inventory, although the post-Cold War situation and experience from the Gulf Conflict was leading to lots of new thinking. Most importantly, Tornado now had, in TIALD, its own highly capable laser designator pod (two pre-production models, 'Sharon' and 'Tracy', had actually served in the Gulf Conflict). This, together with operating Tornados within coalition 'packages' complete with all manner of enabling assets, was changing everything. Stand-off weapons delivery was very much the name of the game rather than overflying the target, so all that was now needed was to get some of those advanced weapons onto the front line.

Five years after leaving the MoD I returned, now as a group captain, and this time working in the air commitments area. The calendar had flipped over to 1996, and SR(A)s 1236, 1238 and 1241 had still not entered service – at least not in their envisaged form. Indeed such had been the delays and so urgent was now the need for a degree of stand-off that what might be described as interim weapons had been procured – the American Maverick missile for the Harrier and the Canadian CRV-7 high-velocity rocket for the Jaguar. Oh, and perhaps I shouldn't claim that no progress had been made – you'll have noted that 'ASR' had become 'SR(A)'. This change was designed to reinforce the notion that control of procurement was a central function rather than a single-service business – but one might be forgiven for perceiving it more as a cosmetic adjustment than as substantive progress.

But not long into that tour we found ourselves in one of those circumstances when, the soothsayers would say, constellations move into conjunction with planets. The spotlight was falling on cluster bombs which, in the case of the RAF's BL755, contained anti-armour submunitions. But other major nations had produced dispensers containing a range of alternative submunition types, some of which were small mines. These were intended to deny use of an area to enemy forces and could be of the anti-armour, anti-soft-skinned vehicle or anti-personnel variety. Unsurprisingly, such weapons had now found their way into the arsenals of third world nations – with the inevitable result that innocent passers-by had had limbs blown off.

In fact it wasn't only mines that were doing the damage. Submunitions such as those in BL755, whose targets were tanks, were designed to detonate on impact. But inevitably, given the spread of the dispenser, most of them missed their targets. They would, perhaps, detonate on the ground. However, at shallow impact angles and on variable surfaces, a proportion could be expected to remain as unexploded ordnance, littering the countryside and lying, ready to trap the unwary, concealed in undergrowth long after the conflict had moved on.

News media and humanitarian organisations began to bring this issue to the attention of world opinion, and before long a substantial head of steam built up, against mines in particular and cluster weapons in general. Prominent personalities, not least the late HRH the Princess of Wales, became involved in the campaign, which eventually bore fruit in the adoption of an international anti-mine protocol. The British signed up, although in the drafting and discussions prior to the signing a most unexpected issue had become apparent. It was HB876.

The HB876 mines in JP233 could in no way be equated to the types of bomblets which the protocol was intended to eradicate. They were huge pieces of kit, standing up visibly (to deter approach) on spindly metal legs. And JP233 was an anti-runway weapon so, even allowing for inevitable aiming errors which could lead to a few being scattered outside the airfield perimeter, one would hardly expect many HB876 submunitions to pose a threat to innocent civilians.

It could have been argued, of course, that JP233 had utility against other area targets such as railway marshalling yards – which would have countered any assertion that its mines would be confined to military airfields. There was indeed some background to this suggestion. The Germans and Italians, who had not bought JP233, had procured a similar weapon, MW-1 (*Mehrzweckwaffe Eins*), which did indeed have a capability against targets other than airfields. But, although I did hear of such employment being mooted on several occasions for JP233, those discussions concerned more a theoretical option rather than a serious move to expand the target range. To my knowledge JP233 remained, to the RAF, strictly a counter-air weapon.

So it might have been possible to argue exemption for JP233 from an anti-mine protocol which was, primarily, targeted at eradicating anti-personnel mines. It was even suggested that JP233 could, if necessary, be modified to carry just the cratering submunitions (the mines were carried and dispensed from a separate container, so this should not have been impossible). But this option was swiftly discarded; the craters made by the primary submunitions were relatively small and, although there would, it was hoped, have been many of them, it was reckoned that, without the harassing effect of the mines, repairs sufficient to make the strip operable again could be effected fairly quickly.

All in all, it might have been possible to save JP233 – given the will. But the fact was that there was little love in the RAF for the weapon. Many weren't persuaded by the efficacy of flying straight and level at low level across a heavily defended enemy airfield. And in any case, weapons technology was now developing to the extent that it was possible to find better ways of carrying out the counter-air role than destroying the operating surfaces. Advances in precision guidance were making it possible to target HASs with a high chance of hitting them; and, because it was now possible to shape trajectories to optimise impact angle and velocity, a hit would usually now mean a kill. The other variable in the equation, the believed impossibility of reaching a heavily defended target at anything other than ultra-low level, was also being affected by vastly improved intelligence, electronic countermeasures and defence suppression. Not to mention that, with the collapse of the Warsaw Pact, the primary target was now perceived to be quite different.

So JP233 was, in the eyes of many senior RAF people, not worth fighting for. And here's where further chance came into play. The air staffs had been dearly wishing for years to bring SR(A)1236 to fruition. Given that the service would now, for reasons beyond its control, have to relinquish Tornado's primary heavy weapon, the urgency of a replacement was reinforced – even to those in the MoD and the Treasury who had hitherto been intent on delaying matters. Although SR(A)1236 was by no means a direct equivalent to JP233, obstacles to its progress suddenly evaporated, and CASOM accelerated towards service entry. Truly, it was an ill wind ...

The kind of damage that can be done by PGMs, nowadays, to 'hardened' aircraft shelters.
These HASs are on a Kuwaiti airfield which was attacked during Gulf War One.

There were other fortuitous twists in the story. Not only the mine, or unexploded ordnance, connection, but also the lack of stand-off and general ineffectiveness, was now making BL755's position increasingly untenable, reinvigorating the urgency of SR(A)1238/1241. Remember Hellfire, the Apache helicopter's anti-tank missile? Well its British derivative, Brimstone, eventually fulfilled 1238 (by now a requirement for a powered, stand-off weapon) when it entered service in 2005 – twenty years after the project had first come to my notice. By this time there were no more Jaguars and would soon be no Harriers, and against all the odds Tornado was picking up the close-air-support task. Some expected the Cold War nuclear bomber to be unsuited to this role but, in its GR4 guise, Tornado excelled.

Moreover Brimstone, with several modes of employment, has become the weapon of choice against many targets other than armour. Besides its great attribute of stand-off, its extreme precision and small size make it ideal in situations where it is of the utmost importance to avoid collateral damage. Thus, in its several versatile variants, it has found gainful employment in Afghanistan and Libya. As well as, most recently, in Iraq and Syria in operations against Islamic State (also known as ISIL, ISIS and Daesh) forces. Indeed, during November 2015's parliamentary debate and division which preceded the Syrian phase of these operations, the weapon's (and the GR4's) excellence was seemingly on the lips of every MP, media commentator and coalition commander.

The question of avoiding collateral damage has, since Gulf War One, been of paramount importance, not least because current conflicts are conducted so much in the spotlight of the world's media gaze. And this was one benefit of advanced laser-guided bombs. The Tornado began with Paveway II, a relatively crude LGB, but the later models Paveway III and IV brought tremendous accuracy and the ability to shape trajectories to optimise weapon effects. While PWIII is a heavy, 2,000-lb class weapon, PWIV is, at 500 lbs, much smaller, minimising the likelihood of collateral damage. Indeed it is remarkable to note in this respect that, during the Iraq War of 2003, a number of weapons equipped with the full guidance kit on practice, inert weapon bodies were dropped. So in particularly sensitive operations it was possible to do the job using purely kinetic energy, eliminating the collateral effects of high explosive.

Another great development has been the introduction of GPS guidance as an option for these weapons, thereby enabling attacks to be made when weather precludes other forms of guidance. CASOM, the erstwhile SR(A)1236, is a major beneficiary of this, giving Tornado GR4 a stand-off, all-weather heavy weapon. As we've already chronicled, Storm Shadow achieved an initial operating capability in Gulf War Two, bringing with it the other major characteristic of being capable of penetrating the most heavily-hardened targets before detonating. Hence the extraordinary post-strike recce pictures showing, sometimes, only a small, neat hole on the surface – betraying nothing of the carnage deep inside.

At service entry the Tornado was already an extraordinary machine. But with Storm Shadow, Brimstone, Paveway III and IV, the complementary sensors and designators – and of course the upgrade to GR4 standard itself – the Tornado has achieved a capability never envisaged in the beginning. It's been a long and winding journey from precision to even greater precision.

The RAF originally had eleven squadrons of GR1s plus the conversion units. Remotely piloted air systems have already taken on some of the load, while the two remaining GR4 squadrons were scheduled to be replaced in 2018/19 by a small number of F-35 Lightning II aircraft. But plans continually evolve. With the current operational commitment against the Islamic State putting such a strain on those two squadrons, a third has been run on to help spread the load. In this unstable world, who would bet against further changes?

So it's too early for an epilogue, but it's already easy to see why the 'Fin' attracts such respect from its operators. No wonder, either, that the Tornado boys and girls continue to regard it with such pride and affection. It has already undoubtedly proved to be one of the great strike/attack aircraft – and indeed reconnaissance and close air support aircraft – of modern times.

GLOSSARY OF TERMS

AAA   Anti-aircraft artillery
AAR   Air-to-air refuelling
AFC   Air Force Cross (medal)
ADV   Air defence variant
AEW&C Airborne Early Warning and
           Control (force)
AFB   (USAF) air force base
ALARM   Air-launched anti-radiation
           missile
AOC   Air officer commanding (of an
           RAF Group)
ASR   Air staff requirement (later SR[A])
AST   Air staff target (later ST[A])
5ATAF   5th Allied Tactical Air Force (Italy)
ATC   Air traffic control
AWACS   Airborne Warning and Control
           System
AWC   Air Warfare Centre

BAC   British Aircraft Corporation
BAe   British Aerospace plc
BBMF   Battle of Britain Memorial Flight
BDA   Boom drogue adaptor, making
           USAF boom-fitted tankers usable
           by probe-equipped receivers.
BL755   Hunting CBU
BOZ   Chaff and flare dispenser
Brimstone Stand-off missile in several
           variants, primarily for anti-armour
           use but useful against multiple
           target types.

CBU   Cluster Bomb Unit
C-in-C   Commander-in-Chief (of an RAF
           command)
CND   Campaign for Nuclear
           Disarmament
CNN   Cable News Network

DDR   *Deutsche Demokratische Republik*
           (East Germany)
DFC   Distinguished Flying Cross (medal)
DGM   Deputy director general
Doolally Originally 'Deolali', from
           the town of that name, known
           for its Indian army transit camp
           and sanatorium. (slang)

DR   Dead reckoning
dry   Maximum power without reheat
power
DSO   Distinguished Service Order
           (medal)
Dumb   Unguided bombs (slang)
bombs

E-scope   Radar display showing range and
           elevation
ECM   Electronic countermeasures
ECS   Environmental control system
EFA   European Fighter Aircraft (later
           Typhoon)
EW   Electronic warfare

F3   Tornado F3 (air-defence variant)
FAC   Forward air control(er)
FAF   French air force
FBI   Federal Bureau of Investigation
           (US)
FOB   Flying order book
FTG   Flight test group
FTI   Flight test instrumentation
FYROM   Former Yugoslav Republic of
           Macedonia

GDT   Ground defence training
GLO   Ground liaison officer
GMR   Ground mapping radar
GPS   Global positioning system
Gulf   The Gulf Conflict (slang)
War One
Gulf   The Iraq War (slang)
War Two

HAS   Hardened aircraft shelter
HB876   Mine submunition in JP233
HIRTA   High intensity radio transmission
           area
HR   Human resources
HUD   Head-up display

IAF   Italian air force
IDS   Interdictor/Strike (Tornado
           bomber version)
IFF   Identification friend or foe
           equipment/selective identification
           feature (radar transponder)

ILS	Instrument landing system		Panavia	Manufacturing consortium formed between Aeritalia, BAC and MBB
IN	Inertial navigation (equipment)		Paveway	(PW) family of laser-guided bombs
IP	Instructor pilot		PBF	Pilot (or protected) briefing facility (hardened building)
IR	Infra-red (imagery)			
IS	Islamic State (also ISIS, ISIL, Islamic State of Iraq and Syria / the Levant or Daesh)		PJHQ	Primary Joint Headquarters
			POW	Prisoner of war
			PSO	Personal staff officer
ISO	International organization for standardization		PSP	Pierced steel planking (temporary surface)
ISTAR	Intelligence, surveillance, target acquisition and reconnaissance		PWII	Paveway II LGB
			PWIII	Paveway III LGB
IWSO	Instructor WSO		PWIV	Paveway IV LGB
JEngO	Junior engineering officer		Q	QRA (colloq)
JNCO	Junior non-commissioned officer		QFI	Qualified flying instructor
JP233	Runway attack weapon		QRA	Quick reaction alert
JTAC	Joint terminal attack controller		QWI	Qualified weapons instructor
kipper fleet	RAF maritime patrol aircraft (slang)		RAAF	Royal Australian Air Force
			RAPTOR	Reconnaissance airborne pod for Tornado
LGB	Laser-guided bomb		RBSU	Radar bomb scoring unit
loft	Attack with bombs released in a climb and 'tossed' towards the target.		RHAG	Rotary hydraulic arrestor gear
			Rhein-dahlen	HQ RAF Germany (as well as HQ 2ATAF, HQ BAOR and HQ Northern Army Group)
Marine-flieger	German navy air wing		RIC	Reconnaissance intelligence centre
			RN	Royal Navy
MASS	Master armament safety switch		RSAF	Royal Saudi Air Force
MBB	Messerschmitt-Bölkow-Blohm		RSO	Range safety officer (weapons)
MBDA	Multinational missile manufacturing company formed mainly from elements of Matra, BAe and Alenia		R/T	Radio telephony
			RTB	Return to base
			RV	Rendezvous
Mineval	Mini evaluation – station-generated exercise		S-60	Soviet-supplied 57mm anti-aircraft artillery unit
MoD	Ministry of Defence (UK)		SACEUR	(NATO) supreme allied commander, Europe
MPC	Missile practice camp			
MRCA	Multi-Role Combat Aircraft (eventually Tornado)		SAG	Surface action group
			SAM	Surface-to-air missile
mud movers	Air-to-surface attack crews (slang)		Scud	Soviet-supplied SS-1 surface-to-surface missile
			Sea Eagle	Sea-skimming anti-ship missile
NAMMA	NATO MRCA Development and Production Management Agency		SEAD	Suppression of enemy air defences
			SEngO	Senior engineering officer
NBC	Nuclear, biological and chemical		Side-winder	AIM-9 air-to-air missile
NVGs	Night-vision goggles		Sky-shadow	Response electronic jamming pod
OC	Officer commanding (of a unit)			
OCA	Offensive counter air (role)		SOP	Standard operating procedure
OCU	Operational conversion unit		SNEB	French unguided rocket pod
OTF	Overseas training flight		SNCO	Senior non-commissioned officer
			Squinto	Squadron intelligence officer

staish   Station commander (slang)
Storm   Conventionally armed stand-off
Shadow   missile (UK)
Strike   Nuclear attack (role)

TACAN   Tactical air navigation equipment
Taceval   Tactical evaluation (NATO
            operational readiness audit system)
TF   Terrain following (flown using
(auto-TF)   autopilot)
TFR   Terrain-following radar
TIALD   Thermal imaging and laser
            designation (pod)
TISMT   Tornado in-service software
            maintenance team
TLAM   Tactical land attack missile
TTTE   Tornado Tri-National Training Unit
Turbo-   International engine
Union   manufacturing company
            comprising elements of Rolls
            -Royce, MTU and FiatAvio.
TWCU   Tornado Weapons Conversion Unit

USAF   United States Air Force
USAFE   United States Air Forces Europe
            (command organisation)
USMC   United States Marine Corps
USN   United States 65

WMD   Weapons of mass destruction
Wild
Weasel   Aircraft armed with anti-radiation
            missiles (USAF)
WLSO   Weapon (nuclear) load supervising
            officer
Wobbly   Squadron warrant officer (slang)
WRAF   Women's Royal Air Force
WSO   Weapons system officer (RAF
            tactical aircraft – second
            crewmember, formerly navigator)

INDEX